ALSO BY RHONDA ABRAMS

*The Successful Business Plan:
Secrets & Strategies*

WEAR CLEAN UNDERWEAR

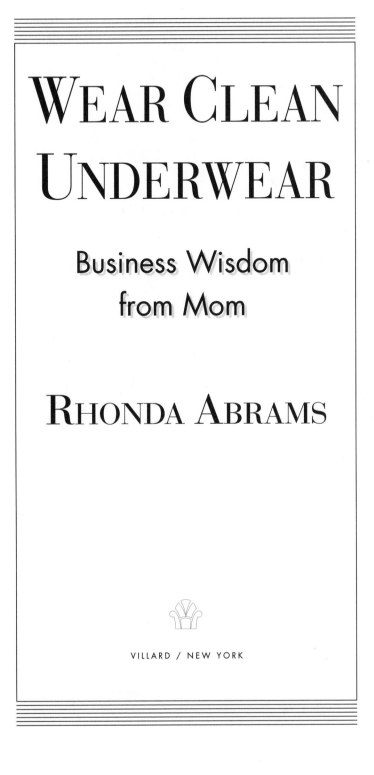

WEAR CLEAN UNDERWEAR

Business Wisdom from Mom

RHONDA ABRAMS

VILLARD / NEW YORK

Library of Congress Cataloging-in-Publication Data
Abrams, Rhonda
Wear clean underwear: business wisdom from Mom / Rhonda Abrams.
p.   cm.
Includes bibliographical references.
ISBN 0-375-50192-4
1. Creative ability in business.   2. Success in business.
I. Title.
HD53.A27   1999
650.1—dc21   98-33310

I have been blessed with a close and loving family and many wonderful friends. This book is dedicated to them, with particular gratitude and affection to four who have been my daily support system for many, many years:

Cathy Dobbs Goldstein

Janice Abrams Hill

Edward M. Pollock

and Dr. Raquel Newman, my personal patron of the arts.

CONTENTS

Introduction		xi
1.	Why the Time Is Right for Thinking like Mom	3
2.	How Do You Know You Don't Like It When You've Never Tried It?	13
3.	If You Keep Making That Face, Someday It Will Freeze That Way	30
4.	I Don't Care Who Made This Mess, Just Clean It Up!	39
5.	If All Your Friends Jumped off a Bridge, Would You Jump off One Too?	51
6.	Don't Get Too Big for Your Britches	74
7.	Say You're Sorry	85
8.	Don't Judge a Book by Its Cover	102
9.	Share	118
10.	It's Not the End of the World	135
11.	Remember Where You Came From	151
12.	Quit Picking on Each Other	170
13.	Eat Your Vegetables, or You Don't Get Dessert	186
14.	Wear Clean Underwear; What If You Get into an Accident and Somebody Sees It?	201
15.	What I Learned from My Mother, Susan Abrams	216
	Acknowledgments	219
	Bibliography	223

INTRODUCTION

What Does It Mean to Be "Businesslike"?

In 1986, I began a management consulting practice, working with entrepreneurs to help them plan and improve their companies.

From the start, fledgling business owners would sheepishly confide to me their desire to do something personally meaningful with their businesses. They knew it wasn't very *businesslike*, but they didn't want to work just to make money. They wanted to do something intrinsically worthwhile *in addition to* making a profit. The specifics varied from one person to the next: one wanted to give a percentage of profits to environmental causes, one wished to share power and decision making with employees, one wanted particularly to hire low-income single mothers. All were noble goals.

But I was having no part of it. I was new to consulting, but I knew what my job was: to help my clients build better *businesses*. Not social work agencies.

"Save those activities for your private lives," I advised them. "Keep your business focused on business. If you want to give money to the environment, write a check with your own money. If you want to help low-income mothers, volunteer for a local charity. Share profits? Well, maybe after you've been successful, but never, ever give up *any* control. The purpose of a business is to make money. You've got to be businesslike."

There was nothing unusual or mean-spirited about such advice. It just took me a long time to realize that it was *wrong*. (Still, I'm not giving any refunds to those clients now.)

The fact that I was wrong dawned on me slowly, through an evolution in my thinking of what enables a company to be successful, distinguish itself from its competitors, energize its employees, and withstand the changes and changing fortunes it faces over time.

In my early days as a consultant, I helped my clients focus on their companies' basic operations and marketing: how to let customers know you exist; how to ship product out the door; the nitty-gritty, the nuts and bolts, the day-to-day realities of running a company. And I gave them good, solid helpful advice that enabled them to make more money. (That's why there won't be any refunds.)

My business grew, and as I began to work with larger companies with more complex problems as well as with entrepreneurs, I realized that a company needs more than just good operations and marketing. As the business world gets more competitive, to survive, a company needs a *strategic position,* a meaningful way to distinguish itself, its products and services, from its competitors'. I'm not talking about just an advertising slogan but a real distinction—a particular place in the market. Having a strategic position makes it easier for a company to understand its markets and how to choose to expend its resources. This was a more sophisticated approach then just nuts and bolts.

While a company could certainly be successful, particularly in monetary terms, by focusing on operations, marketing, and developing a strategic position, those were merely the basic necessities. If your goal is to build a great company, an exceptional company, that will survive over time, your company needs purpose and passion. A great business, it turns out, isn't a *thing* at all; it's a living entity, and it needs a heart, a soul. It needs values, standards, and responsibility.

Increasingly I came to realize that it is the passion, the values, the standards you hold that give a person, a company, an organization its strength. It's what has traditionally been called "character."

Character! Character is what holds you together through good times and bad. Character is what determines your behavior and shapes your goals. Character frames your decisions. And if you want to build a great company, you have to develop and nurture its character, just as Mom develops and nurtures her child's character.

My own belief in the importance of a company's character was further strengthened when I read *Built to Last,* a truly important business book that I highly recommend to anyone in business. The book's authors, James Collins and Jerry Porras, both business school professors, studied *visionary* companies, comparing them to other companies in the same industries. They looked to see what factors make a company great, able to succeed for generations. What Collins and Porras concluded was that what sets these companies apart is *values.* To achieve greatness, the authors realized, a company has to have values other than just making money. They have to have a passion and a purpose.

This point was finally driven home to me by, of all things, nonprofit organizations. For many years, I had worked with nonprofit groups as a board member, volunteer, and a professional. Increasingly, I noticed a trend: executives at these nonprofit organizations eagerly sought to make their agencies more "businesslike." Over and over, I'd hear someone comment, "We have to run this more like a business."

So these nonprofit organizations, which had been established to achieve noble ends, came to spend most of their energies on their operations rather than on their heart and soul, their mission. I would go to a one- or two-day retreat and we'd discuss leadership development, volunteer retention, and fund-raising methods, but we wouldn't spend even one hour examining how we could better achieve our mission, better nurture and develop our core values.

Here I was, working professionally with businesses and realizing the importance of values, purpose, passion—while volunteering with nonprofits that were intentionally paying little attention to the values that were the very reason for their existence. And I realized something about both:

They didn't value their values. It was like building a beach house without any windows: you ignore a million-dollar view to sit staring at the wallpaper.

No, You Haven't Picked up a Work of Fiction

"I love my job."
"I've got the best job in the world."

"I look forward to Monday morning."
"Everyone at work treats me with respect."
"I would do anything for my boss; he's the greatest man in the world."
"This job is paradise."

Believe it or not, I've heard all those effusive comments, and many more like them, while doing the research for this book. I spent months traveling around the country, visiting and spending time at some of the most respected companies in the nation—some very well known, some I had never heard of before.

At almost every company I visited, employees would spontaneously tell me how much they liked their work, their boss, their company. One man literally pulled me out of the hall as I was passing by to tell me he would lay down his life for his boss. It got so I started checking my watch to see how long it took before someone just had to tell me how happy they were. The record, a tie, was less than five minutes.

How could this be?

I can already hear you saying, "It's all just for the publicity, Rhonda; they knew you were writing a book, and they wanted to impress you." But I had done my homework on these companies; it had been very difficult even to be permitted these interviews, and besides, I have a fairly well developed "B.S. detector."

But I don't blame you for your doubts; it's easy to become cynical about the business world these days. After all, we've all read reports of heartless corporations downsizing in the midst of record profits. Or CEOs getting corporate jets while employees get pink slips. Indeed, one day, having just come from a truly wonderful company, I read a news story about a federal agency needing to clarify the labor laws: businesses not only had to *have* bathrooms for their workers, they had to allow the workers actually to *use* them. It seems that some companies don't allow employees any bathroom breaks all day.

Reprehensible practices such as these have formed a lot of the public's view of business. It's a picture that focuses on companies putting profits before people, shareholder value before human value. A picture that portrays everyone who runs or manages a business as being interested in one thing alone: the bottom line. And many of us have worked for companies that reinforce that image.

a contract with Villard, a division of Random House. You can't get more respectable than that. And my previous book had been given positive reviews by leading publications, such as *Forbes* and *INC*. I didn't just crawl out from under a rock. But I had to spend months continually pursuing some of these companies. 3M was a virtual hermit. It took six months of almost weekly contact to get an interview with Nordstrom, and they said I was only the second book author they had given permission to. Six months!

What's up with this? I wondered. Companies generally love publicity. But these companies don't like to bring that much attention to themselves, especially about their values. Some are reasonably concerned that such coverage means they'll be held to a higher standard than companies that don't aim as high. We like to pull down companies that shout their virtues from the rooftops.

But these companies weren't shouters. They felt uncomfortable talking about issues that were so close to their core, to their heart. Some expressed astonishment at getting attention for simply doing the right thing. Almost all felt they weren't doing anything special or extraordinary.

Please let me underscore that none of these companies is perfect. They don't claim to be perfect. They don't even strive to be perfect.

As Mom knew, no one's perfect. No company's perfect either. The companies in this book make mistakes. I'm sure there will be those who could point out instances when these companies don't live up to their stated values. Do any of us?

What these companies do is *try*. They've remembered the fundamental values that Mom taught all of us, and they *try* to live by them and work by them. What these companies do is set importance on goals in addition to money. They make mistakes, sometimes awful ones. They're *ordinary* companies trying to achieve *extraordinary* goals. And they affect the lives of so many in numerous positive ways.

And they're not alone. There are, I'm certain, tens of thousands, maybe hundreds of thousands, of companies that bring Mom's fundamental values to the workplace. They just don't get a lot of coverage in the national news. After all, they don't do it for image, they do it because it's part of their character.

I chose to eliminate companies that have been covered extensively: Ben & Jerry's, Levi Strauss, Malden Mills. I felt honor-bound to eliminate both Gannett and Costco, both of which are regularly included in lists of great places to work or best places for women to work, since I write for them. I then, naturally, felt it only fair to eliminate their direct competitors, such as Knight-Ridder and Wal-Mart, which are also often listed among top places to work. As much as possible, I looked for a range of companies by size, geography, and age, to show that being values centered works in Brooklyn or Boise, whether your company has 75,000 employees or 75.

Very early on in my plan for this book, I identified Disney as an outstanding example of a company that had learned the importance of its core values—"eating your vegetables"—when it resurrected animation. (I interviewed Michael Eisner and Roy Disney prior to Disney's acquisition of ABC/Cap Cities.) I selected two other companies in a "backward" fashion: Kinko's and Zingerman's Deli. My theory is that a company with consistently great products and service probably has consistently good management. I had been a customer of Kinko's for more than a decade, and I knew they had to be doing something right. And my former assistant Ann Smitherman raved about Zingerman's, which proved, after investigation, to be one of the most impressive, and certainly valued-based, companies I've ever seen. And I don't even like pastrami!

I then spent months visiting and interviewing these companies. In most cases, I had a chance to interview the founder, chairman, or CEO, as well as a number of employees. Generally, I directed each company as to the kinds of employees I wanted to interview rather than having it choose its "model" employees, and sometimes I wandered around and interviewed employees at will. It wasn't a scientific process, but I believe I got a good sense of the companies. One of the truly surprising aspects of this whole endeavor was how extremely *reluctant* these companies were to be interviewed, to be included in this book. I was taken totally by surprise; I'm used to companies beating on my door seeking publicity.

Frankly, I have impeccable credentials for getting in the door at most companies. I've had my own business column with Gannett News Service since 1992; my experience in all those years is that I just say the word "Gannett" (owner of *USA Today*) and my calls get returned. I already had

I wanted to be able to encourage and support my clients when they confided that they longed to build companies that provided meaning as well as money.

So how did I select the companies I included in this book?

I started by listing those qualities I valued and that I had seen contribute to success in a business setting. Another person might come up with a slightly different list, but I think the values I identified are fairly universal.

These included such things as a unifying sense of purpose, a willingness to try new things, loyalty, honesty, a belief in the innate worth of individuals, trust, tolerance of failure, personal responsibility, sharing of financial gains, recognition of employees' critical contributions, treating everyone with respect. In other words—integrity.

Then I added one other crucial ingredient: the ability to run a profitable, successful company. Anyone can run an unprofitable company, after all, with or without great values. The challenge was to find those who could run a profitable company *with* great values.

I didn't want to focus just on *programs;* I wasn't interested so much in policies and programs, the things that most organizations rate companies on. Part of the reason was that that information is already out there. Robert Levering and Milton Moskowitz identify programs as part of their rating of the one hundred best companies to work for (see Bibliography). But mostly, I wanted to focus on the values at the core of a company.

And that's just as well: some of these companies certainly wouldn't win any contests for their employee programs. Take 3M, for example. There's no child care center, no gym, no free soft drink machines, none of the amenities we've come to expect (at least here in Silicon Valley). In fact, the single most desired perk at 3M is a *parking space.* To get a covered space at 3M takes about seventeen to twenty years on the waiting list. 3M is in St. Paul, Minnesota. Yet 3M has managed to keep employees happy while making them walk long distances in minus-35-degree weather. Go figure!

I next identified a number of companies that I suspected incorporated those values. I'd been collecting files for years. I then collected as many of the "100 Best Companies" types of lists and recipients of various business awards. Next, I solicited input about companies from business colleagues, investment groups, and organizations that monitor businesses for social responsibility.

There's a common perception that the only way a company can succeed is to behave in just such a fashion. After all, the business world today is so competitive and profit margins often so thin that we easily believe that companies must do everything they can, however objectionable or mean-spirited, to squeeze every penny out of every dollar if they're to survive.

But they don't have to. For much of a year, I visited many wonderful companies that had found a different way to succeed—companies that create nourishing, creative, supportive environments for their employees, deal fairly and honestly with their customers and suppliers, and are good citizens of their communities, while still making great profits year after year. I've referred to them as *extraordinary companies,* but they are extraordinary only in how much they achieve, not because they're alone.

Great companies all over the country, all over the world, have realized that the way to achieve success—the key to creating a truly great company—is to build a business on a solid foundation of *core values* that drive a company's behavior and decision making, and to have a bigger goal than merely increasing profits or enhancing shareholder returns.

They learned, long ago, that the way to get ahead in business, as in life, is by embracing the timeless values we all learned when we were young—sharing, taking responsibility, and not picking on one another—the lessons we learned from Mom. These companies run their businesses in ways Mom could be proud of.

And it's time their stories were told, so we can all learn that the best way to run a company is the way Mom advised, by *wearing clean underwear.*

So How Did I End Up in Waterloo?

I had been wanting to write this book for years. I'd been eager to have a chance to examine companies that strove for goals higher than just the bottom line, companies that made a sincere effort to treat employees with respect and to give them the opportunity to grow, businesses that valued their reputation and dealt with everyone honestly and fairly. I knew that such companies existed. As a business writer, I wanted to share those examples. As an entrepreneur who has started a couple of businesses myself, I wanted to learn more about these great companies. And as a consultant,

This Job Is Paradise

The time I spent working on this book has been the most professionally satisfying time in my life. Every day I dealt with people who were happy to go to work. Every day I saw people being treated the way all people should be treated—with respect, trust, and belief in their abilities and essential goodness.

And it's a good thing that I was enjoying myself, because, let me tell you, it could have been hard to take all those happy employees if I hadn't been so satisfied as well. In fact, I hope I don't depress any readers by making them realize that it is actually possible to enjoy going to work. Instead, I hope I encourage business owners and managers to realize the potential of building an extraordinary company by using Mom's fundamental lessons.

So I want to thank the people at Villard for giving me this opportunity, and the people at the companies in this book for sharing their stories.

When Andy Ouderkirk of 3M said to me about his work, "This job is paradise," I was honestly able to reply, "Mine is too, Andy. My job, too, has been paradise."

WEAR CLEAN UNDERWEAR

1

Why the Time Is Right for Thinking like Mom

We all remember familiar sayings and lessons from our mothers:

"I don't care who made this mess, just clean it up!"
"Eat your vegetables, or you don't get dessert."
"Wear clean underwear; what if you get into an accident and somebody sees it?"

Hearing them again, we may smile—or perhaps grimace—when we catch ourselves saying them to our own children. But we rarely imagine these sayings could apply to us as adults, particularly in a business setting.

But lessons from mothers offer a unique and memorable response to finding new ways to understand business as we approach the twenty-first century. In a time of great change, Mom's timeless wisdom, her fundamental values, are not only desperately needed, but are also enormously effective, in business life today.

Moms everywhere have developed an almost universal language to achieve their goals and instill common values. Virtually everyone's mother at one time or another said, "Clean your plate, children are starving in China"—or whatever country happened to be in the news. Think about all the lessons in that one little line: don't waste your resources, realize that you are more fortunate than others, empathize with those who have less. Mom could teach you a lot just while getting you to eat your green beans. Mom still has a lot to teach us, even how to help us run our businesses.

Who Can I Turn To?

Many years ago, I found myself sitting on a stool in a friend's kitchen, perplexed. I had been in charge of a staff for about a year: making the decisions, enforcing the rules, setting the tone. I was in my twenties, a young woman in a job usually held by a man, trying to prove myself. It had been a rough year.

When I had started the job, I had found an office in disarray. People showed up and departed at any hour; work was sloppy; the financial picture was gloomy. For the first two weeks after my arrival, whenever I'd make a suggestion for an improvement, I'd get the reply "That's not how we do it around here." Well, I quickly had enough of that. I called a staff meeting and laid down the law: "The way I want it done *is* the way we do it around here. No ifs, ands, or buts. This is not a democracy."

Shortly thereafter, my secretary quit.

Playing the tough guy, however, didn't feel natural or right to me. I just wasn't that kind of person. And this "my way or the highway" mentality meant I ended up spending my time enforcing rules instead of getting the staff to do a great job.

So after a while I softened up, shifted in the other direction. I not only stopped telling employees *how* to do their tasks, I also hesitated to tell them *what* to do. Instead, I became friends with staff members, socializing outside the office, sharing personal problems and intimacies while at work. We became more like a club, a bunch of friends getting together. The workplace was enjoyable, but a lot of time was wasted.

One day, a staff member (with whom I went to dance class every week and swapped stories about dating and boyfriends) came and told me she was going to take her vacation at our busiest time of the year. Yikes! We couldn't afford to be shorthanded just then; I told her I wouldn't approve her vacation request. She was stunned and hurt by both the interference and the rejection. After all, she'd come to think of me as a friend, not a boss. What right did I have to disrupt her vacation plans?

Shortly thereafter, she quit too. I wasn't doing too well at this boss thing.

That's how I ended up in my friend's kitchen that December. I was seeking his advice on how to be a manager. "How do you manage people so you have authority and respect without being a policeman? How do you motivate people to want to do the work and do a good job, not just make them afraid? How do you create an inclusive workplace without letting everyone walk all over you and just do what they want?" We talked over the issues for hours, and then I set about looking for answers.

Role models were hard to find. Popular business books were no help. They advised me to emulate Attila the Hun or behave like a shark; to win through intimidation or spend only one minute managing. At four feet, eleven inches, I could hardly play the role of an intimidating, sharklike Hun. And that hardly reflected my personality or my value system.

Looking around, I had a hard time finding answers in the companies and managers I saw in real life. At that time, even small businesses and nonprofit organizations were structured to emulate big business: one of the managers' primary goals was to make certain their "underlings" carried out corporate directives. Decisions were made at the highest levels, and *obedience* was a highly valued employee trait. Managers often focused more on whether a report was filed than on the work the report was reporting about. In a not atypical example, I once received a memo from a boss reprimanding me for using a paper clip rather than a staple on an expense report; he sent copies of this to five different departments, including one for my permanent personnel file.

Okay, so I knew what not to do. But where was a role model that spoke to me? I desperately needed a new kind of role model that fit both my life and my business needs. I wasn't alone.

Homegrown Leadership

So I turned to a role model of a leader who is so close, so familiar, that we often fail to consider her a *manager* at all: Mom.

Generally, when someone talks about Mom as a manager, they think of Mom handling the household budget, getting the meals on the table and the kids out the door. Mom definitely has those kinds of management responsibilities. But I'm talking about Mom as a role model of a group *leader*, not merely the family's chief operating officer.

Think of some of the words we now associate with business: growth, development, maturity, incubating (a new business), and, increasingly, nurturing. These are all words we also associate with mothering. Today's business leader has the same goal as a mother leading her family: to encourage the individual members of a group to maintain common values and standards yet to successfully act autonomously in diverse situations, and also pull together as a cohesive unit, assisting others in their development.

The role model of mother as manager clearly differs from the traditional view of manager. *Managing* is when you try to impose an outside order, regardless of someone's internal nature. Mothers who *manage* their children do only a very small part of their job; it's usually what they fall back on only when things are about to get out of control. A mother's goal is not to manage; it is to teach, nurture, sustain, guide. Mom also monitors her group's interaction and communication, making certain stronger or louder members of the group don't overpower the weaker or quieter. Mom recognizes and develops the unique contributions and strengths of each individual and makes every member feel valued. Mom celebrates successes and consoles when there are failures. That's a pretty good job description for a business manager today.

Clearly, the time is right for thinking like Mom.

Hell, No, We Won't Go!

Have you seen the bumper sticker that says "Question authority"? Odds are, it's a baby boomer who had that bumper sticker plastered on an old VW bug.

In my father's day, employees went to work, did their jobs, and gave their loyalty and, more important, their *obedience* to their employer. You listened to your boss, who listened to his boss, who listened to his boss, who listened to the man in charge. (They were all men.) That's how work got done.

Then a revolution in social thinking occurred in the 1960s and 1970s. Baby boomers, the huge group of children born after World War II through the 1950s, grew up with a different relationship to those in charge. Rules were suspect; authority was to be challenged. "Don't trust anybody over thirty" was the mantra. Hardly the ideal employee for a 1950s-style corporation.

And what happened when the boomers with the bumper stickers became the authorities they'd been questioning all those years? The responsibility of management didn't fit well. Baby boomers were uncomfortable with the traditional role of rule-enforcing manager.

Today, Generation Xers are similarly restless as they move into leadership. Even more than their boomer parents, those in their twenties and early thirties were raised to believe in thinking independently rather than taking orders. They don't want to create or accept management structures based on obedience. In fact, over the last century, the concept of obedience has been replaced by the value of independence. In 1890, 64 percent of parents said that obedience was one of the three most important character traits for a child. In 1978, only 17 percent of parents valued obedience that highly. Conversely, in 1890, only 16 percent of parents wanted their children to be independent; by the late 1970s, 75 percent of parents felt that independence was the most important character trait.

If you keep trying to put an independence-seeking workforce into an obedience-demanding workplace, something has to give.

The Knowledge-Based Economy

Fortunately, the business world changed too. The nineteenth and twentieth centuries saw the world of business evolve from small groups into big corporations and back to small groups again. Before the Industrial Revolution, work was almost always performed by small units: families, communities. Most industries were cottage industries. In a nonmechanized, nonindustrialized economy, there was little advantage to or purpose for large organizations. Being big brought no economies of scale.

The advantages of big business developed along with the industrial and technological inventions of the nineteenth and mid-twentieth centuries and the concept of interchangeable parts and the assembly line. The goal of such businesses was to produce consistent, uniform products as quickly, cheaply, and efficiently as possible. The aim of management was to control individuals' behavior so each participant acted identically in a carefully designed environment. With such an objective, it was not necessary or desirable for individual workers to think. Thank you, Eli Whitney!

These businesses looked and behaved a lot like the military. Historically, in an army, foot soldiers have been required to follow orders, not think. So large industrial businesses took the military as their role model. Corporations were structured as top-down hierarchies with orders from "generals" on high being relayed through layers of management, the "lieutenants" and "sergeants." A typical management organization chart looked like this:

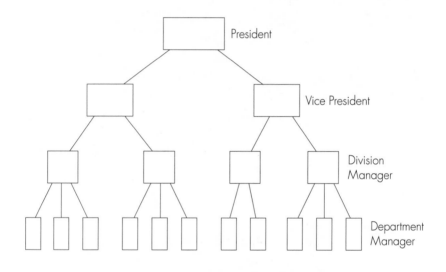

Technology changed all that. Technological innovations radically altered both the nature of what businesses produce or sell, and the way information is shared throughout a company.

Today, much of what companies sell is not a product at all but information—knowledge—or a service. Think about software; what is the product? The floppy disk the software comes on? The CD-ROM? Those have virtually no value in and of themselves (in fact, you can download software from the Internet and never have a tangible product at all). The value is in the functionality, the data, the *knowledge*. To produce a knowledge product, employees must think. Employees who create or interact with data and knowledge, who do the work itself, often know far more than their bosses. (Ask any software programmer or budget analyst!) In a business where the product is a *service,* employees themselves often create

What Scott Adams Learned from His Mother, Virginia Adams

My mother gave me one of the most useful life tips I've ever gotten. I remember it vividly. When I was a little kid, she'd be making dinner, and I'd be watching TV. She'd turn to me and ask, "Scott, do you want peas or corn?" We had both, and they both came out of a can and were equally easy.

I'd say something like, "I don't care." And she'd stop everything she was doing. "There'll be no dinner until you make up your mind. Life is full of decisions; many of them are random, and you have to learn to choose."

My mother taught me how important it was to make a decision and just get on with it. I'm the world's most decisive person on unimportant matters. I've got a keener sense of what to ignore and what to take time deciding than anyone I know. My mother grew up on a farm in upstate New York, and I worked on it when I was little. The farm mentality was just to make a decision and get on with it.

I constantly deal with people who can't choose a meal off the menu or, when they go to an ice-cream shop, can't decide from the myriad of choices. I've got a pool table in my office, and I've had guests who, after the break, can't decide whether they want the solids or stripes.

My mother taught me that 99 percent of everything you do is unimportant. You may think it's important at the time, but you have to step out and look at it from 35,000 feet. Ultimately none of those choices matter.

---

the product, frequently on the spot, or are themselves the product. (Ask any hairdresser, lawyer, or auto mechanic!) These employees, too, must think.

The Information Age depends on knowledge and creativity, not uniformity. The old hierarchical models of business don't fit. Companies instead need flatter, "horizontal," distributed management structures, where decision making and authority are close to those who must act on these decisions. So once again, the best way to organize work is in small groups or teams, each with a great deal of autonomy.

But employees and teams shouldn't be completely independent and isolated from the organization as a whole. In this age of the "empowered worker," managers have a new goal: to make certain everyone in the organization understands and maintains common goals and standards while acting independently and creatively. Managers help team members communicate with one another and with the larger organization. And a manager has to help employees learn how to think—hardly a model of a general issuing orders to his troops!

Take Me Out to the Ball Game

Next, business resigned from the army and signed up for football. Today's popular analogy for an organization is a sports team. Companies are now organized in "teams." Managers have become "coaches." We all switched uniforms, trading in fatigues for jerseys. Whew! That's a lot more comfortable.

The analogy of sports, with their teams, coaches, and opponents, offers many advantages over the militaristic analogy of soldiers, generals, and enemies. On a team, we recognize individual members' contributions and abilities; they're not uniform foot soldiers. Teams work together, pull together. There's team spirit, and teams get to have fun. Coaches don't just issue orders; they guide, assist, develop. They are more helpful, more buddylike, more equal. They may run plays, but they don't call all the shots. Sports is definitely a more positive, upbeat, friendly model than the military.

The problem with the sports metaphor is that it still focuses on beating someone else. Yes, you may now want to crush the competition instead of killing the enemy, but your focus is still primarily outward. The goal is to *win*. This orientation doesn't focus on the long-term health and well-being of a business, just on getting a higher score in today's game. It's focused not on developing the skills, talents, and resources of your own group, especially over time, but on taking away the strength of your opponent. Each time one side wins, the other loses. Such a competitive orientation eats up, instead of building up, your internal resources.

Perhaps most important, with a competitive orientation, your business and your actions are fueled not by your own values, but by a desire to beat the other guy. That makes for some fairly hollow victories. You better get a pretty terrific Super Bowl ring.

Today, people in business want more than just to win for winning's sake. They seek a bigger victory than just beating a competitor, landing a end of the day, you told her you'd had fun. Mom could help you overcome your fears by being there for you, pushing you a little, encouraging you a lot, and applauding your success.

Making things less scary for *you* was the easy part. But when risk was involved, Mom had her own fears to overcome. Watching you ride your first bike, cross your first street, or drive your first car was tough on Mom. Sure, she wanted you to grow, but she also wanted you to be safe. Sometimes, to help you get over your fears, Mom would have to conquer her own. The hard part was making it less scary for *Mom*.

I remember how I felt watching my niece Adeena when she was about five years old. Adeena and I were at a playground, along with Adeena's mother, my sister Karen. Adeena quickly scrambled up the stairs of the slide, leapt from one rung to the next on the crossbars, and gleefully climbed to the top of the jungle gym. Watching her, my heart was pounding, and I found myself holding my breath because I was so scared. Karen, however, offered Adeena only encouraging words.

"Aren't you afraid she'll fall?" I asked Karen.

"Sure," Karen admitted, "but if I don't let her take some chances, she'll never be confident."

Growing in capabilities and confidence requires trying new things, taking risks. Trying new things—whether spaghetti or skiing, supervising or sales—can be pretty scary, pretty "yucky." But risk is a part of all life and a critical part of business life. We need someone to make the world a safer place for us to take risks. Like kids, we need a helpful push, support when we fall, applause when we succeed. We need Mom gently encouraging us, "How do you know you don't like it when you've never tried it?"

A Business Quiz

You're the CEO of a Fortune 500 company with a large research and development budget. One of your company's scientists, a brainy physical chemist, invents a new product. This scientist is also working on a number of other important scientific developments. He has no marketing or product management background. This particular new product appears to have the potential to make your company billions of dollars. It is so versatile that the possible uses are mind-boggling, spanning industrial, commercial, con-

2

How Do You Know You Don't Like It When You've Never Tried It?

"One bite. Take just one bite."
"No."
"C'mon, just one bite. Spaghetti tastes good."
"I don't like it. It's yucky."
"I'll take a bite first. Yum, delicious."
"No! I don't like it."
"How do you know you don't like it when you've never tried it?"

You can't grow if you don't try new things. Mom knew this. But new things are scary. Mom knew this too. She understood that when you said, "I don't like it," often what you meant was "I'm afraid." Mom knew it was part of her job to help you overcome your fears and broaden your experience. Sometimes it was a battle—why couldn't she just leave you alone? But if Mom had never gotten you to try spaghetti or pet a dog or put your face into the water while swimming, your life would be a lot more limited and a lot less fun.

Mom made things less frightening for you by creating an atmosphere, an environment, that encouraged experimentation and risk taking. Before you went to your first day of school, Mom talked to you about it days or weeks ahead, maybe read you a book about school or took you there to look around. She went with you the first day and held your hand. She understood why you were frightened and showed her delight when, at the

What If I Don't Like My Mother?

I am, of course, using Ward and June as the archetypes for Dad and Mom. Very few of us had the Cleavers as parents. All parents are flawed, and our own were no exception. Most of us have some conflicts about our parents, and some of us had just plain bad mothers. You don't have to have liked your mother to understand the value of Mom's lessons. You don't have to value motherhood—or apple pie, for that matter—to want to bring values and integrity into your life and the lives of others.

This book isn't about *your* mother—it's about the *archetype* of mother. The Mom in this book is the idealized mother, the one who, if we could have designed her, would have wanted us to be our best, truest selves. Who believed in us and gave us confidence. Who was quick to praise and slow to blame. Who cared about us. The lessons in this book reflect the fundamental values of Mom, who taught us right from wrong, who taught us to think, to care, and to be decent human beings.

This book is about the kind of mom who taught us to "Wear clean underwear; what if you get into an accident and someone sees it?" Mom wasn't really worried about an ambulance driver checking out your BVDs. What she wanted was for you to do the right thing, even when no one could see.

Companies, too, need to do the right thing; they need to get back in touch with the timeless wisdom as expressed by Mom. Mom's fundamental values, it turns out, are the best guidelines for a successful business—successful not only in terms of profits but in the contributions they make to their employees, their communities, and the happiness and well-being of their owners.

Now more than ever, in our personal lives, our political lives, and our business lives, we see that Mom was right all along. Mom's fundamental values build extraordinary character. They build extraordinary people. They build extraordinary businesses. The time is right for thinking like Mom.

customer, or reaching a sales goal. They want work they can believe in, an extension of their values. They want pride—a pride that comes not just from winning but from feeling good about what they do and what their work contributes to the world. They want integrity. They want to get back into touch with the fundamental values they learned from Mom.

Do We Have to Wear Pearls?

"What do you have to say for yourself, young man?"—Ward Cleaver
"Ward, when you talk to Wally, will you let him know you're on his side?"—June Cleaver

In two lines from that classic business reference *Leave It to Beaver,* Ward and June demonstrate the difference between the old-style manager and today's manager; a patriarchal style of leadership and a style with Mom as role model.

Ward is the traditional authority figure. He comes home from his day at the office and demands that everything run smoothly, the way he wants. He's established rules; Wally and the Beaver (and, to a large extent, June) must follow them. When they do, they're rewarded; when they don't, Ward administers punishment or sends a reprimand to their personnel file.

June builds the group. She's there when the Beaver needs her. She monitors the family dynamics. She keeps Wally from browbeating or teasing the Beaver. She gives Wally, the Beaver, and Ward individual attention, and she's far more understanding than Ward when the Beaver expresses his own unique personality. June gets everybody talking to one another, soothes and smooths problems. June doesn't judge; she helps, she guides, she mothers.

Ward wants Wally and the Beaver to do what he tells them. But June knows there will be many times when neither Ward nor she will be around and the kids will need to have internalized the values underlying Ward's rules. They had better be able to think and act independently in a wide variety of situations. And they had better *want* and *accept* the standards, not just be afraid of punishment. June knows she can't just rely on the threat "Wait till your father gets home."

sumer, and medical applications—*everything from computer components to surgical room equipment to toys to sporting goods to Las Vegas lighting.*

As CEO, you need to put someone in charge of this groundbreaking product. Do you:

1. *Assign the product to the aggressive and brilliant senior vice president who spearheaded your company's last major successful product launch, building an experienced marketing, scientific, manufacturing, and administrative team around her?*
2. *Hire the best management consulting firm in the country to determine which markets to pursue based on a thorough competitive analysis of each major potential product line, including detailed financial projections and pricing structures?*
3. *Let the product stay in the hands of the brainy, bookish chemist-inventor, a few other scientists, and a young marketing executive, allowing them to choose markets for the product based on their judgment and what they think is "cool"?*

Keep reading. I'll give you the answer shortly.

How to Think like an Entrepreneur

A few years ago, I put together a training course for a Fortune 500 company on "How to Think like an Entrepreneur." Like many major corporations, they had come to realize that in today's business environment, companies and their employees must be able to act entrepreneurially, regardless of the size of the business. Today, whether we run a large corporation or a small business, we want our employees to start thinking like owners—nurturing customer relationships, controlling expenses, initiating solutions, taking responsibility.

During my training program, I taught many key concepts of entrepreneurship: identifying and evaluating business opportunities, anticipating and responding to various types of change, understanding and targeting markets, developing strategic and competitive positions. I covered the essential concepts and skills necessary to react quickly to changing market conditions and to bring new approaches to old problems.

But what I couldn't teach, couldn't develop, at least not in a two-day session, were the essential *attitudes* of entrepreneurship. An entrepreneurial organization requires entrepreneurial people and an entrepreneurial culture. You can't just plop a book down in front of an employee (even, dare I say, one of *my* books) and suddenly expect a twenty-year veteran of a large corporation to start acting and thinking like the owner of a business start-up.

Getting employees to act entrepreneurially is the corporate equivalent of getting a kid to try spaghetti. It can look pretty yucky. After all, entrepreneurs take risks, try lots of new things, and do what needs to be done, regardless of job title or training. Entrepreneurs stuff their own envelopes, make their own sales, clean their own floors. If we want employees to "Act as if you own the business," we can't just issue a directive. Like Mom, we've got to create an environment, build an infrastructure, that makes it safe to try new things. We have to help employees become comfortable being entrepreneurial. We have to help them try it.

A Business School Professor's Nightmare

One of the basic tenets of business strategy is that you must understand your core business. You've got to know what business you're in if you're going to compete effectively. But as I went around 3M, I repeatedly asked people to tell me what business 3M was in. After they paused and thought about it, the answers were usually on the order of "We make stuff." Sometimes they were somewhat more explicit: "We make *new* stuff." One person managed an even more clearly articulated position: "We make *new* stuff *that makes money.*"

Now, I have to tell you, if a client came to me with a company mission statement consisting of "We make new stuff that makes money," I'd tell that person to come up with a new mission statement.

3M does indeed make stuff. Lots and lots of stuff, 50,000 different products. And I mean *different*—the range of 3M products is daunting. Driving out to the 3M campus, I started thinking about a few of the 3M products surrounding me at that moment: the safety film in my car's window, the reflective material on the traffic signs, the Thinsulate lining of my gloves, the Scotchgard I had sprayed on my shoes, possibly some adhesive in my dental work, and, of course, my beloved Post-it notes. This from a company that started by making (and still sells) sandpaper!

You'll notice that there is no rhyme or reason to these products, no apparent common denominator. It's just a lot of different stuff. Good stuff that still outperforms its competitors. And still makes money.

But at 3M it works. It works because 3M is defined not by product lines or a vague statement of mission but by a clear, strong set of values and a very powerful corporate culture. Because while 3M fits into no specific business category, the company knows exactly what business it is in: "innovation." 3M's stated vision is to be "The most innovative enterprise in the world."

3M has put a number on that particular goal: at least 30 percent of each year's sales must come from products introduced in the previous four years. This means they must constantly reinvent themselves. And they've raised the bar even higher: new products must be *new*. 3M's "Pacing Plus" program requires each business unit to create at least one breakthrough product *that changes the basis of competition*. In other words, each unit must develop a product so new, so different that it revolutionizes the business they are in. So they've not only to invent a lot of new stuff, but to invent a lot of *exceptional* new stuff.

You don't think up exceptional products or services by doing a lot of market research or conducting focus groups. Customers may be able to define problems, but you have to come up with solutions. Customers may be able to suggest refinements to products; truly innovative products have to come from within your own company. Innovation is homegrown, not the result of a poll.

"Innovation is about doing what delights the customer, not just satisfying the customer," observed Geoff Nicholson, 3M's staff vice president of corporate technical planning. "It's giving the customer something they didn't expect. They can't ask for it because they can't know what it is before it is created." But sometimes, as with masking tape, Scotch tape, or Post-its, once it has been invented, customers can't imagine ever having lived without it.

But you can't invent revolutionary products in a conservative environment. You have to let people think and act outside their corporate "boxes," unlimited by job descriptions, corporate ladders, or organizational hierarchies. You have to create an atmosphere of innovation.

Surprisingly, the word I heard employees use repeatedly to describe 3M's environment was "nourishing." Over and over, employees told me how "nutritious" it was working at 3M. Since there was no evidence of even so much as a cup of coffee, let alone a carrot stick or cookie, outside the employee cafeteria, I doubt they were speaking of 3M's culinary offerings. No, I think what 3M employees were referring to is the atmosphere that encourages them to taste new intellectual and business offerings; to fill up on information and assistance from whatever source they wish; to take a bite whenever something appeals to their appetite. Go ahead, is the message they get—try it. You might like it.

Even a Diamond Hurts

Andy Ouderkirk doesn't look like a risk-taking entrepreneur. Meeting me, Andy seemed to involuntarily shrink down his six-foot, one-inch frame, almost embarrassed to be so tall. He is unfailingly polite, quiet to the point you have to strain to hear him, diffident. He chooses his words carefully, making certain nothing reflects poorly on his employer, 3M. Sitting in his nondescript beige office, Andy seems the ideal employee—loyal, hardworking, easygoing; the kind of guy who knows exactly how much he has in his 401(K) and how many months he has before retirement. Seeing him in Minnesota, it's easier to imagine Andy as a model citizen of Lake Wobegon rather than a role model in Silicon Valley.

Looks, however, can be deceiving. In fact, it wasn't easy being Andy Ouderkirk's boss. Ask any mom. She'll tell you her most adventurous child was her biggest challenge. The obedient children are easy. It's the spunky ones who make you tear your hair out; one minute you want to hug them, the next you want to kill them. And you never quite know whether the spunk is going to lead to greatness or grief.

The same was true with Andy. Beneath his mild-mannered exterior, Andy had an inquiring mind and a restless spirit that were uncomfortable with corporate protocol and bureaucracy. In many companies, Andy would have been either causing trouble or in trouble, if not both. If it hadn't been for 3M's policy of allowing employees to use 15 percent of their time on projects of their own choosing, Andy might never have been able to fit into corporate life at all. As it was, he was often a handful for his boss, Yvonne Cadwallader.

"There were always reports to be written," recalled Yvonne, her voice still reflecting her frustration. "I had to chase Andy down, and he wasn't always easy to find. Time sheets? He was late every month. He was always

---

What Andy Ouderkirk Learned from His Mother, Ruth K. Ouderkirk

My mother is an artist. She was always teaching me not to be afraid, to try anything, learn everything. She told me to experience everything you can in as many different areas as you can.

In particular, my mother taught me a tremendous sense of experimentation with food. She and I formed a team to try interesting things. I particularly remember when I was eleven years old when we were in Mexico, at Isla de Mujeres. She ordered octopus for us. Only she and I ate it, not my father or brothers. It was great, tasted like beef.

My mother is an excellent cook, and she taught me to cook. She taught me, "Never cook anything the same way twice; always experiment, always improve."

I think this influenced my choice of chemistry as a profession. I'm always trying to influence what things do. That's just like cooking. I'm trying to create a certain result rather than just waiting to see what happens.

---

like that. I once told him, 'Andy, you're a diamond. But even a diamond in a shoe hurts.' "

Andy is a good example of the tension that occurs when you put inventive, entrepreneurial people into a corporate culture. If you don't find an appropriate outlet for their creativity, there's going to be a whole lot of chafing going on. On both sides.

In 1991, Andy was working in 3M's central corporate lab on what sounds like a scintillating assignment: trying to find a new adhesive for a film backing for tape. As part of this search, Andy was taking one thin layer of film and heating it with a laser to see what happened, how it might be useful as an adhesive.

But like all true, trained scientists, Andy was a careful observer. Looking at the now-melted film backing, Andy noticed a reflection. Echoing almost the exact words of Art Fry, the inventor of Post-its, Andy recalled, "It was such a huge effect. It had to be good for something." A true entrepreneurial attitude: give me something new, and I'll build a business around it.

Andy showed me the original piece of film. Now, I couldn't see anything that was "reflective," certainly nothing huge. But Andy's the scientist, not me. Andy then turned the film to reflect the light, and he pointed out a teensy bit of iridescent color, the type of shiny reflection you would see if there were a tiny drop of oil in a puddle of water in a parking lot.

Andy didn't have any idea what this reflective ability might be good for. But he was curious. And 3M's culture encourages people to pursue ideas they find interesting. 3M's "15% Rule" allows employees to use 15 percent of their time on projects of their own choosing, regardless of assignment. Andy wondered what would happen if you put hundreds of layers of this laser-melted film together. He knew that the best mirrors are made from multilayer technology. What was the possibility of this material being really reflective if you layered it? Why not try it?

What Makes Silicon Valley "Silicon Valley"?

Now, here's where a culture that encourages employees to try new things, act outside their "boxes," makes a difference. Andy was able to line up the resources he needed to pursue his ideas without any involvement of the 3M corporate hierarchy. If he wanted to try something, he could just go ahead and try it. No approvals needed, no official channels to go through.

I live in Silicon Valley, and I know that communities all over the world want to create another Silicon Valley. Surprisingly, and without knowing it, 3M provides many of the same nutrients for their internal new developments as does Silicon Valley for theirs.

One of the striking things about Silicon Valley that enables it to produce the innovative breakthroughs that it does is a willingness to share information and an ability to secure the resources needed to pursue ideas. Most people identify Silicon Valley's infrastructure as the universities, the availability of venture capital, and the established high-tech firms. The formal stuff. But there's a larger informal network. Not only are there dozens of organizations in which budding entrepreneurs assist one another, but there's a general willingness to help entrepreneurs get started. I found this out when I was starting an Internet business. In early 1995, I heard Andrew Anker, then president of HotWired, speak at a Software Forum event. I went up to him afterward and asked if I could take him to lunch one day and get some advice. Andrew's response: "Sure, I can do that." I found the same helpfulness repeated over and over by people such as Bill Rollinson of the Internet Shopping Network, Mark Gorenberg of the venture firm Hummer Winblad Venture Capital, and Randy Haykin of Yahoo. At the time, I didn't know a URL from a UFO, but the people I met were open, helpful, and approachable.

3M has its own version of this same sharing culture, and that's what makes big payoffs possible. There are many formal ways of exchanging information, such as "Tech Forums," to disseminate new developments from one part of the company to anyone else who's interested. But more important, there's a commitment to sharing information informally, without regard to rank. At 3M, anyone can talk to anyone else; everyone helps everyone else. When your phone rings at 3M, you pick it up, and if a colleague needs help or advice, you give it, even if you're busy. It doesn't matter what department or division, what level, what discipline. It doesn't matter if that person has a formal assignment or is working on "15 percent time." Everyone talks to one another. It's part of your job, your company, your family. You share.

Andy knew that. "At other places, there's a hierarchy, an organizational chart," he recalled. "If I was going to contact a person [in another department], I had to work through the management chain. If you did other than that, you were at risk."

At 3M, the Tech Forums are particularly good ways for employees to meet one another, cross-fertilize their ideas, share information, and assist one another. Andy said he hadn't been planning to fool around much with the multilayer reflective film idea, but then he had gone to a Tech Forum where James Jonza, who was in the Verification System Laboratory, was speaking. Afterward he went up to Jim, showed him his laser-melted, reflective film, and said, "Could you put a bunch of layers of this stuff together for me?" (not in those exact words, of course), and Jim said, "Sure, we can do that." Andy was on his way.

You Light Up My Life

The result of putting together all those layers was a really, really shiny film. This was getting exciting. Andy started looking for a couple of other people to help out, asking them to volunteer their 15 percent time, and the team gave the film the code name Stratus. Stratus presented a lot of scientific and technical challenges. For smart guys, this was really fun. And rewarding. They came up with what Andy, a truly modest man, calls "the world's best mirror."

Let me transmit to you a little lesson I learned from Andy about light. Light can be either transmitted, absorbed, or reflected:

A window mostly transmits light.

A black dress mostly absorbs light (and makes you look thin).

A mirror mostly reflects light.

A mirror reflecting light looks shiny because light bounces back at you instead of being absorbed or passing through. Not all mirrors reflect the same amount of light. Those horrible mirrors made out of metal (so they couldn't break) in your junior high school bathroom absorbed a lot of light, so they weren't very reflective or shiny. Remember how gray they looked? That wasn't all dirt.

Stratus reflects an amazing amount of light; it is 99 percent reflective. (A sheet of Stratus looks like Mylar film, but a whole lot brighter.) So when you shine a light on it, a lot of light bounces back at you. This means you can use Stratus to make a little bit of light seem a whole lot brighter—as in a computer screen, on a traffic sign, in a light fixture. Unlike regular mirrors, Stratus reflects light without also reflecting heat—it's a "cold mirror," so you can use it to reflect light in places where you need the light but heat is harmful, such as in medical surgery or food displays. And one of Andy's fellow scientists, Mike Weber, discovered ways to make Stratus in any color, so you can use it for decorative purposes such as wrapping paper or for graphics. The possible uses are mind-boggling. It's a really bright invention.

Did that shed enough light on the subject for you?

And the Answer Is . . .

So now Andy had this great material, Stratus. It had the potential to be a major technology for 3M, possibly worth billions of dollars.

Remember our Business Quiz? Who should 3M put in charge of this new technology? "1," the hotshot VP? "2," the management consulting firm? "3," the brilliant, bookish chemist?

Obviously, either 1 or 2 is less risky. That's in the short term. If Stratus is going to be the only product 3M makes for the next ten years, perhaps they should take it away from Andy. But if you want to build a culture of entrepreneurs, if you want to create hundreds of breakthrough products, you've got to let your employees take risks. You've got to let them take ownership. You've got to let them climb jungle gyms even if you have to hold your breath. You've got to let them try it.

That's what 3M did, and the answer, of course, is "3"—Andy Ouderkirk, entrepreneur.

Just Trust Me

As is normally the case at 3M, Andy now had to head up the show, wear all the hats, while still doing his "real" job. This fits the classic mold of an entrepreneur—following a dream while not quitting your day job. Like any other real entrepreneur, Andy had to grow his invention, prove his market, line up resources, show it could be big. 3M helped by giving him a couple of grants. And he needed a little push from Mom.

Andy's boss, Yvonne Cadwallader, recognized that Stratus was getting too big for her group, and it didn't belong there anyway. Stratus wasn't about adhesives; Andy had set off in another direction.

"3M has this philosophy of letting people try new things, but at some point you have to give a program priority and resources," said Yvonne. "That didn't fit our charter. Carol Fatuzzo [Andy's technical director] and I were proud of Andy. We knew even then, and would say to each other, 'One day he'll be thought of like Art Fry,' but he didn't belong here anymore."

Andy had to make a choice. He had to either move to Stratus full-time or give it up and go back to work full-time on his responsibilities in Yvonne's area. It was Andy's choice to make. Even though 3M already believed in Stratus enough to give it two grants, the company's entrepreneurial culture means that a product has to have a real champion, a visionary, just like in the real world. Other companies might have dictated that Andy pursue Stratus—or have taken it away from him. Either way, Andy would have been resentful, and other inventors would have taken notice and been discouraged from pursuing their own visions. At 3M, Mom, in the form of his supervisor, Yvonne, gently pushed.

"The problem was, Andy didn't want to leave. So I had to make it easier for him. First I promised him he could keep his office here. We'd list him as on a sabbatical from this team, and he could keep his office here. Then he spent more and more time away. Finally, I said to him, 'I need your office for somebody else now. Can I move you? Andy, I need you to move out of your office.' He said, 'I don't want to. All my reasons are emotional. I don't want to go.' So I told him he could keep a couple of file cabinets here.

"It's like kicking kids out of the house," Yvonne observed. "You know it's good for them, but it can be painful on both sides. A lot of people in big corporations are more risk-averse than being out there [in the larger business world]. We like to stay where it feels good. Andy had all that. But it didn't mean it was the best place for him."

Yvonne had to make it easier. She had to push. She sounded a lot like Mom when she finally made Andy get Stratus established as a separate project. She told him, "Get out of here and just trust me. Everything will be all right."

A Revolution in Glitter

Andy was now running his own small business within 3M. 3M's philosophy is to start small and prove a market. You don't have to do a big market research study; you can just be interested in something.

This is unusual for big companies. I spoke with an executive at Kodak who had formerly been employed by 3M and a few other research-oriented major corporations. He told me that the thing that made 3M so inventive, so innovative, that set it apart from all the other companies he had been with, was that at 3M groups were allowed to play around, start small, and build a market. At the other companies, before setting up a project, a market research study would be done to demonstrate the market potential, then a big team would be established. At 3M, employees can just try things. Take just one bite. And then another. Of glitter, for instance.

One day, Lee Whitney, who was working with Andy on Stratus, was playing around with a sheet of the stuff and said, "Hey, I bet this would make great glitter."

Glitter? This is 3M, maker of adhesives and abrasives and industrial supplies. Glitter? Andy wasn't particularly interested, and neither was

The Glitter Girl

Michelle Bellanca was on a fast track when she got sidetracked by a tennis shoe. In 1995, the ink was hardly dry on Michelle's brand-new MBA when she was hired as a member of 3M's special "fast-track" program. If she stuck with it, after three years she would be guaranteed a product manager position with direct P and L responsibility.

Then someone told Michelle about a small volunteer group and she joined "eight ragtag guys," playing around with ways to develop sporting goods applications for 3M products. One day the team leader said, "Oh, Bill Coyne's interested in helping us out." Bill Coyne is 3M's senior vice president of research and development, one of the ten highest-ranking people in the entire company.

Now, Michelle is from Virginia. She's the kind of southern girl who still calls men "Sir" and women "Ma'am." But she was on her way, at twenty-six years of age, to meet the executive VP.

"I was sweating. They're like a teacher when you're a kid. I never imagined I'd have any interaction with someone at a director's level, let alone this level of the company. And then he walks in, just this happy, laid-back guy."

Over the following months, Michelle got used to Bill being part of the group's effort. He didn't come to all of the meetings, but he'd be there for certain milestones, and the meetings were casual, straightforward, and candid. From time to time Bill would pick up the phone to ask advice of one of them, or they'd call him. "You look at 3M, and it's this large company. But I'm part of this team. I've only been at the company three months, and the executive VP is asking my advice. It's astounding."

Once she started working with Stratus, Michelle knew what she had to do: she jumped off the fast track. Captivated by the product, the people, and the entrepreneurial risk taking, Michelle asked to be assigned to Stratus.

Besides, Stratus looked good on her. At a demonstration of toy products, Michelle held some of the prototype toys. Some of the Stratus glitter came off on her hands, and she unconsciously kept rubbing her face. Pretty soon, she was covered with gold, silver, and blue glitter. And Stratus glitter is very shiny; you can't miss it. Michelle was stuck with the glitter for a long time. And she's still stuck with the nickname "The Glitter Girl."

anybody else on the small team. In fact, they all laughed, but Lee thought it would be cool. So he went off to make glitter. It turned out that making glitter out of Stratus is not easy; it's hard to grind. But Lee stuck with it because he thought it would be really cool.

Finally, he made up a bunch of glitter. It *was* cool. It was really, really great glitter. So Lee picked up the phone and found the country's biggest glitter people (there are, I learned, glitter people), and he brought them in to see different-colored Stratus glitter. They took one look, nearly jumped out of their chairs, and cried, "*This* is a revolution in glitter!"

It turns out that there's a big glitter market. Glitter is used in, among other things, paints, cosmetics, toys, and security applications. 3M may eventually have a huge piece of the glitter market, all because Lee thought, "Hey, I bet this would make great glitter." Cool.

Does It Take a Rocket Scientist to Make a Barbie Dress? Or, Cross-Dress for Success

One of the noticeable things about 3M is that there isn't a lot of talk about employees' "cost effectiveness." No one ran a bunch of numbers to come up with 15 percent for the amount of time to be given to employees to pursue their own projects. Twenty-five percent just seemed like too much; 5 percent seemed as if the company didn't take the idea seriously.

The 15 percent Rule means that people don't have to spend all their time just in their own fields. Employees can get onto any project, cross any discipline. 3M's history is replete with people crossing disciplines. Dick Drew was a low-level lab technician working on sandpaper samples when he invented both masking tape and Scotch tape. Later, another salesperson would invent the dispenser that enabled Scotch tape to become a household item. It's not your job title that counts; it's whether you're open to solving problems, looking at things a different way, trying new things, taking a bite.

Certainly no one would consider it cost-effective to deploy a high-level theoretical physicist to design a Barbie dress. But that's what 3M did.

Early on in the development of Stratus, an engineer picked up a sheet of Stratus and started playing around with it. He rolled it into a tube and, being a guy, pretended it was a sword. It looked a lot like a laser sword from *Star Wars*. So he decided to add a flashlight to add more light. Wow! This really showed off Stratus's reflective qualities, and the team started using this to demonstrate the film at internal 3M forums. Pretty soon, someone asked a natural question: "Why not pursue the toy market?"

The fledgling Stratus team realized that if it was going to convince toy makers of Stratus's potential, it would have to show actual uses. So they'd need to create toys using Stratus. They needed someone to make toys.

Dr. Leland Whitney is a rocket scientist. Literally. No one at 3M would tell me exactly what Lee's assignment had been before coming over to the Stratus team, just that it had been on "a high-level government maximum-security project involving very sophisticated physics." But trust me, he's a rocket scientist. That assignment had come to a conclusion just as the fledgling Stratus team needed someone to invent toys. Lee was available and interested. Why not him?

When I first went past Lee's office, I noticed a Barbie doll. I thought it was someone's plaything. But no, it was research. Lee had spent weeks roaming the aisles of Toys "R" Us, Target, and the like looking for inspiration. He played around, goofed off, experimented. He loved it.

"We're shortchanging ourselves if we don't employ the whole person," said Yvonne. "Lee might be a theoretical physicist, but it doesn't mean he didn't play with toys as a kid."

By the time the big annual toy fair came around, the Stratus team was ready. Andy, Lee, and the others put on demonstrations for Mattel and Hasbro to show how to use Stratus. They received a standing ovation at each meeting.

One of Lee's very first toy creations utilizing Stratus was a product now on the shelf: the dress, halo, and wings of "My Size Barbie." The fabric of Barbie's dress was invented by a chemist (Andy), and the dress itself was designed by a rocket scientist (Lee). Barbie's got some pretty fancy duds. And Yvonne isn't far wrong when she observes, "If we could just make this fabric flexible and breathable, we could make every prom dress in America."

This Should Have Been Invented Here

The cross-fertilization of disciplines and ideas at 3M isn't limited to scientists making toys. It works across all fields and in all directions. Ph.D.s clean test tubes, and lab technicians help on science. Entrepreneurs clean their own floors, remember?

Before coming to 3M, Andy worked at another big research company. At that company, one day someone held up a Post-it and said, "This should have been invented here." But it couldn't have been, Andy told me. Employees would have had to go through too many layers of bureaucracy to get approval. Employees at that company talked to managers, not to one another. They couldn't try new things, experiment, grow, change.

Challenge and growth may ultimately be the most rewarding things you can provide an employee. "Young people want to measure their performance against other people, the time to their promotions, to pay increases," commented Yvonne. "But there's only one thing that's really worth measuring: opportunity. 3M is full of opportunity. You can learn a new technology, work in manufacturing. People here will say, 'I changed jobs.' But no, they didn't leave 3M. It's a sandbox full of opportunity. You can literally change the direction of your career unlimited times. I don't know many places you can do that."

Yvonne calls it "The frog-kissing stage" ("You've got to kiss a lot of frogs before you find your prince"). At 3M, you get to try a lot of different things. After all, how do you know you don't like it when you've never tried it?

If You Allow Them to Fall, They May Learn to Fly

There is no way to fully measure the financial impact of a good idea. How much was masking tape, Scotch tape, or Post-its worth? How much will Stratus be worth?

More important, how much did a company *lose* because a breakthrough product *wasn't* invented there because employees with good ideas were frustrated or disheartened by not being allowed to try them because that wasn't part of their job assignment? Because they had to stick with adhesives when they had a different bright idea?

Good, clear thinking is good, clear thinking whether you're a salesperson or a scientist. And sometimes the best ideas come from the most challenging employees, like Andy Ouderkirk. You just can't get innovative products without innovative people. That means you have to encourage, support, and sometimes push people to try new things.

"If you look at a flock of geese, there's always one or two who are out of formation," Yvonne observed. "They'd die flying in formation. But notice one important thing: they're all headed in the same direction."

Letting people take risks is the only way they're going to grow; it's the only way your company is going to grow. Not every employee wants to take risks. For some employees, that will be fine. You need some employees like that. But for many more, you'll need to encourage them to take risks, try new things, even when they think they don't like it. And with the adventurous ones, the Andy Ouderkirks, you may have to learn, like Mom, to hold your breath and overcome your fears. Try it. How do you know you won't like it?

By the way, my niece Adeena, the one I watched in the playground years ago, is now a beautiful young woman in her early twenties. She's certainly confident. Adeena has lived in foreign countries amid bombings, confronted congresspeople on tough issues, and sung in front of eight thousand people and the president. And she can still climb a jungle gym.

3

IF YOU KEEP MAKING THAT FACE, SOMEDAY IT WILL FREEZE THAT WAY

You're in a bad mood. It's hot. You're crowded in the backseat between your little brother and the dog, and the seats are sticky. You got a D on your spelling test and were picked last for the softball game at recess. Nothing has gone right all day. At the red light, Mom turns around and reminds you that tonight it's your turn to take out the trash. Yuck! You scrunch your eyes, nose, and mouth into the ugliest contortion you can imagine.

Mildly, Mom warns you, "If you keep making that face, someday it will freeze that way."

It's not that Mom isn't sympathetic to your plight, it's just that Mom knows we become what we do. If what we do is ugly, we become ugly. If what we do is beautiful, we can become beautiful. How we react to life's day-to-day ups and downs inevitably forms our personality and character. How we act determines what we are. Our "verbs" eventually become our "adjectives." If you start making faces every time you have to deal with the trash, one day you'll freeze that way.

The same is true in business. The face a business keeps making is the face the business eventually becomes. If a boss treats employees with patience and respect, employees are likely to treat their managers, coworkers, and customers with patience and respect. I'm always amazed when I see abusive managers who expect their employees to be able to turn around and smile at customers.

What Paul Saginaw Learned from His Mother, Helen Saginaw

My mother taught us that it was more important to be kind than clever. If I was trying to point out to my sisters how stupid they were, she would tell me that. At the dinner table, if I was being overly sarcastic, if I was teasing my sisters, she'd tell me, "Pauly, don't be such a smart-ass; it's more important to be kind than clever."

My mother was an only child who led a very overprotected life. She was bound and determined that her children wouldn't be that way. So we had an enormous amount of freedom growing up to do things: travel at an early age, do a lot of things without any parental oversight. She was not a hovering mother at all. She encouraged us to leave the nest. The other message I got a lot from my mother and my father was to be your own boss.

My mother's father, Benjamin Sherman, was a major influence in business. He was a remarkable man, very generous. He would say to me, "If you're successful, you should help make your friends successful. Half of what you own belongs to those who need it."

I worked for my friend's father Al Rosenberg, a kosher caterer, all through high school. He taught me about customer service. He loved catering, felt he dealt with people at their moments of joy. He taught me about quality. He'd say, "If you wouldn't serve it to your mother, you shouldn't serve it to your customers."

My mother is currently dying of cancer.* She lives outside Detroit, and my sisters live away, so I'm the closest physically. At the [Zingerman's] partners meeting, I told them she was dying, and I wanted to take time to be with her, spend more time with her. I got support from them in taking over projects I was working on. Later, I got feedback from them: "That was real leadership you demonstrated [by taking time to be with your mother]. You're a good role model."

I learned sacrifice from my mother. She was so willingly devoted to her parents. She showed me what a good marriage is. My mother has three happy, successful children who enjoy being together. She has shown me countless lessons about people and their potential.

Being with my mother, I have been struggling to come to terms with my own mortality. I talk with her: What were your hopes and dreams? What's it like to know you're going to die? I give her my time. And I'm learning from her in her struggle now.

*She died in July 1998.

Like people, companies get to choose, to a large extent, which face they turn to the world. It all depends on what a company is willing to work toward, where it is willing to put its efforts, what face it keeps making, day after day.

One company I visited chose to make a face of respect and patience, of belief in the ability of people to grow and change. I was amazed at the results.

A Lot More Than Mozzarella

At Zingerman's Deli in Ann Arbor, Michigan, there's a sandwich on the menu called "Nic's Opportunity." Zingerman's occupies an historic building with what appears to be about 1,000 square feet of retail space. But there's a lot more to Zingerman's than meets the eye, just as there's a lot more to that sandwich than mozzarella.

Nic Schoonbeck would never get a job interview at most companies. He started using drugs at the age of fifteen. By the time he was seventeen, he had two felonies and two misdemeanors on his record, and the police had found a sawed-off shotgun in his apartment. He spent a little time in jail. He admits to having used marijuana, mushrooms, acid, cocaine, even crystal methamphetamine. Nic was no Boy Scout.

But beneath that description Nic was—and is—an enthusiastic, smart, hardworking, ambitious guy who needed the right environment to bring out those qualities. Fortunately, Nic stumbled into the right place: Zingerman's Deli.

Nic's background didn't present a problem for Zingerman's. Like many food companies, Zingerman's hires from a high-risk group, mainly sixteen- to twenty-five-year-olds, most on their first jobs, many living away from home for the first time.

Looking around Zingerman's, I saw a staff with a disproportionately high number of pierced body parts, vividly colored hair, and clothes that I would charitably describe as "individualistic." And that's just fine with Zingerman's owners, Paul Saginaw and Ari Weinzweig.

When Paul and Ari founded Zingerman's in 1982, they started with $25,400—a small business. But the partners didn't have small aspirations. Paul and Ari chose to aim for greatness. They wanted a company where the food would be great, the service would be great, and it would be a great place to work. They wanted a business that made a face filled with pride.

Over the years, the two owners developed a set of Guiding Principles by which they'd run their business. One of the key principles, taught to every employee, is that at Zingerman's, they give great service to one another as well as to customers. They support one another.

"Nobody Throws Plates at You"

"Supporting one another" is an unusual aim for a business, but Paul and Ari knew they wanted that attitude to be central at Zingerman's.

"From day one we've taken great pride here in creating a workplace that is supportive of the people who are a part of it as they move along on their personal journey through life," said Ari. "We work to create an open and rewarding workplace for our staff, one where they can find meaningful and challenging employment, where they can make a difference."

What does "supporting one another" mean? The basis is respect. This may show in little ways: "Nobody throws plates at you." When Nate Oswald started as a dishwasher, he noticed the difference: "In other restaurants people throw stuff at you. Here, even if you've only been on a shift for two hours and someone's coming off theirs after ten hours, if you're stacked up, they'll stay and help you."

"Supporting one another" shows by encouraging employees to pursue their careers and dreams, even if it takes them away from Zingerman's, and it shows by giving people the time to learn from their mistakes.

This doesn't mean that Zingerman's is a social welfare agency; far from it. Zingerman's is a very serious food business. While Zingerman's 1,000-square-foot retail store may look like just a little deli, behind that store is a major operation. Zingerman's is now a collection of five companies with more than $11 million in annual sales and three hundred employees. Zingerman's is thriving financially and consistently profitable, and food companies from all over America attend its training classes.

"Supporting one another" simply means that at Zingerman's they consistently treat one another with respect and display belief in each individual's potential. "Supporting one another" means that Paul and Ari understand that everyone's work, whether that person is a baker or a banker, plays a big part in shaping their destiny and self-esteem. Paul and

Ari consciously decided that Zingerman's would play a positive part in forming that destiny.

Paul remembers an incident that helped shape this desire. When he was much younger, a cynical child of the 1960s, Paul commented to his grandfather that the world was so messed up that one person couldn't make much of a difference. His grandfather pointed to a neighborhood wino he'd just bought a meal for, saying, "It made a difference to him." Our daily actions, however small, do matter.

"The way we deal with people is about being nice, listening, letting them know they're valuable. Having confidence in them, letting them go and do their job, and, even when they fail, thanking them," said Ari. "Our basic belief is that everyone has within them some of the ingredients for success."

"I could motivate my employees with fear. I could motivate my employees with incentives. What I have chosen to do, though, is to motivate by offering the opportunity for growth and change," said Paul. "When you offer the opportunity for growth and the chance for someone to change his life, you have an employee who is working with you, someone who sees your goal and his goal as the same one. Such an employee brings an enthusiasm to the workplace that is hard to equal."

Zingerman's keeps making this face of encouragement and support to each and every employee, every single day. Even guys like Nic Schoonbeck.

"What Can We Do to Fix It?"

Zingerman's runs an extensive training program, and Nic took advantage of lots of classes. One class all employees take after one month on the job is called "Day Thirty-one." It consists entirely of a one-on-one meeting of an employee and a supervisor, in which the supervisor asks, "What do you like so far; what don't you like; and what can we do to fix it?"

What Nic didn't like was that not everyone worked as hard as he did. He wanted to know how he could get other people to perform. So Zingerman's sent him to their classes "Train the Trainer," "How to Be a Supervisor," and "How to Be a Manager." Although Nic had been there just a month, making sandwiches, wearing a torn shirt, with his long hair pulled back, Zingerman's paid him to take classes on managing. It was money well spent.

Nic blossomed. Within six months, he moved up to supervisor. When Ann Arbor's annual Art Fair, the major community festival, rolled around, Nic was made head sandwich maker, a big responsibility.

"That's How My Boss Talks to Me"

Nic clearly learned a lot. Zingerman's turned a face of support and belief to Nic, and he in turn learned how to treat others the same way. He shared with me an example that could be a model of employee training. Remember, this comes from Nic, a twenty-four-year-old with little education other than what he learned on the job and a background that's hardly typical management material:

I needed this guy today to learn when he takes meat out of the [big] steamer and fills the little steamer, he [also] needs to take the [meat] out of the cooler and put it in the big steamer so it's constantly hot. We need the meat hot.

Now, when he messes that up three times in a row, during the lunch rush, I could turn around and [say], "You dumb fool, you have no idea what I'm talking about, do you? The meat needs to be hot! Are you stupid?" But I'm not going to do that.

I'm going to say to him, "Listen to me, dude. This is the fourth time I'm going to tell you." And I stop. I put my knife down. I stop thinking about the tickets. I stop thinking about the customers. I don't listen to [my] anger, but I turn around and I look him in the eye, and I say, "So, what I need you to do is start remembering to get that [corned beef] and put it in the steamer 'cause I need the meat to be hot." Then I make him taste a hot piece and taste a cold piece, and say, "See, it tastes better hot; that's why we serve it hot. So do me a favor and just focus on that."

And then I'll tell him, "All day today you've been slicing meat, and I tell you what, you're doing an excellent job. The meat is thin; it's going to break up in the customer's mouth, like we taught you. You're cutting off enough fat, but not too much fat, 'cause that's where the flavor is," and you continue to educate him, and it also calms you down.

I'm saying all these things that he already knows, as well as telling him, "You're not in trouble, I just want you to learn something new because you know what, you learned all the other stuff I told you. So let's go back over it again. We'll both stay calm. . . . Do me a favor and start watching that meat." And he'll start watching it.

Servant Leadership

A growing management philosophy with increasing impact on corporations worldwide is the concept of "servant leadership." Based on the teachings of Robert Greenleaf, servant leadership is based on leadership through *serving* rather than *managing* or *controlling*. Servant leaders work for the well-being and growth of all employees and are committed to creating a sense of community and sharing power in decision making. Those with the most authority in an organization have the most responsibility to serve.

Like many other companies in this book, Zingerman's advocates "servant leadership," and co-owner Ari Weinzweig explains how the company views its obligations:

> You're not dropped down onto the earth with this given right to have as much as you can possibly get. . . . You have a responsibility to pass it on to the next generation in better shape than it is now. . . . That means thinking of success—personal success or business success—not as what you're going to gain or accomplish for yourself, but what you're going to contribute. Whether that's to your employee, your organization, or your community. If you do that, then it's a lot easier to see yourself as successful. You're working with what you believe in, you're connected on a very deep, personal level to your humanness, and so it puts a lot more meaning in what you're doing.
>
> The traditional business theory is straightforward: there's a market need, fill the market need, and drive for as much profit as possible. That was okay when we were a society of farmers and merchants. But businesses are social institutions that have enormous impact on society. Filling a market need is not the same as delivering a social good. A great example would be drug dealers. They're filling a market need, but I don't think anyone would argue they're delivering a social good. Our responsibility as a business is that we should be responsible in everything we do.

And he started doing it today. . . . I'm looking over my shoulder while I'm making sandwiches, and when I see him empty one tray and go get the second tray, I say, "That's what I'm talking about. That's what I wanted you to do, man. That's what I'm talking about. Thank you."

And then, at the end of the day, I say, "Hey, thanks for finally doing that. Let's try not to forget next time. But thank you for doing it. And did you see how much smoother it went after that? Nobody's yelling at you, 'Can I have some more meat in the steamer'. . . . You see how nice that was?"

And then they see it. You know, they see it, and they can feel it, and they understand, and they know that you're not mad.

How did a guy like Nic learn this? "That's how my boss talks to me."

Nic saw the face Zingerman turned to him, and it's the face he now turns to others. Zingerman's kept making a face of respect and pride until it "froze" that way. And it's a beautiful face.

Nic's Opportunity

That brings us back to the sandwich on the menu, "Nic's Opportunity." Zingerman's has a long sandwich list—115 sandwiches. But it still takes a lot to get a sandwich on the Zingerman board. Nic started experimenting with different ingredients, trying to create a sandwich. Eventually, his boss decided it was good enough to put on the menu. Usually, a group of managers names the sandwiches. But this time they asked Nic what he wanted to name it. He called it "Nic's Opportunity."

"I'm just some street kid, you know, from New York," said Nic, "who went through a whole bunch of shit and was strung out on drugs and is just trying to get his life together. . . . When you get a reward like that—'We're going to put *your* name up on *our* menu. And we're going to tell people, "That's the guy who created the sandwich. You want to order [Nic's] sandwich? He's right there. He'll make it for you." '—it's a good feeling."

And why "Nic's Opportunity"? "My name, of course. And the fact that Zingerman's gave me so many opportunities."

Nic later left Zingerman's to go back to New York to be more involved in his daughter's life. He timed his departure so he could attend her preschool graduation. His former boss, Tommy York, says that he wishes Nic would have never left and said he got a call from Nic's father to thank him for taking such good care of Nic. "Nic's Opportunity" sandwich is still on the menu.

Nic Schoonbeck is proof that Zingerman's, by continually making a face of respect toward its employees, makes more than great profits; more than great pastrami; it makes great people.

Sometimes You Just Want to Scream

To keep making a positive face in your business isn't easy. Real business life is filled with stresses and pressures that challenge our patience, and real employees continually challenge our best intentions.

As you sit here comfortably reading a book, it's nice to think you're always going to believe the best about your employees. But then you return to work only to discover your computer programmer forgot to run a backup and lost critical data, your janitor broke your new $2,500 copier trying to fix it, and the receptionist told your most important client that you've been gone all day and no one has any idea where you are. You just want to scream.

"Giving people respect . . . is just as hard as any other hard job." Even Nic understands that. The truth is, this takes a lot of work and a lot of commitment. It's not easy; it's tough. And sometimes—many times—you won't succeed as well as you'd like.

But it pays off. Zingerman's turnover is less than one third the industry average, and their sales per square foot are in the top 1 percent. They are growing and consistently profitable. And Paul and Ari can rightfully derive great personal satisfaction from the impact they have had on others.

"We have no secret formulas. We carry no exclusive products," explained Paul. "What we have are employees who feel personally responsible for the success of the business. Why? Because we feel responsible for the success of our employees, each and every one of them. Sometimes the process is long and the reward not immediately apparent. . . . But I believe Zingerman's is successful because we have a compelling vision in which we have chosen to develop the human potential that surrounds us and not discard it."

Zingerman's is a business success. It is also, unquestionably, a human success. And it's also a successful lesson Paul learned from his mother. When Paul would tease his sisters, calling them names, particularly calling them stupid, Paul's mother would chastise him: "It's more important to be kind than clever." Zingerman's proves you can be both.

4

I Don't Care Who Made This Mess, Just Clean It Up!

We've all been there. You approach a business with a problem, and the employee you speak to passes the buck: "It's the shipping department's mistake." "Contact the manufacturer; there's nothing I can do." "You'll have to take that up with June in accounting, and she's off today."

You feel just like Mom coming home to find the house torn apart, with toys all over the living room and the kitchen coated with chocolate syrup, while you and your brother or sister pointed to each other: "She did it." "He did it."

"I don't care who made this mess," screamed Mom, "just clean it up!"

Mom wasn't interested in your excuses or finger-pointing. She didn't care who made the mess, and she didn't care how it all got started. She just wanted the house cleaned up. Now! Mom got you moving.

Where's Mom now when you have a business mess? Whether it's a rush order of beach balls for Brazil or a customer receiving 144 purple pans instead of purple pens, employees often act like a kid on the couch watching TV while there's a pile of laundry to be folded. They avoid responsibility, evade extra effort, and place blame instead of taking action ("That's Seth's job; why don't you get him to clean it up?"). "Why," we silently scream, "can't I get anyone else to clean up this mess?" As we stand there, up to our neck in Brazilian beach balls or purple pans, we wonder, what did Mom know that we don't?

Shoot the Messenger

A few years ago, a client complained to me about his employees: "Why don't they just use common sense? Why do they turn to me for every little thing?" I was sympathetic. Nothing frustrates managers more than employees who won't take the initiative to solve even minor problems. But as we worked together, I watched my client. He continually interrupted our meetings to hover over his employees, popping up to check their work, constantly correcting, intervening, reproving.

Many people in business act like my client. They say they want their employees to take more responsibility but won't give them any room to make decisions. And when someone makes a mess, they're more interesting in finding the culprit than cleaning up the mess. The result is frustrating for everyone.

Take, for example, an incident I saw at a large drugstore in Ashland, Oregon: An elderly woman stood in line to return about two dozen neatly cleaned empty Coke cans for a refund of the Oregon bottle deposit (five cents).

"I can't accept those," the cashier told the woman. "We no longer sell Coke."

"But I bought these here," said the older woman, clearly confused.

"Well, we stopped selling Coke."

"But I just bought them here a couple of weeks ago."

"Well, the store policy is not to accept Coke returns anymore. I can't take those back." The elderly woman left the store, clearly tired and frustrated, leaning heavily on her cart still filled with the empty cans.

Now, in the same shopping center as the drugstore is a supermarket that sells Coke. If the drugstore clerk had been allowed to use her common sense, she could have accommodated the elderly customer, given her the refund, and returned the cans to the market later that day. Instead, for a measly $1.20, the store alienated a customer.

The cashier might have been just as frustrated as the customer, but what could she do? Reaching into the cash drawer and taking the money was against the rules and might have gotten her fired. Even reaching into her own purse for the $1.20 might have resulted in a reprimand. She couldn't solve the customer's problem without facing blame.

Many companies take this kind of "shoot the messenger" approach to problem solving. I've seen an accounting clerk reprimanded for suggesting a way to reduce interest charges, a program director yelled at for pointing out a problem in another area, and a secretary berated for coming up with a way to save money on mailings. The message: Keep your head down and your mouth shut.

"Shooting the messenger" happens even when companies are responsive. Let's say an employee knows of an inexpensive software program that will help the company process orders faster and more cheaply. "Great," says the boss. "I'll pay for the software if you'll install it." No extra pay, lots of extra work. Lesson learned: Keep your mouth shut, or you'll lose your weekends.

Restrictive rules. Reprimands. Shooting the messenger. It's no wonder nobody wants to pitch in to clean up a mess.

Most of us didn't learn from Mom. Mom might have been really mad; she might even have known who had made the mess; but she was more interested in getting the problem solved than fixing blame. Mom wanted *action,* not excuses, so she shifted the focus away from *retribution* to *solution.* Remember what Mom did first; she let everyone off the hook, saying, "I don't care who made this mess."

The Tire Story

One of the country's best-known customer service stories centers on the Seattle-based retailer Nordstrom and has become a business legend.

One day a customer came to a Nordstrom store to return a set of defective tires. The department store's return policy is so liberal, and they are so eager to accommodate customers that they cheerfully refunded the customer's money—even though Nordstrom has never sold tires!

Sounds ridiculous, yet this episode has been repeated so often that it is widely believed. But is it true or merely a legend?

Whether it's fact or fiction, Nordstrom's customer service definitely deserves legendary status. Get a group of Nordstrom shoppers together, and you'll hear anecdotes of exceptional service. Some stories almost defy belief, like the "wedding dress" story told me by Susana Higuera Lerner, internal investigator at the San Francisco Centre Nordstrom.

I've known Susana more than half her life, so I'm inclined to believe this account.

A woman had just come from picking up her bridal gown for her up-coming wedding, just three days away. She stopped in the Nordstrom shoe department for a little last-minute shopping. While trying on shoes, the woman placed her gown, wrapped in a large plastic bag, on a chair. When she left, the nervous bride-to-be forgot the dress. About an hour later, she realized her mistake, but the dress was gone, evidently stolen by another shopper. A bride's worst nightmare! Nordstrom, sympathetic to her plight, replaced the wedding dress at no charge. Generous? Yes. But here's the critical detail: Nordstrom does *not* sell bridal gowns. Nordstrom employees contacted the store where the bride originally bought her gown and worked with them to make certain she would have another gown ready for the wedding. Then Nordstrom paid for it.

Heroics like these have earned Nordstrom a virtually unmatched repu-tation for customer service. Other corporate executives will often state a goal of making their own company "the Nordstrom of . . ." (whatever their industry is). Indeed, Nordstrom is so frequently used as the stan-dard that when I interviewed Paul Orfalea, founder and chairman of Kinko's, he turned the usual comment on its head; he said his goal was to provide such outstanding customer service that Nordstrom would refer to itself as "the Kinko's of department stores."

There are so many stories of customer service "heroes" (Nordstrom collects them monthly) that no one episode has received the notoriety of the tire story. Some certainly could. One comes from the Tysons Corner, Virginia, Nordstrom store in the early 1990s.

A traveling businessman needed two suits urgently. One he had to take with him immediately, and one he needed two days later in New Hamp-shire. A young salesman sold him the suits, arranging for the second suit to be shipped to New Hampshire. "I'll get it to you on time," said the salesman. "I guarantee it."

A day and a half later, the businessman called, distressed; the suit had not arrived in New Hampshire. Nervous, the salesman dropped every-thing and tracked down the whereabouts of the suit, only to discover it was still in the store. "What are we going to do?" the frantic salesman asked the manager.

"What did you tell the customer you'd do?" was the manager's reply.

"I said he'd have the suit today."

"Well, then," said the manager, "if there's any way to do it, you'd better get it to him."

So the salesman, at Nordstrom's expense, purchased an airline ticket, flew to New Hampshire, rented a car, drove out into the country, and arrived at the customer's door around midnight, suit in hand. How about that for cleaning up a mess?

Stories like these reinforce—to both Nordstrom customers and employees—that when something goes wrong, it will be fixed. Nordstrom has managed to develop a corporate environment where, when someone makes a mess, employees jump in to clean it up. They must have learned something from Mom.

Creating an Action Atmosphere

When you're an executive making large, strategic decisions, it's easy to forget the power and pride that come from being able to affect your world, if only in small ways. An employee at Zingerman's Deli, describing how Zingerman's showed him respect, said they had taken his suggestion about changing the paper cups used by employees. They used to use the same cups as customers, printed with the company name. He realized they could save three cents a cup if they used plain paper cups instead. He was extremely proud that Zingerman's had taken his suggestion—and this had happened three years earlier!

You can unleash an immense amount of employee problem solving if you nurture an atmosphere where employees know their ideas are valued, they are trusted, and they are encouraged, expected, and allowed to act whenever they see an opportunity to save some money, serve a customer, or clean up a mess.

But you have to make it easy and painless for employees to think and act. You have to build in what Sam Stern, coauthor of the book *Corporate Creativity*, calls a "bias toward action."

As an example of this, Stern and his coauthor, Alan G. Robinson, relate what happened when the Eastern Region of the U.S. Forest Service changed the way it handled employee suggestions. Under the old system, employees had to submit a four-page form and wait for the administration to respond. In four years, the administration had received 252 ideas

---

What John Whitacre Learned from His Mother, Hazel Mae Whitacre

My grandmother, Alma Dorothea Moore, was the first woman to climb Mount Rainier. I'm very fond of women athletes. . . . I was always in athletics, which was a very male environment. I later coached both boys' and girls' sports teams, and I really like the way the girls compete. . . . They combine buff and brains. . . .

My mother was good to everyone. Throughout literature, there's the unconscious Christian, and my mother is what I call an unconscious Christian. Like [James Fenimore] Cooper's character in *The Deerslayer* Judith Hutter. That's how I think of my mother. She just can't imagine people would do things that are dishonest or mean-spirited. My mom wants to meet people—understand them—with an open mind.

My mother was always my biggest fan. When I was in Little League, she had this kind of cheer she would do: "Whoo, whoo, whoo!" I hated it. But all the other kids loved it because she'd always be there no matter what happened. Whether we won or lost. She was the ultimate cheerleader.

One thing I learned from my mother was the passion for competition and the sheer joy of competing. To this day, she just loves competition. But the minute the competition is over, she's total mother: if you lose, she'll make you feel better. She's always right there with words of encouragement.

---

from a staff of 2,500 employees. When it revamped its system, it adopted a very simple, one-page form. And here's where the Forest Service turned the process on its head: if an employee submitted an idea that didn't break any laws, if that person didn't receive a response within thirty days, he or she could just go ahead and do it!—it was automatically approved! The number of suggestions skyrocketed, going to 6,000 in the first year alone. Thus a company's structure and policies can either encourage or discourage employees from cleaning up when they see a mess.

Use Good Judgment

Nordstrom's employee handbook consists, in its entirety, of the following:

Welcome to Nordstrom. We're glad to have you with our Company. Our number one goal is to provide outstanding customer service. Set both your personal and professional goals high. We have great confidence in your ability to achieve them. So our employee handbook is very simple. We have only one rule. . . .

Our only rule: Use Good Judgment in all Situations.

Please feel free to ask your department manager, store manager, or personnel manager any question at any time.

That's it. No thick rule books. No manuals on how to greet customers or how many times to smile. No demands that employees check with their supervisor before making a decision. The one phrase "Use Good Judgment" even covers Nordstrom's return policy; many customers believe Nordstrom accepts all returns. Not so; employees can use their own good judgment. Through their employee handbook, Nordstrom liberates employees to take action.

But such encouragement would be meaningless in an atmosphere of blame and retribution. It's not enough merely to give employees the freedom to take action; they must be confident that when they do, supervisors will be accepting rather than accusatory, and that when they make mistakes, as we all do, they'll be treated with patience rather than punishment.

Not Just Crying over Spilt Milk

Nordstrom calls mistakes "spilt milk," and when speaking with Nordstrom's chairman and chief executive officer, John Whitacre, I was reminded of an episode I had seen of the children's television show *Mr. Rogers' Neighborhood*. At one point, Mr. Rogers spilled a glass of milk. In his calm, patient way, Mr. Rogers wiped up the milk and swept up the glass, all the while talking about how accidents happen to everyone. There's no reason to get upset, he reassured his accident-prone young audience; what's important is to clean things up.

While he may not welcome the comparison, Whitacre sounds a lot like Mr. Rogers: "Every day we're doing something wrong. . . . You're going to fall down; you're going to make mistakes." Whitacre recognizes that great service can be hit or miss; the important thing is what happens when something goes wrong. Nordstrom wants to free employees from worrying about the reaction of their boss so they can focus on pleasing the customer. "If something isn't going the way it should, we want to know, and we want to try and do our best to fix it.

"We don't care what's gone wrong," he continues. "We just want to know about it and deal with it, and learn from it, and use that as an opportunity for growth. . . . We don't want to have too much spilt milk, but if something gets spilled around here, five people will rush to clean it up and help with it."

That's a critical part of Nordstrom's success in customer service—they're eager to know when something is messed up. Employees who learn of a problem, or who cause a problem themselves, can feel confident going to a manager for help finding a solution. They're not afraid of being blamed.

One incident happened just the week before I interviewed Seattle store manager Jeff Greer. A salesperson asked him to take a dress to a customer on his way home from work. Alterations had messed up; it had sent the dress to the wrong store, and the customer needed it that weekend. "The fact that a salesperson came to me and asked if I could deliver it pretty much shows the servant mentality that exists in this company," explained Greer. "I wouldn't have responded any differently if it had been Whitacre down here asking me to take the dress or if it was Irene from Encore [another department]—'Yes, I can do it, of course.' She wasn't afraid to come up here. It's not like 'You know what? You screwed up, you've got to take care of it.' "

Nordstrom's organizational structure encourages this kind of supportive management, "servant leadership." The company is organized as an inverted pyramid, with salespeople at the top and the copresidents, chairman, and board of directors at the bottom. (See figure on page 47.)

Managers aren't supposed to hand orders "down"; they're supposed to help hold salespeople "up." Virtually all Nordstrom managers and executives began in sales, so they understand a salesperson's pressures and needs. Whitacre, the first non-Nordstrom family member to hold the chairmanship and CEO position solo, started as a shoe salesman. When strangers ask what he does for a living, he says what all Nordstrom family members say: "I sell shoes." (Nordstrom was founded as a shoe store in 1901 and didn't sell general apparel until 1963. The company likes to emphasize its roots as a shoe store because "there is no other place where you get on your knees for customers.") Six Nordstrom cousins serve as

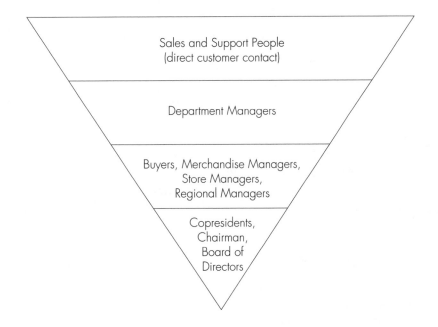

copresidents, but Nordstrom family members don't start in sales. No such luck: Nordstroms must begin their careers in the stockroom of the shoe department, literally cleaning up other people's messes.

Celebrate the "Baby Steps"

All this sounds simple. First you create a structure that permits employees to make decisions; then you next cultivate a blame-free atmosphere so employees are encouraged to act. But what happens when some employees make bad decisions, take less-than-ideal actions? It's easy to say "Use good judgment," but, let's face it, some people have better judgment than others. This presents a real challenge for managers, who have to both help employees cultivate good judgment and learn to live with the honest mistakes of their employees while they grow in experience.

Whitacre tells a personal story to illustrate: When his son was about eight or ten years old, Whitacre gave him the responsibility of mowing the lawn. But there are, he quickly learned, different versions of what it means to mow a lawn. At first, his son mowed randomly, cutting every corner. Whitacre didn't know how to handle this. Should he reprimand him? Coach him?

When You Hear Gershwin, Thank Mom

One of Nordstrom's signature features came straight from Mom. At the beginning of the Christmas holiday season, Nordstrom stores open one night for employees and their families, so they can shop and party.

When John Whitacre, now Nordstrom's chairman, was manager of the Bellevue, Washington, store, the mother of one of his employees suggested something she thought would add more atmosphere and enjoyment to the holiday party: Why not have a piano player in the store? One of the employees' wives worked at a piano store and could lend them a grand piano for the evening.

It was a hit! Everyone enjoyed the piano playing, and Mom suggested they keep it at the store throughout the holidays. They soon extended the piano playing to other times throughout the year and finally kept it year-round. Almost all Nordstrom stores now have a full-time piano player and a grand piano—thanks to Mom!

"I decided instead to celebrate the fact that he got the mower out of the garage, he got the motor running, he didn't cut any toes or fingers off," Whitacre recalled. "He has the reward, the great experience of 'Hey, I mowed the lawn!' We were joyous in the fact that this occurred, with the hope that we would return another day.

"A lot of managers are so quick to want to show employees how things should be done, rather than celebrate the little baby steps as they go," concludes Whitacre. Instead, he counsels patience; "Sure enough, as my son has gone along, he's developed and matured. So we existed with his version of how to mow the lawn being different than mine. But over time, he's gained an appreciation for how he wants it to look. And from time to time, we might call attention to the yard a day or two afterward and say, 'Oh, look what you missed.' But if you try and intercede too quickly, you lose your audience, you lose your ability to help them grow and learn."

If your goal is to get your employees to be willing to clean up a mess, perhaps even to jump in and clean it up without first being asked, prepare yourself: at first you may have to live with a pretty broad definition of "clean."

Authority and Expectations

All this doesn't mean you can't have standards and expectations. Like most of the companies in this book, Nordstrom gives a lot of authority and responsibility to its employees, but it also demands a lot from them.

Nordstrom is focused on sales. It's a competitive, pressured environment. Each pay period, the company posts every salesperson's average sales per hour. You know exactly how you stack up. There's a lot of pressure to do well. Top salespeople can make over six figures a year, and there's national recognition for the top 10 percent of all salespeople. That's the upside.

But there's a downside. If you consistently fall below department averages, you'll find your manager suggesting that you transfer to another department or a nonsales job, or perhaps leave Nordstrom altogether. Salespeople are expected, if not required, to put in extra effort to stay in touch with customers and provide personal service. (This made Nordstrom the target of an attempted union action over the issue of the time spent on writing notes or telephoning customers after "work" hours. Nordstrom employees didn't agree with the union, however, and they decertified it.)

The result is very high productivity: Nordstrom has one of the highest sales per square foot in its class. But the competitive atmosphere is certainly not the right fit for everyone, and employees tend to either love Nordstrom or leave it.

Just Clean It Up

When something goes wrong, our first inclination is to find the culprit. This doesn't make us bad people, it just makes us human. Part of it comes from the fact that we're angry; when we're mad, it's easier when there's a focus for that anger. Part of it is shame; even when we know things are our own fault, it's comforting to think that someone else had a hand in them. Part of it is a natural, human need to understand a situation better by retelling it; when we look for the culprit, we get a chance to dissect what's happened. So we focus on placing blame, and that's how we end up knee-deep in Brazilian beach balls or purple pans, pointing fingers at each other and sounding like kids: "He did it." "She did it."

If we're in charge, we may decide that the best way to avoid future messes is by putting tighter controls into place, giving employees fewer chances to make mistakes. "I can keep everything clean and tidy," we imagine, "if I have really strict policies and procedures." You can't make a mess if you can't move around. The result is a company organized to avoid failure, not to produce success.

The truth is, you can't avoid messes, especially in today's business world of constant change. Employees have to have some room to think, to act, to make mistakes. If you want your messes cleaned up, and cleaned up fast, you've got to remember how Mom handled it. First, she got away from blame: "I don't care who made this mess." Next, she made her expectation clear: "Just clean it up." And then . . . she let you do it. She walked away. She let you have some time to clean up the mess your own way. You knew she'd check to see how well you did, but first she gave you a chance to put things right.

Oh yes, about the tire story—the one in which Nordstrom supposedly refunded a customer's money on a set of tires. Nordstrom executives hate this story, which has been widely circulated and published. They're not going to be pleased that I'm repeating it now, because they don't want customers under the impression that Nordstrom will refund money on merchandise purchased elsewhere; they won't. Nevertheless, the facts are that in 1975, when Nordstrom opened their first stores in Alaska, they took over three locations from another store, the Northern Commercial Company. As is their usual practice, Nordstrom closed the stores, revamped them, and reopened them as Nordstrom stores.

A while after the reopening, a man walked in with a set of tires to return. He had purchased them at the Northern Commercial Company store at that location. He evidently did not realize that the store had changed hands. Wishing to accommodate the customer, a Nordstrom salesperson gave the man his money back. The company, to this day, has never sold tires.

5

If All Your Friends Jumped off a Bridge, Would You Jump off One Too?

When all the other girls wore short, short skirts, Mom wouldn't let you. A bunch of the guys pierced their noses, but Mom put her foot down. "Aw, Mom," you'd plead, "all the other kids are doing it." Mom, with her usual common sense, frustrated you with the irrefutable rejoinder "If all your friends jumped off a bridge, would you jump off one too?"

Companies, too, want to be just like all the other companies, do what the others do. Downsizing is in? Cut out a division. Management by objectives? Let's spend two days dissecting the differences between a *goal,* an *objective,* and a *strategy.* TQM?—adopt it, whatever it is. And how about those new team uniforms and the home-run posters since we turned our managers into "coaches"?

But even those who recognize such trends as just "management fads *du jour,*" may never question whether the "normal" way of doing business isn't also just a matter of following the crowd. *Conventional wisdom* is all too often viewed as *wisdom* instead of just plain *convention.*

One piece of conventional wisdom widely imitated in business is that if you choose to position your company to compete on the basis of price—if you intend to distinguish yourself in the marketplace by being the low-cost leader—you *must* keep wages and benefits low. Price-based business strategies depend on high volume, rather than high profit margins, for success. With narrow margins, a business has to look for every angle to save money, and conventional wisdom says the first place to look is at labor costs.

So many businesses have quickly adopted trendy ways to reduce labor costs: turn full-time careers into part-time jobs—that way they won't have to give employees benefits or overtime. Then hire teenagers or others who will be the least dissatisfied with the lack of opportunities for advancement. Finally, standardize every job responsibility—"dumb down" all tasks—to accommodate the high level of employee turnover such working conditions create.

Like kids mimicking the behavior, however objectionable, of their peers, executives argue that this is the "normal" way to behave: "All the other companies treat employees this way; if we want to succeed, we've got to do it too."

Mom wouldn't agree. She knew that bad behavior is just plain bad behavior, even if "everybody does it." Moms know that the best—the healthiest—way to grow is by developing your own unique character and your own sense of right and wrong, not by blindly following the crowd.

Mom was right. I've seen a company that proves you can not only succeed, you can excel, by following Mom's advice. I've seen a company that operates in an area of such tight price competition that their rivals match their prices *within minutes.* Because such a large proportion of their costs are substantial fixed expenses—involving extremely expensive equipment—they have limited ways to achieve savings over their competitors. They have every reason to keep wages and benefits low.

Yet they were selected as the *number one* best place to work in America, with good pay, great benefits, and outstanding opportunity. This company has been consistently profitable when its competitors have not. Executives of Fortune 500 companies name it as one of the handful of most admired companies in the country, and its CEO has been called the best CEO of all.

How did they do it? Not by jumping off a bridge just because "all the other kids are doing it." Instead, they developed their own unique philosophy, unheard of in any business school. They built a company on "love."

I'm Going to Love You Like Nobody's Loved You

When I started work on this book, I made a list of some of the qualities, values, and practices I thought made for an extraordinary company. And

I made a list of some of the fundamental values that Mom taught us—characteristics such as integrity, open communication, fairness, a willingness to take risks and to accept our failings with grace.

Sex wasn't one of them.

Next, I started researching companies. I listed companies that I knew from personal experience exhibited extraordinary attributes; I asked business colleagues, venture capitalists, and corporate executives I knew to recommend companies and tell me what they thought made a company exceptional.

No one mentioned love.

I contacted various business organizations, business journalists, and groups that made awards to outstanding companies on the basis of social, community, and business criteria. I sought their suggestions for companies and descriptions of what makes a company exceptional.

No one mentioned sex. No one mentioned love.

But then came Southwest Airlines. Now, if you're putting together a list of outstanding companies, Southwest Airlines is impossible to ignore. It makes almost all the "100 Best" lists. In 1998 Southwest was selected as the number one best place to work in America in a study for *Fortune* magazine.[1] Even though it's heavily unionized, Southwest has great relations with its employees, and it's almost impossible to get a job there. Turnover is ridiculously low.

Southwest is clearly also a business success: it's not only the most consistently profitable airline, but other *Fortune* studies showed Southwest to be one of the ten U.S. companies most admired by CEOs[2] and the most admired airline.[3] Herb Kelleher, Southwest's chairman and CEO, is regularly selected as one of the best CEOs in the country.[4] And there's no question that Southwest does its job well. In virtually every ranking of airline performance and customer satisfaction, Southwest comes out on top year after year after year: in on-time performance, safety, least lost luggage, fewest customer complaints. Even the *Los Angeles Times* asked, "Is

---

1. Robert Levering and Milton Moskowitz, "The 100 Best Companies to Work For in America," *Fortune,* January 12, 1998.

2. *Fortune,* March 3, 1997.

3. *Fortune,* January 1997.

4. *Industry Week,* November 20, 1995; Kelleher was second most respected CEO following only Bill Gates; *Fortune,* May 2, 1994.

this the perfect company or what?"[5] If you're looking for extraordinary companies, Southwest is impossible to ignore.

Obviously, Southwest does something right—a lot of things. Consistently. Now, I know that when a company does a lot of things right over a long period of time, it's more than a matter of just being a well-run company—there has to be a strong set of core values holding the company together. Looking at all of Southwest's accolades, I knew there had to be a value system, a philosophy, guiding Southwest, keeping them grounded (although perhaps that's not the right term for an airline). I had to see what was up.

At Southwest's headquarters in Dallas, I expected to find that one key to Southwest's success is that Southwest has a clearly articulated and well-communicated business strategy that gives them a competitive edge—that they know their market and their strategic position and focus on those first. They eat their vegetables. I was right; they do.

I further expected that many of Southwest's extraordinary achievements would stem from their commitment to sticking with their strategy regardless of popular trends in airline management. They're not always looking to see what other airlines are doing, and they're not blindly following. I was right; they aren't.

When Mom told us not to jump off bridges, she wanted us to use our heads. But Mom also wanted us to use our hearts: to do the right thing, regardless of the crowd. And that's where Southwest took me by surprise. I went to Dallas expecting to find a company that survived by its strategy; I found a company that triumphed through love.

What Is This Thing Called Love?

Nobody starts out to build a company on love—at least nobody rational! It's certainly not taught in business schools. Can you imagine the course listing? "Managing Through Love 201," upper division; prerequisite: "Managing Through Mild Affection."

With all the fear of sexual harassment suits, people at work are afraid to say they even like one another; they certainly wouldn't want to openly

5. Jesse Katz, "Southwest Is the Zaniest, Savviest Company on Earth," *Los Angeles Times,* June 9, 1996.

What Herb Kelleher Learned from His Mother, Ruth Moore

Basically, all my values come from her; she was the only one there when I was growing up. I was ten years old in 1941, when my brother was killed in the war. My mother was very strong. She lost a son and, within a year, lost a husband. Her other children went off, and she was left with just a little squirt, little jerk. She was both mother and father to me. My mother never faltered.

My mother and I would sit up till four in the morning talking about business and politics and philosophy. We'd talk a lot about what was true and what wasn't true, who was really trying to do good and who wasn't, who was putting on a show and who was a phony.

She was wonderful. She told me a lot of things that formulated my perspective on life. She told me that position and title meant nothing, that you should never honor anybody just for their position or the title that they had. She taught me to be a behaviorialist; pay attention to what people do instead of what they say.

My mother taught me that every person was important. There were no unimportant people in the world, no matter who they were or what they did. That they were all to be treated with courtesy and kindness and you were not to allow people to pick on them. She told me a story: My father was working at the Campbell's Soup Company, and farmers used to bring the tomatoes in on horse-drawn carts. When my father saw a farmer beating his horse, he got angry and knocked the farmer out. Consequently, he had an assault-and-battery charge against him. But my mother just said you shouldn't treat horses that way.

She was a housewife but loved to talk about business and how one should conduct themselves in business. You should never seek after money. Money was a by-product of being excellent. If you were excellent, the money would come, and if you were lousy, you shouldn't have the money. Money was not significant; it was your character and how you behaved that was significant.

As to going my own way, my mother taught me, first of all, think about things. Secondly, when you're right, don't let anybody else convince you you're wrong.

promote love. It's not just the fear of being misunderstood about sex, romance, or harassment. Businesses naturally and appropriately want to be able to discipline and fire employees. They'd be afraid that if they talked about *love*, employees would feel as if they couldn't be fired. *Love* just leaves too much room to be misinterpreted.

Today's business atmosphere, especially in large corporations, is contrary to the concept of love. The new employer/employee relationship, openly stated, is that of a team with a free agent: We hire you. While you're here, you're part of the team. We keep you as long as we need your skills and talents. You stay as long as you think being here helps your career. Then you move on, transfer to another company's team. It's the ultimate transactional relationship. You are indeed a human *resource*.

Love is really different. Love is about valuing you as a human *being*.

The philosopher Martin Buber described the difference in his book *I and Thou*.[6] In an "I-It" relationship, you view the other person as something to be used, a thing, an "it." The other person is interchangeable with a machine, existing to be used by and interact with you. When you restore the humanity of the other person, you go from an "I-It" to an "I-Thou"[7] relationship, in which the other person is now viewed as truly human, a person with real feelings, concerns, and needs of his or her own. That person has an existence that is distinct from yours and does not exist merely to serve your needs.

"I-It" interactions are *transactions;* each side constantly measures how much is given and how much is received. Is this a bargain? Is this person meeting my needs? Am I getting too little, giving too much? Can I get a better deal?

"I-Thou" interactions are *relationships;* each person acts with genuine concern for the well-being of the other. We relate to the whole of each other, not just the small portion that we need. We don't measure; we don't keep score. We care. "Is this person okay? Happy? Growing? How can I help?" Only "I-Thou" relationships can be the basis of love.

But why love in business? Why an "I-Thou" relationship in the workplace? After all, isn't business the ultimate transactional setting? We refer to the business world as the "marketplace"; a marketplace is where things

---

6. Martin Buber, *I and Thou*, trans. Walter Kaufman (New York: Touchstone, 1996 [1970]).

7. "Thou" is an archaic version of the second-person familiar, which no longer exists in modern English. We would now call this "I-You," with the most personal connotation of the word "you."

are exchanged, bartered, sold. Transactions are transacted. The people in my business are not my flesh and blood, they are not my spouse or life partner or mate. Generally, they're not even my in-laws. I didn't fall in love with them. They are people I *hire*, I use. Isn't it only a matter of reality to view an employee as an "It"? Not necessarily. Because if we check our humanity and, more important, our employees' humanity, at the office or factory door, what else gets left behind? What happens to trust, commitment, loyalty, a willingness to go the extra mile? Can people do their best work if they are not allowed to bring their full selves to their jobs?

We can all cite examples of businesses that treat employees as *things*. A colleague once told me what happened when she informed her boss she was pregnant. She had worked in the company for a number of years. She and her boss were very friendly; they had taken many business trips together and worked long hours side by side. She was a valuable, dedicated employee. Her boss had met her husband on a number of social occasions. But when she came in, glowing, to tell her boss she was pregnant, his only response was "How long will you be out? If you're not going to come back after your maternity leave, could you just quit now so I can replace you?" It took a week before he thought to offer congratulations; to him, this pregnancy just made his human resource less valuable. She was an "It." From that moment on, her dedication to the company plummeted—as did that of others who heard her story. Unfortunately, this is hardly a rare example.

In a new economy, our businesses depend on the knowledge, creativity, and initiative of our employees, often acting independently. If we treat employees as "It"s instead of as "Thou"s, if we fail to deal with them as real human beings, if we stop caring, we may soon find they stop caring too. How can I ask my employees to put their heart into their work if I'm not willing to give them mine?

What's Love Got to Do with It?

Sex.

That's what it was all about. Let's be clear. Southwest Airlines didn't start out to build a business based on love. They started by building an airline based on sex. Forget hearts and souls; they were focusing on other parts of the anatomy.

In the early 1970s, the struggling young airline was spending most of its time and money battling its competition in courtrooms instead of in the air. The other major airlines in Texas threw one legal roadblock after another in their way. This ate up much of Southwest's financial backing, and they had little money for advertising and promotion. Southwest needed to get the most mileage from their limited marketing dollars. Recognizing the need to capture attention quickly and generate free publicity, they decided they better do something different. Something outrageously different. Something the public couldn't miss.

Sex.

Southwest may now try to sugarcoat the fact, but it was sex, not love, that they sold in those years. I know because I was living in Texas at the time, and Southwest's message was unambivalent: sex, sex, sex.

Now, there's nothing particularly remarkable about using sex to sell things. It's a time-honored advertising tradition. Ever go to a car show? Even today, long-limbed lovely ladies lounge lasciviously on the latest Lexus. In the early 1970s, sex was everywhere; it was certainly in the air. Other airlines used suggestive double entendres—"We really move our tail for you" and "Delta is ready when you are"—but nothing came close to rivaling the taboo-shattering scope of Southwest. They got noticed: tongues as well as tails were wagging.

The hostesses (no flight attendants here, not even stewardesses) were referred to as "Jet Bunnies"; they wore tight, bright orange hot pants and knee-high go-go boots. Help-wanted ads for hostesses said, "Dear Raquel Welch: We'd like to offer you the position of a hostess with Southwest Airlines. . . . You typify the girls we're looking for . . . warm, personable, and great-looking in hot pants. . . . We have a lot to offer—good pay, a training program, and airplanes full of terribly interesting men." The first chief hostess, in charge of training the Jet Bunnies, had formerly been the chief hostess on the *Playboy* jet.

The free and plentiful drinks were called "love potions," peanuts were "love bites," and Southwest's three-city service area (Houston, San Antonio, Dallas) was called the, um, "Love Triangle." Later, Southwest would name their instant ticket machine the "Quickie Ticket." Nothing subtle here.

This was also at the height of the women's movement, which had a strong impact in Texas. A woman was nearly elected governor; San Antonio elected a woman mayor. In living rooms across Texas, women were holding "consciousness-raising sessions," learning to resist being seen solely as sex objects. Pedestals were coming down, and the Equal Rights Amendment was coming up.

And here came this upstart airline, openly pushing sex, sex appeal, and how hot their hot pants were. Southwest became the subject of cocktail party (actually, beer-and-barbecue) debates. People were talking about Southwest, and the airline even made the cover of *Esquire* magazine in 1974. Southwest had needed a strategy to stretch their marketing dollars, and they succeeded. Sex sold. And Southwest sold sex.

It never hurts to show a little leg.

I Can't Help Falling in Love with You

As so often happens, what started as a purely sexual attraction turned into love.

Oh sure, even from the early days, Southwest talked about *love* when what they really meant was *sex,* but then again, so many do. (But perhaps we should stick to our business, not personal, lives.) It took a while for sex to evolve into something deeper.

Southwest had a good reason for throwing the word *love* around. That's because Southwest lived on Love. Literally. Southwest's headquarters were located at Love Field, the downtown Dallas airport. When Southwest started operations, the Dallas/Fort Worth International Airport was soon to open. Even though all the other airlines were moving to DFW—all the other kids were doing it—Southwest knew DFW was one bridge they didn't want to jump off.

DFW is a long drive from downtown Dallas. Southwest's business centers on short-haul flights, for example, Dallas to San Antonio. The idea is that if you can offer customers the opportunity to fly nearly as cheaply as driving and it's faster, they'll beat a path to your door. But they won't if your door is an hour away. Southwest recognized that they had to be convenient.

Staying at Love Field was critical to Southwest's success, and it would be the focus of most of their litigation for the next decade. Being convenient was a key competitive and marketing advantage. The same was true in Houston, where Southwest landed at the downtown Hobby Airport rather than the distant, enormous Houston Intercontinental Airport. (A rumor at the time had it that, in true Texas spirit, Houston officials had lobbied NASA to land the space shuttle at least once at the new Houston airport so they could name it the Houston Intergalactic Airport.)

Southwest wanted to emphasize its connection with Love Field, so, in addition to sex, *Love* was featured everywhere. The company took a heart as its corporate logo. They dubbed themselves the "Love Airline," their slogan was "Somebody Else Up There Loves You," and when Southwest eventually went public, the stock exchange symbol they chose was "LUV."

All this talk about love was starting to have an effect. Southwest's advertising was helping crystallize a management philosophy. Their slogans were actually shaping the company's sense of itself. *Love* became a corporate mission as well as a corporate motto.

Now, it wasn't marketing alone that contributed to the evolution of *love* as the description of Southwest's core value; marketing just put a word on it, a word that other companies would have been afraid to use. Southwest had other key allies helping to develop what would turn out to be their greatest advantages—their competitors.

Remember, Southwest's competitors were determined to keep them from operating in Texas. Southwest fought one legislative battle after another, one court case after another. Chairman Mao said that nothing brings people together like a common enemy, and Southwest's employees certainly had that. Under constant siege, fighting for their very existence, Southwest's employees rallied. Every new battle brought an increased esprit de corps: "We survived despite the odds." "We're in this together."

Southwest's corporate culture evolved rapidly. Other Southwest employees weren't merely coworkers, they were your battlefront buddies, your partners, your family. These were the people you could count on to stand by your side when times were tough—the people who loved you.

"Love was handed to us," recalls Southwest's executive vice president, Colleen Barrett, the number two person at the airline. "We served Love Field in Dallas and had a heavy-duty sex thing in 1971. Now, we're not silly and stupid. As time went on we softened that, and by then we had our family culture. We started using the word for that. We used that word when talking to employees, at events. It fit our culture. We treat you like family. Families talk about love."

At first "love" was promotional; later it became philosophical. As Southwest's corporate culture evolved, benefits and employee relations evolved too. They paid competitive wages even though they had to keep fares very low. They offered good benefits and developed a strong commitment to training and promoting from within. Southwest introduced the first profit-sharing plan in the airline industry.

Southwest started by doing something Mom warned us against: using sex to get attention. But over time they matured and figured out how to offer their customers and employees a more meaningful relationship.

Southwest started with sex, and fell into love. Southwest still uses the same company logo, but now they really do focus on the heart rather than other parts of the anatomy. Mom would definitely have approved.

Shower the People You Love with Love

As I went around visiting the companies for this book, one thing became clear: little things mean a lot.

At Kinko's headquarters, employees strongly expressed their opinions on the flavors of soda in the *free* vending machines. At Hewlett-Packard, they're still talking about the fact that they no longer get free donuts every day. And that practice stopped in the 1970s!

We all choose and keep our jobs because of the big things: satisfaction, challenge, pay, benefits, opportunities, the goals and values of the companies we work for. The big things have to be right for a job, a company, to be right. But sometimes what makes us love a job or a company are the small things.

If we stop and think about this, we know this is true in our personal relationships. It's the small considerations that endear someone to you—bringing you coffee in the morning and remembering how you take it; sending you an article about your favorite artist; turning on your radio station in the car. Little gestures that show that person thinks about you and wants to please you.

It's also true in business. Little things mean a lot. Little things can mean the difference between a merely satisfied employee and a dedicated one. Little things make us feel loved.

"Other people try to make sense of what makes Southwest work," says Herb Kelleher, Southwest's charismatic chairman and CEO. "I always tell our people that the intangibles are much more important than the tangibles. . . . We're going to provide you with the highest-quality service for the lowest price—and we're going to infuse that with the warmth, the hospitality of *love,* if you will, a spiritual element that says, 'Boy, we're really happy to see you. We like customers.' [Our competitors] may be able to duplicate the airplanes, they may be able to duplicate the ticket counters, they may be able to do a lot of other things we do, but that spirit is going to be really hard for somebody to equal. . . . It requires attention in terms of behavior to a thousand different things every day. It's not formulaic. It's not programmatic. It's very difficult for somebody to go back and say, 'Let me tell you the essence of Southwest Airlines, it's $E = mc^2$.' They just can't say that."

Colleen added this insight: "It's just like raising a family; it's got to be something you do every day."

Southwest pays a lot of attention to the little things, the gestures that show they remember you're a human, not a thing. In fact, Southwest doesn't have a personnel director or human resources manager; they have a *"vice president for people."* Finally! Mom never understood what a human *resource* was, anyway.

My Heart Belongs to Daddy

The day before I was to meet with Herb Kelleher, I saw him walking down the hall of the company's Dallas headquarters. "Walking" is perhaps the wrong verb; striding, glad-handing, parading, effusing, *campaigning* might all be more accurate. As he passed, employees reached out to shake his hand or, more typically, hug him, and he'd hug back. He addressed people by name, often asking a personal question, inquiring about a golf game or illness or vacation. The connection might have been for only ten seconds, but there *was* a connection, a human one.

Herb certainly doesn't look like other CEOs. It seems as though he spends more time in costumes than in regular clothes. He shows up at company events dressed as Elvis, one of his favorite personae, and the brochure listing Southwest's leadership shows Herb dressed as: a gangster, an old-fashioned golfer, a German fräulein, a violet-clad matron, and some other costumes impossible to figure out. While dressed in drag, Herb drags on his ever-present cigarette, stopping only to enthusiastically kiss employees, both men and women, and drink whiskey with gusto. Herb may have come from New Jersey, but he sure knows how to be a Texan, to be larger than life.

If Southwest is a family, there's no doubt whatsoever that Herb Kelleher is the benign, beloved dad. The kind of dad who dispenses good advice and terrible jokes. Who helps with your homework and cries at your wedding. The kind of dad who, if you call when your car breaks down in the middle of the night, picks you up without giving you a lecture.

The business press and stock analysts often place the credit for Southwest's top performance solely with Herb. But at Southwest's headquarters, the other ubiquitous figure is the woman who plays the role of Mom, Colleen Barrett.

Colleen was Herb's secretary back in his law office in San Antonio when Herb and Rollin King came up with the idea of starting an airline, and she's been through all of the company's trials and tribulations. Inside Southwest, Colleen gets most of the credit for setting the company's tone and maintaining the family culture.

Together, Herb and Colleen do the things Mom and Dad do in a family, letting family members know they're loved—individually, as people. All current Southwest employees and many past ones, as well as frequent fliers, get birthday cards from Herb and Colleen, many with personal notes included. If employees have any significant event in their work or personal lives—a promotion, an illness, a new baby, an award from a community organization—Colleen sends a card or a note. But Herb and Colleen's family has 26,000 members. How do they keep track?

Colleen has established a method of gathering information from both official and unofficial channels to see what's going on with employees personally. Not job performance; life performance. In addition to receiving copies of employees' status forms showing medical leave or extended illness, Colleen has a network of contacts at each of Southwest's fifty-two locations. It's their (unofficial) job to keep her informed. Someone getting married? Having a baby? Parent ill? Child a valedictorian? Tell Colleen. She'll send a note.

Colleen spends about 40 percent of her time maintaining personal relationships with employees or customers. Although the birthday cards are computer-generated, Colleen herself spends four to six hours a month going through the list and pulling out cards on which to write personal notes. She dictates notes all weekend long. A mother's work is never done.

And They Called It Puppy Love

As in any family home, the walls at Southwest's corporate headquarters are covered with family pictures. I'm not talking about baby pictures pinned on the inside of employees' personal cubicles but pictures all along the corridors and hallways throughout the buildings.

Now, a lot of companies put up pictures of their "Employee of the Month," usually formal, eight-by-ten glossy black-and-white photos. Some companies, like Kinko's, may even have photos of employees wearing shorts and tossing Frisbees at the company picnic. But at Southwest you see real family pictures, the same kind you'd hang on your wall at home.

Walking around, you can see what your fellow Southwest family members looked like as kids, with their prizewinning dahlias, or pitching in the softball championship last year. You see wedding pictures and baby pictures and Grandma's pictures and pictures of Chris from accounting going to her prom. Real people doing real things.

But my favorite part of Southwest's family photo album is the "Pet Wall." Only it's not a wall; it's a whole corridor of photos of Southwest employees with their pets: dogs, cats, goats, birds, horses, pigs, and other creatures. If Fido didn't already have a pic ready for framing, not to worry: Southwest brought in a professional pet photographer, and you could bring in your pet for a pose. Herb, of course, came to greet the other-specied members of Southwest's family (and naturally he remembers many of their names and asks about them when he sees their human owners). I didn't find out if Southwest has a vice president for *animals.*

The family atmosphere at Southwest extends to actual family. Nepotism is in vogue. It's very hard to get hired at Southwest, but they tend to look more favorably on employees' relatives (except that no child or spouse of a company officer can be hired), believing that a positive, fun attitude runs in families. When I visited Southwest, there were more than 960 married couples, and they were eagerly trying to reach 1,000. Libby Sartain, the vice president for people, joked that she had her eye on someone for Kristin, the cute PR coordinator. Is matchmaking in a human resources director's job description? No. But it is in Mom's.

Some People Want to Fill the World with Silly Love Songs

Giddy. That's how you feel when you're in love. One of the best parts of being in love is that it's fun. Every day seems better, happier. You laugh a lot. You play jokes on each other. You goof off. You celebrate each other's successes. The same is true at Southwest—in spades.

Every day's a party. While I was at Southwest's headquarters, there was an ice-cream party for the baggage handlers, Southwest's "official" birthday party for the whole airline, and a party party celebrating the dedication of the new dispatch center. Party on, Herb.

Southwest knows how to have a good time and doesn't take itself too seriously. Frequent passengers on Southwest have become accustomed to the jokes and songs of flight attendants. Flight attendants have been known to hide in overhead compartments to surprise unsuspecting passengers. They wear costumes on Halloween.

Fun is an openly stated corporate value and objective. A sense of humor is one of the key traits Southwest looks for when hiring. You don't have to be able to tell jokes (although it helps), but you had better look on the lighter side of life. After all, this is a company that paints its planes to look like whales, and the annual employee newsletter looks like the *National Enquirer* with stories such as "Seven-Headed Alien Invades System." When Southwest acquired Morris Airlines, they staged a "wedding" in Las Vegas with an Elvis impersonator presiding over the "ceremony." To settle a legal dispute with another airline, Herb arm-wrestled the other CEO (Herb lost).

Their humor extends to their ads. One of my favorites is the one on the next page. One of the reasons I particularly like this ad is that I know it would be almost impossible to get an ad like this approved at most other corporations. I've worked with a lot of big companies, and there's always a pervasive concern with not offending anyone, not being sued, not being misunderstood. That's why so much of corporate America is bland.

That's one of the things you notice about all the fun and games at Southwest. They send a message to everyone—employees, customers, stockholders—that Southwest is different and is going to continue to be different. They also give Southwest a distinct personality. When I happened to mention to a friend that I was working on a chapter about Southwest Airlines, she said, "I like Southwest; they're *human.*" That's the idea.

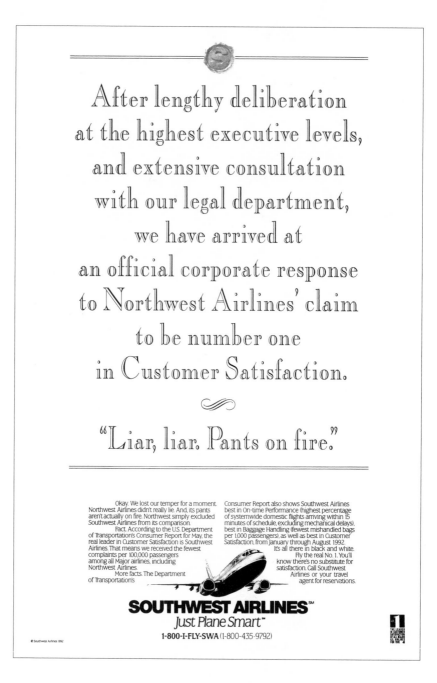

After lengthy deliberation
at the highest executive levels,
and extensive consultation
with our legal department,
we have arrived at
an official corporate response
to Northwest Airlines' claim
to be number one
in Customer Satisfaction.

"Liar, liar. Pants on fire."

Okay. We lost our temper for a moment. Northwest Airlines didn't really lie. And, its pants aren't actually on fire. Northwest simply excluded Southwest Airlines from its comparison.

Fact. According to the U.S. Department of Transportation's Consumer Report for May, the real leader in Customer Satisfaction is Southwest Airlines. That means we received the fewest complaints per 100,000 passengers among all Major airlines, including Northwest Airlines.

More facts. The Department of Transportation's Consumer Report also shows Southwest Airlines best in On-time Performance (highest percentage of systemwide domestic flights arriving within 15 minutes of schedule, excluding mechanical delays), best in Baggage Handling (fewest mishandled bags per 1,000 passengers), as well as best in Customer Satisfaction, from January through August 1992.

It's all there in black and white. Fly the real No. 1. You'll know there's no substitute for satisfaction. Call Southwest Airlines or your travel agent for reservations.

SOUTHWEST AIRLINES℠
Just Plane Smart™
1-800-I-FLY-SWA (1-800-435-9792)

© Southwest Airlines 1992

Your Love Keeps Lifting Me Higher

Now, here's where I think Southwest's attitude toward their corporate culture gets really interesting: at some point, Southwest recognized that the culture itself, the feeling of love and family, was in and of itself a valuable corporate resource. Like any other critical resource, the company culture needed protection, tending, enhancing. All this lovey-dovey stuff wasn't just icing on one of their ubiquitous cakes; it was vital to the airline's success.

Colleen, like any good mom worrying that the kids won't keep in touch now that they're grown, knew she had to do something to keep the family spirit as Southwest expanded. She selected about fifty employees who she thought exemplified the Southwest spirit and created the "Culture Committee."

The Culture Committee's role is to extend the Southwest spirit throughout the airline and show employees they're loved. For instance, committee members heard that maintenance teams working in the middle of the night felt like "stepchildren." So committee members visit them, send them notes, go out and cook for them as a group at two in the morning. The committee, now with more than a hundred members, meets four times a year and develops its own plan of activities. All its members are *volunteers.*

"Doesn't a lot of this just seem hokey?" I asked. They laughed. "We even have Hokey days." It turns out that "Hokey" is the name of the small vacuum cleaners used by flight attendants. (One of the ways Southwest turns flights around faster is that as passengers leave the plane, flight attendants start vacuuming from the back of the plane, using a small handheld vacuum cleaner called a "Hokey.") Once a year, the airline has Flight Attendant Appreciation Day, and someone from the Culture Committee meets every plane and vacuums it for the flight attendant. Yes, it's Hokey; it's also very nice. Loving. A little thing. It matters a lot.

What I Did for Love

With all this loving, does any work get done? You bet.

Southwest works its people very, very hard. Instead of squeezing employees on wages, it concentrates on productivity. Southwest flight attendants and pilots get paid only for time in the air, not for time on the

cision that passengers would rather get to their destination on time than have coffee. At this, according to my friend, the passengers broke out in a round of applause. Just a little loving does beat a cup of coffee.

On the Wings of Love

During my visit to Southwest, I walked in to the dedication of the new Flight Operations Control Center, a room with a bank of computers and huge screens to track and control the plane routes. Of course, they were having a party. Milling around, I stopped and talked to a group of three men. One, it turned out was Jim Kolkmeier, now retired from Southwest, who had dispatched the first Southwest plane in 1971. The others were Dave Jordan, director of the control center, and Paul Sterbenz, VP of flight operations, under whose jurisdiction the control center fell.

I spent about twenty minutes with this small group, talking about the company's history, funny occurrences with charters, how planes were dispatched differently by Southwest than by other airlines. I eventually asked what happened when bad weather or other factors forced changes in the schedule. Dave said that the most important thing he thinks about is how to inconvenience the fewest number of passengers.

"No matter what the cost?" I asked, knowing that everyone at Southwest is trained to think about costs.

"No matter what the cost," said Dave.

"I myself cost this company millions to save customers inconvenience," echoed Jim.

Up until then, I had been facing away from Paul, and I now turned to ask him, since it was his budget these guys were spending so freely, "How about you? Do you agree that it's not about cost?"

As he started to answer, I was surprised by his voice, which was choked with emotion, and I saw tears welling up in his eyes. I had obviously touched some nerve. "Safety," he said hoarsely. "I think about safety. In twenty-seven years this airline has never had a fatality, and I think about that record every morning first thing when I wake up. I think about safety."

"Why?" I asked in my most hard-bitten business reporter manner, not letting him get away with such a sentimental response.

Pausing and regaining the clarity in his voice, Paul said, "First, it would really damage us in the market. An accident damages you in the market-

How's Your Tripod?

Hanging around Kinko's, you may overhear a coworker say, "My tripod's out of balance." They're not talking about a paper jam in one of their copiers. They're speaking "Kinko-ese."

According to Kinko's founder and chairman, Paul Orfalea, three ingredients form the foundation of a happy life. They are:

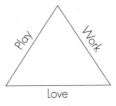

Paul, who created the tripod believes these three elements must be in balance to stay healthy.

All Kinko's employees are introduced to the concept of the tripod early in their orientation and training. They are reminded that Kinko's philosophy is that "We trust and care for each other." As such, Kinko's coworkers are encouraged to develop and maintain all three aspects of their life and are cautioned not to let work overwhelm their humanity. "Your life needs to be happy," one group of new employees was advised during orientation, as they were taught about the tripod. "We need you to be round people. Balanced people."

Kinko's managers regularly ask their employees, "How's your tripod?" And from time to time a coworker will go to a manager and say, "My tripod is out of balance." That means they need some time off to catch up on the play and love components of their tripod. They've got to get a life.

Work, play, and love. Three pretty good basic elements of a happy life. How's *your* tripod?

place, and it also damages a company internally, in the emotions of its people." But as he continued, his voice once again choked with emotion, and he literally fought back tears: "But mostly it's because I couldn't bear it if something happened. This is my family; those people in our planes are my family. I want to keep my family safe."

That's a love airline.

It's Almost like Being in Love

Only two companies I visited overtly use the word "love" as a mandate for their management style. Most companies are uncomfortable with that word. Instead, like Southwest, many use the term "family" to describe their corporate culture, to convey the sense that people are cared for as people. Southwest, of course, was one of the two that use "love." The other one took me by surprise.

As I was interviewing Yvonne Cadwallader, she offhandedly mentioned that when she had been in management training at her company, they had said that love was part of her job. "If you don't love the people who work for you," Yvonne remembers being taught, "you don't deserve to be a manager at 3M." *3M???*

Had I heard her wrong? 3M, after all, is a hundred-year-old midwestern company with 75,000 employees that primarily makes industrial products. Its employees are engineers, scientists. Lutherans. It's not some Californian, touchy-feely, New Age commune. I called Yvonne back.

Yvonne remembered her training quite distinctly. Tom Vaaler, a senior VP in human resources, had talked about the importance of dealing with employees as whole human beings with needs, feelings, and problems. "It's your job to get involved, to care if they have problems at home with alcoholism or drugs, with stress. You've got to love your employees," she recalled Tom saying. "And if you've got trouble with the 'L' word, you better really, really like them."

Still disbelieving, I tracked down Vaaler, now retired from 3M. Did he mean it about love at 3M?

"If you don't really care for the people you're responsible for, it's an empty existence," he responded. "I'm talking about the whole of the person. You need to differentiate yourself and people from machines and other resources. If you look at 3M's principles, it says the most important resource 3M has is its people; it doesn't say our patents, financial resources, or products are the most important; it says our people are the most important resources. A business is only as valuable as its people."

But even Vaaler got nervous speaking about *love:* "Twenty years ago I might have used the term *love;* in the last decade I probably substituted the word *caring.* But it is a consistent behavioral part of 3M, one of the reasons 3M sustains itself, grows itself. . . . We need caring more than ever because the world we live in is giving us all sorts of examples of an absence of caring. Companies are shutting down. Wall Street is telling employers they have to shave head count. Boards of directors listen to Wall Street. 3M could probably increase its value on the stock market if Desi [Livio DeSimone, the CEO] came out and said, 'I'm going to cut 10,000 people,' but he understands his greatest resource is the people of 3M." He didn't jump off that bridge just because Wall Street said all the other kids were doing it.

The World Will Always Welcome Lovers

When Mom refused to let you do something just because all the other kids were doing it, she was giving you a valuable lesson about setting your own standards. Mom wasn't trying to get you to be different just for difference's sake but so you'd have your own sense of how to behave, of how to do the right thing, even if you were the only one who did. She was helping you define yourself and be comfortable with who you are. A confident company, like a confident individual, can go its own way, especially if it's a way that brings more caring, more thoughtfulness, more love to the workplace.

Love is a decision, not a feeling. It's choosing to treat the people in our lives, whether in our private or business lives, as full human beings with their own feelings, needs, and vulnerabilities, as well as their own strengths, ideas, and dedication. That doesn't mean turning the workplace into a giant social hall or social work center. You can still demand hard work. After all, work itself is an important—I believe crucial—part of being human. But it does mean recognizing each individual's humanity.

"People think there are complicated secrets if they could just figure them out," remarked Colleen. "But it's just basically, practice the golden rule and treat people the way you want to be treated; *enjoy one another.*"

When that happens, people stop keeping score all the time. Southwest employees willingly volunteer an immense amount of extra time. When that happens, work becomes fun. When that happens, you not only bring your brains to work, you bring your heart. That would certainly make Mom happy.

6

DON'T GET TOO BIG
FOR YOUR BRITCHES

"I'm five and a half."
"I'm seven and three-quarters."
"In two months, I'll finally be a teenager."

When you're young, you can't wait till you're older. You eagerly anticipate every birthday. You imitate adults: wearing Mom's high heels or "shaving" with Daddy's empty razor. As you reach adolescence, your attempts at acting older get more daring, and you imagine all your problems would disappear if only you were grown up.

Now you look back with amusement and wonder why you were in such a hurry: high heels hurt, and shaving's a nuisance. And you're not nearly so eager for your next birthday to roll around. Mom was right when she warned you not to be in such a rush to grow up.

Many business owners think the same way as kids. They imagine that if only they were bigger—had more revenues, more employees, more products or services—their problems would be if not totally solved, at least greatly reduced. They attribute most of their difficulties to being small.

Being a big company seems exciting. Just like other adult pleasures, growth is glamorized in our society. Business magazines feature cover stories on "The 500 Biggest Companies" and "The 100 Fastest-growing Companies." I've never seen one on the "100 Happiest Business Owners." We associate "bigger" with "better."

But size doesn't always count. Sometimes getting bigger just means getting bigger problems. As you grow, whether in business or in life, you have to leave behind many things you can do only when you're small. You may find yourself wishing for the time when everyone in the company knew one another's name or all of you could go on a picnic together. Getting bigger may threaten even more important aspects of your business, including your passions, your purpose, your philosophies. You may find that what you wanted to be is no longer what you are; your company no longer fits your values—you've gotten too big for your britches.

Growth Without Trying

Patagonia, the outdoor clothing manufacturer, learned this lesson the hard way. Founded in 1957 by mountain climber Yvon Chouinard, the company grew slowly for its first twenty years. Chouinard originally manufactured climbing equipment and later broadened Patagonia's offerings to adventure wear. An avid outdoorsman, Chouinard was obsessed with quality. The clothes he made had to be as good as the equipment he built; after all, a mountain climber depends on it under the most severe conditions. When you're at ten thousand feet, you can't run out to the store for another pair of socks.

As a small company with a niche market, Patagonia could manufacture its products to meet Chouinard's high quality standards, set prices accordingly high, and still satisfy its customer base. But suddenly, in the boom years of the 1980s, Patagonia was "discovered." Sales skyrocketed, and the company grew rapidly. Between 1988 and 1991, payroll increased 40 percent, the number of stores wanting to sell the company's merchandise ballooned, and Patagonia was on track to be a $1 billion company within eleven years.

In the midst of this kind of growth, you don't stop and ask yourself, "Is this what we want to be doing with our company?" No, you hustle to fill orders. And you naturally get excited by all that money rolling in.

Patagonia was no different. Indeed, since Chouinard, an ardent environmentalist, "tithed" a percentage of Patagonia's gross sales to environmental concerns, increased sales meant Chouinard could give more money to the causes closest to his heart. It should have been the best of times.

Coors management saw this status as an invitation to expand nationally. But once you could buy a can of Coors at the corner 7-Eleven, the brand lost its mystique and customer loyalty. Coors lost what had made it special. The company now spends millions on advertising trying to build an image of uniqueness, with commercials often featuring tie-dyed hippies celebrating their "score" of Coors.

Wiser heads learned from Coors. When investor Warren Buffett acquired See's Candies, he instructed its president, Charles Huggins, to guard against becoming another Coors. They have. See's carefully controls growth, limiting geographic distribution and opening a new store only when projections show it will have higher profits than the average of existing stores. The goal is not to just add more numbers to See's total sales figures; growth must make See's healthier, not just bigger. This strategy inevitably means slower growth but a more stable, profitable company with a very sweet bottom line.

More Than One Playing Field

But, I hear you saying, if you don't grow big enough fast enough, you'll inevitably be beaten by bigger, richer competitors. The trick is to play a different game.

Like Patagonia, Richard Sawyer was once mesmerized by the idea of growth. The owner of Ricardo's Tortilla Chips in Memphis, Tennessee, Sawyer had a successful company selling tortilla chips to restaurants. But then one day he decided he needed to get bigger. He starting selling packaged chips to grocery stores.

"In the beginning you think you want to be a little Frito-Lay and grow to millions and millions," Sawyer recalled. But suddenly, instead of Sawyer controlling his business, his business was controlling him. He became enslaved by bank loans and big customers, constantly worried about paying off equipment and suppliers. He decided it wasn't for him and went back to his original market.

"I made a decision that we're better off having a business that's controllable and that the bank doesn't own, but that we own," said Sawyer, "and that we can control which products we sell. We'd rather sell a little bit at a good profit than a whole lot at reduced margins.

"Competition is what you make it," Sawyer reflected. "I'm not about to go out and compete with Frito Lay. There's a certain customer who needs good old-fashioned customer service, the guy who only wants fifty cases, not five truckloads. Somebody that just can't buy from larger corporations because they have so many restrictions."

Sawyer understood that big companies often don't want to serve small customers. One large company I've worked with ignores any market segment under $250 million a year; another won't pursue customers who spend less than many millions annually. Many major manufacturers will no longer supply small retailers. That leaves a lot of customers left over.

You can, of course, be *too* small. Without adequate resources to serve your current customers, develop new products, and market and manage the business, you'll soon be both financially vulnerable and emotionally frazzled. You need to reach a size with a manageable level of growth that allows you to survive and adapt. You can't be too small for your britches, either.

Honey, I Shrunk the Company

By 1991, Patagonia's founder, Chouinard, knew his britches were certainly the wrong size. And there were far too many of them! To meet market demand, Patagonia's catalog had 375 different products. Excess inventory was mounting in the company's warehouse.

Fortunately—and the company does indeed now consider it fortunate—Patagonia was in financial crisis. They could no longer afford their rapid growth, and they were forced to examine what they wanted to be.

It certainly wasn't a huge fashion apparel business. Fashion companies are based on changing styles, colors, and trends. The goal is to have consumers buy new things each season. As a sportsperson and environmentalist, Chouinard wanted to make products that people would buy once and use for years and years.

He realized growth was controlling his business. "What we were trying to do in 1990 was grow a single company into a size that was too large for its own britches," he reflected. "There's an optimum size for any endeavor, any business, government, city. If it gets any larger than that, it

Zen Archery

Many companies hire motivational speakers for their annual staff meetings. Patagonia does things a little differently.

At their 1997 company meeting, Patagonia brought in a demonstration of *kyudo,* or Zen archery. Western archery, of course, is aimed at scoring points by hitting the target, particularly the center bull's-eye. Zen archery, on the other hand, is not a sport, nor is it a martial art. Zen archery is a spiritual art, a ritualized formal ceremony. You don't try to hit the target. Instead, you focus on discipline and precision, how you move, how you think, how you relate your body and mind to the bow and arrow. The concept behind Zen archery is that if you forget about the *target* and concentrate on the *process,* you will not only hit the target but achieve spiritual growth.

Patagonia saw Zen archery as a parable of how they wanted to approach business. A Zen archer lets go of his concern for the target, fixing his concentration solely on doing everything the right way, achieving excellence in the execution. As a result, and not as the intent, he hits the bull's-eye. Patagonia, too, talks about letting go of the target—sales goals, for instance—and focusing solely on how they do business, their process and values.

As the Zen archers performed the silent ritual in their ceremonial robes, there was not even a whisper in the large hotel ballroom. The Patagonia staff was mesmerized. "It was very powerful, very emotional. There was true beauty in the simplicity of the movements. It was a physical example of the philosophies of this company," recalled Lu Setnicka, Patagonia's public relations director.

And it captured the essence of Patagonia's desire to put their values at the center of all their business decisions and actions; to concentrate on how and why they do business, not just the financial results. "Every time we have done the right thing, just because it was the right thing to do, it's always been good for us," said director of quality Randy Harward. Or, as Yvon put it, "I don't focus on profits. Profits happen when you do everything right."

doesn't work anymore. The market is a certain size, and that's just the way it is, and you should be a certain size within that market.

"A cancer cell is an unnatural growth. Your cells are growing, but when it becomes a cancerous cell, it grows out of control. That's what happens with most companies. Companies commit suicide. . . . I see so many companies that try to go as fast as they possibly can, and the fastest-growing companies are the quickest-dying."

As a mountain climber, Chouinard knew that Patagonia's increasing dependence on outside financing was dangerous. "One lesson climbing teaches you, or any type of risk sport, you never exceed your resources. . . . It's a matter of living and operating within your means. I've always done that. I've never actually been a risk taker. I don't take any risks. Before I go do a hard climb, I know exactly that I can do it. I've hardly ever hurt myself. I'm just not lazy. I do my homework."

So they shrunk the company. Patagonia dramatically cut back the number of styles, eliminated many distribution channels, reduced the size of the staff. It was a wrenching experience. But it gave the Chouinards back their control, and it gave Patagonia back its soul.

It's My Company; I Can Do What I Want

Staying smaller freed Chouinard and Patagonia to focus on issues other than just financial gain. The most dramatic example is organic cotton.

A few years ago, Patagonia conducted an environmental assessment of the four main fibers they used in their clothing. To their surprise, they discovered that the fiber with the greatest negative environmental impact was cotton. Patagonia's board of directors recommended that the company phase out its use of regular cotton, slowly moving to the use of organic cotton over a number of years. Organic cotton is far more expensive and the supply is very limited, so this would take some time.

Chouinard said no. Patagonia would not phase out regular cotton. They would just stop using it. Now. Not three years from now. As of the next catalog, Patagonia would no longer offer products made with traditional cotton. Boom!

Chouinard could never have made such a decision if the company had been committed to growth; cotton products represented 20 percent of its sales. There wasn't enough organic cotton on the market to substitute for the amount of regular cotton the company used. In the short term, this meant reducing the number of products offered; over the long term, it meant that Patagonia would spend significant amounts of money and energy on research and development of organic cotton products and helping to build the organic cotton supply. It was a very expensive decision. And it was certainly not motivated by the market; Patagonia's customers had never expressed a demand for organic cotton. But it's what Chouinard wanted.

Patagonia is now the country's largest purchaser of organic cotton. When they stopped thinking about the size of their britches, they were free to think about what their britches were made of.

Protecting the Seventh Generation

By 1993 Patagonia was once again healthy, and an investment banking firm approached Chouinard with a proposal to go public. Chouinard would retain control, Patagonia could still be committed to their environmental goals, and the sale of stock would bring Chouinard more than $100 million, with which he could establish a foundation to support his causes. There was only one catch: he would have to be willing to *try* to grow the company 10 to 15 percent a year. Chouinard said no. Growth would never again be Patagonia's controlling factor.

"Having to grow [continually] would kill this company; we wouldn't be here a hundred years from now. . . . I want to run this place like it's going to be here a hundred years from now. If you want to get anywhere near sustainability . . . you have to do your planning for many generations down the line, not just the next two, three years. . . . The Iroquois nation used to have a guy on the council, when they made any decisions, there was one person representing the seventh generation. He was always looking into the future to see if this is a good decision for the long, long term."

What Makes Your Company Unique

The decision to grow—how much and how fast—should be a thoughtful business choice. And you do have a choice. Patagonia could have chosen to go public; Coors could have chosen to stay a regional beer; See's could choose to add fifty stores a year. It's a question of what you gain and what you give up.

All too often, growth demands that you give up your values, your character, your uniqueness. When Patagonia had large bank loans, the bankers wanted Chouinard to stop mountain climbing; they thought it was too risky. Here was a company founded on the pitons Chouinard used climbing and whose heart and soul centered on adventure sports. Asking Chouinard to stop climbing struck at the very personality, the character, of Patagonia.

Being bigger isn't the key to survival. Being healthy and being yourself are. Warren Buffett recognized the value of maintaining a distinct identity with See's. As a result—and I speak from personal experience—See's is almost religiously revered, their shiny white stores seen as temples of temptation by western chocoholics. It need not fear Fannie Farmer.

Limiting growth meant Patagonia could keep what made it unique, what made it special. "How have you changed since you've worked at Patagonia?" I asked Hal Thomson, product marketing specialist.

"I came to Patagonia so I wouldn't have to change. I love outdoor sports, and I wanted a place that would allow me to pursue that. I'm committed to the environment, and I wanted to work at a place consistent with my values. I'm casual, and I wanted to work where I could be casual."

Hal paused, considered, then continued, "If there's one way that I am different, that I have changed, it's that I'm less skeptical. Before coming to Patagonia, I didn't think I could really make a difference in the world. Now I know I can make a difference. And it's nice to have hope."

It's Not the Size, It's the Stamina

In fact, the question is not whether to be a "big" business or a "small" business at all. You have to free yourself from the tyranny of concentrating on growth for growth's sake. Stop thinking about size, and start thinking about health.

Doesn't this just seem like common sense? Why open new stores, serve new markets, add new products if you don't become healthier, more profitable? Yet growth is so enticing that most companies frantically pursue it without ever asking why they want to expand and what will happen if they do. They need Mom to remind them not to outgrow their britches.

The real issue is sustainability. Fast growth is hard to sustain because it consumes resources more quickly than they can be replenished; a company's own income can rarely fuel fast growth. That's why you end up needing bank loans and other outside financing. In addition to money, fast growth consumes a company's resources of energy, attention, and personnel.

A no-growth state, however, can starve a company. Without an infusion of some new resources, some new challenges, you'll soon stagnate or wither away. You need sufficient growth to stay adaptable over time. Staying small doesn't mean standing still.

The goal is to become a "sustainably sized" business with a more natural growth level appropriate to your company's existing resources, needs, stage of business life, and, equally important, character and values.

Becoming a "sustainably sized business" means concentrating on your company's fundamentals, not its growth rate. When you take care of business, growth takes care of itself. Growth becomes a natural product of running your business well rather than a goal in itself.

Sustainability requires long-term vision. You'll occasionally have to forgo some opportunities because they demand too many resources, and you'll have to invest some of today's resources to enable yourself to thrive later. Sustainability requires sacrifice and self-control. And you have to look beyond the next quarterly earnings or annual report. Growth focuses on the short term; sustainability focuses on the long.

This doesn't mean you don't grow; you just don't grow too fast. Always remember Mom's advice and never get too big for your britches.

7

SAY YOU'RE SORRY

"He hit me!"

Remember the mean things you did as a kid? The times you pinched or shoved another kid, called each other names, or snatched your friend's favorite toy? We all did things like that. I wasn't a particularly nasty kid, but when I was about six, I pushed my brother, Arnie, off the bed and knocked his tooth out.

Fortunately—usually before we did too much damage—Mom stepped in. She got us to stop whatever we were doing, made sure the other kid was okay, and then firmly insisted, "Say you're sorry."

Now, you never thought about it, and your Mom may not have either, but Mom knew what she was doing when she made you say, "I'm sorry." An apology—a sincere apology—made the other kid feel better and made it possible for you to go on being friends. But it did more than that. Having to face the kid and say "I'm sorry" also forced you to think about what you had done, helped you empathize with your friend, and made you understand the consequences of your actions.

Companies can also hurt people. It might be a little hurt, like failing to make a delivery on time or mixing up an order, or it may be something very important, but we usually feel much better about the company if they apologize and appear sincerely sorry for their mistake. Apologizing seems such a little thing to do that we can be incredibly frustrated when a company doesn't bother.

A few years ago, I bought a mail-order laptop computer. The first time I had a problem, I discovered that my warranty didn't actually include the on-site service the salesman had promised. "Oh, some of our salespeople get that wrong," said the customer service representative airily. After about ten calls, I finally got the service originally promised, but no one at the company ever said, "I'm sorry." I haven't bought a computer from them since.

Many companies forget the importance of an apology when something bad happens. Companies frequently delay, deny, or derail. They may even blame the victim: "You didn't order blue, you ordered red." "You didn't read the directions." This attitude inevitably adds insult to injury. It's not only that the company wronged us, we feel the company just doesn't care. And if the company doesn't care about us, how can we care about the company? Increasingly, customers, employees, even vendors want to know that they are doing business with people who care—care about their product, care about their customers as individuals, and care about the kind of business they run.

An apology is not just saying words. We all know people who, when pushed to it, will offer a weak, empty "I'm sorry" that can leave us vaguely dissatisfied. We feel that they are going through the motions but the lesson hasn't sunk in. The same applies in a business setting; training employees to routinely express regret when something goes wrong may sometimes make the customer feel better, but it does little to help you improve your company over the long run.

No, a sincere apology should accomplish what Mom intended: looking at your behavior, empathizing with the wronged party, and recognizing your need to change. Believe it or not, problems may offer opportunities for you to improve your business. Apologies are little signposts letting you know that such opportunities exist.

To examine the power of an apology in a business setting, even in the face of a very major issue, I decided to compare how two different food companies responded when their products were implicated in causing serious injury and illness. One decided, for sound business reasons, not to apologize nor to act as if they had done anything wrong. The other chose an entirely different response and tested the power of saying "I'm sorry" even in the face of a tragedy as great as the death of a baby girl.

The $3 Million Cup of Indifference

Whenever people talk about silly lawsuits, they're likely to bring up the case of McDonald's and the hot cup of coffee. In this famous case, an elderly woman was awarded $2.9 million when she bought a cup of McDonald's coffee at a drive-through window, held the cup between her legs while in the car, and then got burned when the coffee spilled. If ever there seemed an obvious abuse of the legal system, this was it. The comics and pundits had a field day. But the judgment actually had relatively little to do with coffee and a lot to do with McDonald's not being sorry.

McDonald's coffee was indeed hot. The fast-food company's market research showed that customers preferred very hot coffee, so they made it company policy to give customers what they wanted—a reasonable business decision. But McDonald's coffee was exceptionally hot. The company's own lawyers found that McDonald's coffee was at least twenty degrees hotter than coffee at other fast-food outlets or restaurants. Sooner or later, people spill coffee, and when they do, they're likely to get burned. The hotter the coffee, the worse the burn.

A lot of people had gotten burned by McDonald's coffee. These weren't necessarily just little burns. In the elderly woman's case, for instance, her burns were so serious that she required hospitalization and skin grafts. Before this suit, McDonald's had already settled more than seven hundred claims for coffee burns and paid out more than $500,000. While that may seem a lot, remember that McDonald's sells millions of cups of coffee and a few hundred injuries and a few hundred thousand dollars may be, statistically and financially, a very small price to pay for satisfying the taste of the vast number of customers.

But the jury didn't think so. What led to the award of millions of dollars, according to jury members, was not the woman's injuries in and of themselves but the testimony of a McDonald's executive. Even in the face of this lawsuit and the previous burn cases, the executive testified that the company had no plans to lower the coffee's temperature. While they knew of the many burn cases, McDonald's had never consulted burn experts about the effect the higher temperatures might have on increasing the severity of the burns. And even after many people were burned, McDonald's decided *not* to warn customers.

One juror said the case was not about coffee but about McDonald's "callous disregard for the safety of the people." As one juror told *The Wall Street Journal,* "There was a person behind every number, and I don't think the corporation was attaching enough importance to that."

The jury was angry because McDonald's wasn't sorry. Even in the face of hurting hundreds of people, McDonald's just didn't seem to care. The company was making a reasonable business decision but not a human, caring decision.

So the jury came to an extremely logical conclusion. First they awarded the woman $200,000 for the actual damages, but since they felt she had contributed to the accident by driving with the coffee between her legs, they then *reduced* that amount by 20 percent. But then, to punish McDonald's for their "willful, reckless, malicious or wanton conduct," the jury awarded the woman $2.7 million—the amount McDonald's makes on coffee in *two days.* (Though the judge shared the view that McDonald's conduct was reckless, callous, and willful, he reduced the punitive damage award from $2.7 million to $480,000. The parties then settled the case for an undisclosed amount.)

The jurors were sending McDonald's a message: they wanted the company to understand the impact of its actions, to acknowledge the hurt they had caused, and to take steps to make sure it wouldn't happen again. They wanted McDonald's to "say you're sorry."

Odwalla—The Party's Over

Tuesday night, October 29, 1996, Greg Steltenpohl was up late celebrating. Greg's colleagues had thrown him a surprise birthday party. But the party was more than just a birthday party; it was a special celebration to honor Greg for his sixteen years of vision and leadership as the founder and chairman of Odwalla, the leading fresh fruit juice company in the country.

The atmosphere at the party was heady. All the senior executives, the board of directors, and longtime Odwalla employees were there, toasting

Greg's phenomenal achievement in bringing Odwalla to the level of success it enjoyed that October. The company was on a roll: sales were up more than 65 percent, the company was expanding, and they had recently gone public, issuing stock on the NASDAQ exchange. As a token, Stephen Williamson, Odwalla's president, presented Greg with a bronzed receipt of the company's first sale: $11.20 from the Cook House Restaurant in Santa Cruz, California. Odwalla's sales were now over $60 million a year.

Odwalla had indeed had humble beginnings. When Greg, along with his wife, Bonnie Bassett, and friend Gerry Percy, founded Odwalla, it couldn't even be called a small business—it was a *micro*business. The three were living in the counterculture beach community of Santa Cruz, and all were committed to doing something socially responsible with their lives. Greg ran across the book *100 Businesses You Can Start for Under $100* and focused on the idea of producing fresh juice. It was a business they could start cheaply, but, more important, they felt they could make a product that was healthy for people, something they could feel good about contributing to the community.

From those inauspicious beginnings, Odwalla rapidly grew into the nation's leading producer and distributor of fresh juices, with operations in seven western states and British Columbia, Canada. Odwalla's growth was far more like that of one of the many nearby Silicon Valley technology companies than of a traditional food products company.

But Greg and Odwalla were focused on more than just growth. From the beginning, Odwalla had developed, and operated around, a set of core values that served as a conscious basis for decision making within the company. The first of these values was "Honesty, integrity, and respect." Others included "Personal responsibility and accountability," "Striving for the essence," "Effective communication," and "Eco-logical leadership and sustainability."

So that Tuesday night, the people of Odwalla had reason to celebrate. But even while Greg was being toasted, Odwalla's fate was being radically altered by scientists a few hundred miles to the north. Within hours of downing his last glass of champagne, Greg would face the most difficult challenge of his professional—perhaps even personal—life, one that would threaten Odwalla's very existence.

"We Have an Issue Here"

When Greg arrived in his office on Wednesday morning, October 30, the air of festivity continued. Then came the phone call. "I was in a meeting, and he [Stephen Williamson] took the call," Greg remembers. "He came in and interrupted me from the meeting and said, 'We have an issue here.'" The call was from the Washington State Health Department with ominous news: it had received reports of thirteen cases of illness caused by the potentially deadly bacterium *E. coli*. Ten of the thirteen patients, mostly small children, had consumed Odwalla apple juice within ten days before becoming seriously ill.

Within hours of that call, Greg and the officers of Odwalla made a critical, costly, and controversial decision: they instituted a recall of almost all Odwalla products. Moreover, they did this as a "public recall," informing the public through public service announcements and press releases, instead of just recalling the products quietly by taking the juice off the store shelves; doing so would have meant that juice previously purchased would have remained in the hands of unwary consumers.

To the uninitiated, Odwalla's immediate recall might seem a straightforward decision. In fact, it is highly unusual for a company to make a decision with such potentially devastating financial and public relations consequences so quickly. Few companies would have dared take such a great business risk, and most would have considered Odwalla's action premature. The conservative position would be to wait for the result of tests. (At this point, no evidence of *E. coli* had been found in any Odwalla product.) Indeed, a few years earlier, when *E. coli* had been linked to Jack-in-the-Box hamburgers, also in the Seattle area, that company had taken a few days before issuing a recall.

"I think the original position they [Jack-in-the-Box] took," according to Carl Osaki, chief of environmental health for the Seattle/King County Department of Public Health, "was to hunker down, be defensive, try to protect the business rather than solve the problem. One of the concerns off the bat was, what does this do to my business, to my stock? Once they realized TV screens in Seattle were showing little kids on kidney dialysis machines, they became more concerned with food safety." Osaki emphasizes that Jack-in-the-Box later became one of the leaders in dealing with food safety in the fast-food industry, but it took a while for the message to sink in.

Not Odwalla. Benefitting from Jack-in-the-Box's experience and, more important, from their own core values, Greg and Odwalla acted quickly. "They [Odwalla] were definitely quicker to respond," said Osaki, who remembered that everyone was also concerned about apple cider being consumed the next night, Halloween. "The recall was done voluntarily by them, in a very rapid manner."

"The question is, if you have a potential problem, how serious is it, and if you wait for confirmation more people can get sick," said Greg. "On the other hand, you obviously have the reputation of the company and the [effect on] sales. . . . We're a publicly held company, we have a fiduciary responsibility to the shareholders. . . . If we act in a way a shareholder can later legally criticize, then we can be sued for a lot of money.

"What's most surprising is that this type of conduct is not the expected and usual conduct for business. . . . I've had this discussion with a number of people, and they say, 'You were jeopardizing the whole company.' And I say, 'Yeah, but if you were a parent and you knew that some company was going to wait an extra week to find out a little bit more because their company could go out of business, and meanwhile your kid got sick, let alone died, would you want to support that company after that?' For us, it wasn't a wisdom thing. It's just we're parents; we have little kids. I don't want them to keep drinking that apple juice. So why would I leave it out on the shelf for an extra week? Even if it's not a problem [i.e., no *E. coli* is later found], who wants that worry?"

Over the next forty-eight hours, Odwalla conducted an aggressive and massive recall effort, removing all its juice from all its shelves, everywhere. This meant that the entire company went to work around the clock, pulling a half-million juice bottles from 4,600 locations in seven states and British Columbia. The one and only positive identification of *E. coli* in Odwalla juice was found a full five days after the recall was announced and three days after the recall had been completed. Had Odwalla waited those five days, who knows how many more children might have become ill?

"Let's Just Take Care of It"

Within a day, Odwalla made another bold move: they apologized. In full-page newspaper ads, Odwalla not only expressed their regrets ("We are deeply sorry for any illness or suffering associated with our products") but offered to pay any medical bills for those who were sick—all this before tests had yet proved the link between Odwalla and *E. coli.*

Much as Greg and Odwalla wanted to make the offer to pay the medical bills, it wasn't really theirs to make. Odwalla wouldn't be picking up the tab; their insurance company would. Before they could make this commitment, they had to convince the insurance company—and its lawyers—to go along.

Insurance companies don't like to make offers that could lead to lawsuits, and they had never before taken Odwalla's approach. "This was way different," recalled Greg. "They were not used to a company that wanted to say we'd pay for medical expenses. They just weren't used to any of this. So there was a trust process that had to happen between us and our own insurance company.

"We tried to avoid the lawyer-to-lawyer thing as much as possible by setting a tone and saying, 'Look, if you or your kids went through this, and we think it was our product, let's just take care of it so it's easy for both of us,' " said Greg. "[This way] you don't create additional trauma around the whole resolution. The insurance company agreed with that. So we just set a policy. Let's just settle claims without . . . trying to make everybody prove it. That worked out for the insurance company. In fact, the insurance company's claim agents said they were more impressed than any case they've ever worked on with the legitimacy, courtesy, and respect they got from Odwalla customers."

Making Changes

Besides the recall, the other major issue Odwalla faced was tracking down the source of the *E. coli,* if any, and taking whatever steps were necessary to prevent a future occurrence. A troop of county, state, and federal regulators, along with personnel from the Centers for Disease Control, were at Odwalla's plant and facilities in Dinuba, California, for eleven days. The agencies would later praise Odwalla for its cooperative attitude throughout the crisis.

Fairly quickly, Greg made another momentous decision for Odwalla— a decision that to this day is controversial within the company. Odwalla changed the way they produced apple juice, adopting a process called "flash pasteurization," which heats the juice to the point where any possible bacteria are killed but retains the flavor and nutrition. "It was a very unpopular thing to do," recalls Greg. Odwalla's founding purpose was to be a producer of fresh juice, and many Odwalla employees and customers are ardent, even strident, believers in fresh-only juices and foods. The decision to go to flash pasteurization struck at the very heart and foundation of Odwalla.

While all this was going on, Odwalla was taking a financial pounding. In the first two days of the recall, Odwalla stock lost a third of its market value. The recall's direct costs alone—just getting the product off the shelves—not including lost sales and indirect costs, would be more than 5 percent of the company's previous year's gross revenue. For a company so small, this was life-threatening.

"Human Beings Who Actually Care"

Within a few days of the outbreak of the illnesses, Greg took another highly unusual step: he visited the families of those who were sick to apologize in person.

Imagine the scene: you're the founder and chairman of a company you started in the hopes of making people healthier, of doing something good for the world, but here you are in the home or hospital room of a family with a very sick child, a child made gravely ill by your very own product. You're also a parent of a young child yourself.

"It's painful even to revisit it," said Greg. "The idea that our products could cause somebody harm was extremely hard to take given the fact that . . . I dedicated my whole professional career to bring products to market that optimize people's health. . . . It was just painful. I was probably like a doctor losing his first patient, a certain sense of failure."

"There is not a lot to say," remembers Greg about what was discussed during these visits. "Sometimes a lot of what we did was, we just sat there . . . talked about little things. . . . When we first acted, all I could do was give them an impression that there were human beings on the other side of the fence, and that we're human beings who actually care. If all else fails, they know that."

One visit would later prove especially heartbreaking—the one to the Gimmestad family in Denver, whose eighteen-month-old daughter, Anna, was seriously ill. "I just wanted them to know that during the time that they were hoping, we were there for them," said Greg. "They wouldn't have to worry about the quality of medical care, [wouldn't] have to make a decision that they couldn't afford a certain doctor. Let them have the best chances.

"When I met them, I was just completely struck by their humility," Greg remembers. "They're a young, Christian couple. Clearly Christian and conscious about their Christian beliefs. . . . The Gimmestad family was so unusual in that they retained enthusiasm for Odwalla all the way through. . . . They just said, 'Look, we think Odwalla's great. . . . We know you guys wouldn't have been conducting yourself in some cheap way. You didn't know better. We just know that. That's not where we're coming from. We think it's a healthful product.' In fact, they served me fresh juice when I went over to their house. They're unusual. Other families, I think, who went through the really serious illnesses had a tougher time [dealing with us]."

"No Mumbo Jumbo"

Within a couple days of that first phone call, Odwalla had taken the following steps:

- They recalled their products.
- They set up phone lines and a Web site to answer questions.
- They changed the process by which they manufactured juice to ensure that the problem wouldn't be repeated.
- They offered financial compensation to any injured party without the party having to prove a link to Odwalla.
- In print and in person, they apologized.

This swift, open reaction started to attract attention, even from the news media, and people started to rally around the company.

"We'd just like you to know we appreciate your immediate response to the recent *E. coli* illness. . . . Rather than making a bunch of excuses or hiding behind a gang of attorneys, you chose to accept responsibility and

What Greg Steltenpohl Learned from His Mother, Benita Johnson

My mother was in the hospitality business. She was first a chef, then later ran restaurants. She loved food; she *loved* food. The thing she taught me about food is presentation. She said, "A good presentation is half the joy of eating." Whenever she made food, she always made it look nice. It started out with just little things like garnish: how you arrange the plate, how you scoop things out and put it on the plate.

When I first got into the food business, one of the things I thought about was the packaging, the design. It's not just how good the juice is, but it's also how I present it. That led to a whole strategy in the company around the merchandising coolers being a showcase presentation for the bottles of juice. That strategy was one of the most successful, and it's still one of the most admired, copied strategies in use. Typically, package companies don't use that, you just get space on the shelf. You don't bring your own container. Coke and Pepsi discovered this concept a long time ago, but for a specialty food company, it was not in much use at the time we started.

That was a legacy of my mother and what she taught me about presentation. That's something I remember—a piece of advice that became part of my business.

My mother also taught me a whole attitude about customers: the personal touch in customer service. I definitely applied that [during the recall] if you look back at the personal visits [I made to the families of the sick children]. If I go into my own psychology, it was necessary for me to have personal contact. That pathway was paved for me because my mother, being a hostess, knew there was a whole personal contact that made people enjoy the food a lot more. Things taste better when people know the person who made it. That's another whole side I learned from my mother— the necessity for a personal touch in business, person-to-person contact.

take positive action," said one of the hundreds of letters and e-mails the company received.

The response buoyed the spirits of the overworked Odwalla staff. "[I was] floored and amazed by the number of people who called in on the 1-800 lines to voice their support of the company," said Odwalla employee Rupesh Shah, who helped answer the hot line. "I was getting calls from people volunteering to come to work for us. For free. They'd call and say, 'If you guys need help, I'll come and work.' "

An Odwalla driver recalled an encounter in a supermarket once he started returning some juice to the shelves: "I met a woman on Saturday while I had my head stuck in a cooler, and she said she had never tried our products before. Her feeling was that Odwalla had handled itself through this crisis with such integrity and that the media had given us a bum rap, that she was going to start purchasing the products to show her support. She then picked up a grapefruit juice, and off she went."

"I was at my bank that first Friday, standing in line with about twenty people. I had my Odwalla shirt on, the one that says, 'No Mumbo Jumbo' on the back," recalled John Kirk, a payroll specialist. "When I got to the front of the line, the guy in back of me said, 'You work for Odwalla?' I said, 'Well, yes, I do.' He said, 'You guys have handled everything really great!' Then the person behind him said, 'Yeah, you guys are doing a great job.' And there were four people in line behind him, all expressing these positive comments about Odwalla. So I just turned around and said, 'You see the shirt? No mumbo jumbo!' You know, that was cool, because it was really stressful that Friday. Here are these complete strangers in line at a bank, and everyone's kind of fuming to begin with, and yet they were able to go from a negative, 'We're in this damn bank' attitude to such positive energy about us. That was very uplifting to me."

Local pizzerias sent complimentary pizzas to Odwalla headquarters. Another Bay Area entrepreneurial venture, Pete's Brewing Company, makers of Pete's Wicked Ale, also sent pizzas with a note signed by seventeen of Pete's "gang": "We have the utmost respect for Odwalla, Inc. and how company management is handling this difficult situation to the best of its abilities."

Even vendors came to Odwalla's aid. A new "T-1" telephone line, to handle all the phone calls, was installed by Pacific Bell, the local phone company, in less than a week, instead of the usual month or more. The phone company also went through all Odwalla's phone bills, looking to find any credit it could give the company, and retroactively lowered the rates on some of Odwalla's regional phone bills. Long-distance provider Sprint gave the company a significant credit "out of the blue."

But perhaps most important, Odwalla's trade partners—stores, restaurants, coffeehouses—were eager to help the company regain its footing.

Because Odwalla's route drivers had regular interaction with grocers and café and restaurant managers, they knew how Odwalla took care of its product. One grocer was typical, and Greg remembered her comment: "She said, 'Look, this company manages its stock better than any company I've ever seen. They're more conscientious about the date code on its product, not just since the recall but since the get-go.' Grocers are enormously practical people; the grocer is another person you don't fool. They see it all, products come and go, trends and fads and lots of promises. You don't win their hearts overnight. . . . They had seen us over many, many years being totally conscientious around the freshness of the product, the quality of what was on the shelf. When it came time that we were in trouble, it wasn't, like, 'Who are these guys, are they just going to try and shuck us?' They knew we were capable of managing our shelf; they knew we were capable of ensuring that the bad product would not be there after the recall. . . . There was that respect, [and] we were a great-selling product. The retailers wanted that business back just about as much as we did."

Anna

One week into the crisis, Odwalla's employees and operations were regaining some equilibrium. And then, on Friday, November 8, Anna Gimmestad, eighteen months old, died.

"It felt like . . . the 1989 earthquake," recalled Santa Cruz route driver Tinker Dominguez. "I had been on the same street—Pacific Avenue—in the earthquake. . . . It was this same sense of the unreal, and shock. . . . On Saturday I went to downtown Santa Cruz—this is the heart of Odwalla—and every newsstand has the headline ODWALLA LINKED TO BABY'S DEATH, and there was a picture of Anna. It was the most horrible day I've ever experienced as a driver. I'd been driving that street for years. People were looking at me with such sympathy—and shock and horror too. So I was delivering this juice and trying not to cry—I'd allow myself to cry in between stops. Then I went into one little café, and there was this small handwritten note on the cooler saying, 'Please support our Odwalla friends.' When I saw that, I started crying."

Anna was from Denver, and the Colorado team got the brunt of the public reaction. "We had a lot of comments about being baby killers, things like that," said Tony Olson, a Colorado manager. "I visited a . . . store in the mountains, introduced myself to the store manager, and he said, 'Did you kill anybody lately?' We got a lot of that."

Perhaps no Odwallan felt the impact of Anna Gimmestad's death harder than Colorado driver Jim McClaury. Jim's wife owns a beauty salon, and one of her regular clients was Christy Gimmestad, Anna's mother. Jim's wife was the person who had originally introduced the Gimmestads to Odwalla, and in a chilling coincidence, it was Jim himself who had delivered the juice to the store where the Gimmestads bought the bottle associated with Anna's death. When Anna died, this was not a nameless, faceless victim but a child of a friend.

Greg, who had visited the Gimmestads when Anna had first become ill, now telephoned them again to express his condolences and concern. They invited him to Anna's funeral.

"That was the worst part . . . that was the most intense part of the whole [crisis]," he said. The Gimmestads embraced and forgave Greg and Odwalla, but others did not. "Many people in their town were very adamant that our company should be vilified. . . . They thought we were a big California company, a [huge] corporation, and these people [Odwalla] were responsible for killing this little girl. They didn't want to see our trucks in their town. It was pretty hard core. So I wasn't sure I wanted to be there [at the funeral]. But I thought, our whole company has an emotional investment in this. . . . I owe it to them, at least the employees, to represent Odwalla and see this thing through. We didn't publicize my attending. When I greeted the family, they all gave me a hug. They were all very gracious and open. The whole family."

"What has helped me feel better is the company's response to the crisis," said Colorado manager Randy Andersen. "We responded with our core values. Another thing that helped was Anna's parents response to Greg's concern and the fact that they embraced him. This was an incredible response on their part, the fact that the parents do not hold anything against us, and they understand the whole issue. [And] Greg's personal attention in visiting them and sharing their grief. He represented the whole company, and we felt really good about that."

The Gimmestads never got a lawyer, and they never wanted money. "We don't blame Odwalla at all," Christy Gimmestad said in an interview with the local newspaper, *The Greeley Tribune.* "They had no bad intentions throughout all of this."

Anna's father, Chad Gimmestad, added, "Our society is always out to get what they can, and we wouldn't want to take advantage of anyone, especially in a situation like this."

Odwalla later made a monetary gift to the Gimmestads to enable them to create something in Anna's name. At least one playground has been built in Anna's memory.

Because Anna's loss was felt so deeply at Odwalla, many employees expressed a desire to make a personal connection with the Gimmestads, and the family graciously agreed to come to Odwalla's headquarters to receive the gift in person. On the day they did, the people of Odwalla met and embraced the Gimmestads, and each one who wanted had a chance to say, in person, for themselves and for Odwalla, "I'm sorry."

Parents to Parents

Of course, nothing is as simple as it seems, and just saying "I'm sorry" didn't mean the end of legal entanglements for Odwalla. The government continued to investigate, and some families of children who became ill pursued lawsuits.

The investigation by the federal government did not conclude until July 1998, when Odwalla pleaded guilty to sixteen misdemeanor charges and paid a fine of $1.5 million. Odwalla readily cooperated with the U.S. attorney's office, which had been seeking ways to become more aggressive with the food industry.

An editorial in Denver's *Rocky Mountain News,* which had followed the *E. coli* case carefully since Anna Gimmestad was from the area, decried the conviction against Odwalla, saying it had been meted out solely to send a message to the food industry, not as a result of Odwalla's actions. "The real point," said the editors, "is to get other people's attention." One of the parents of a child sickened by the *E. coli* added that the penalty had been meant less for Odwalla than for others, "kind of a fine for the industry as a whole, letting the industry know, 'You guys, you got to be a little more careful.'"

When it came to negotiating a settlement with families of five other children who had become ill, once again Odwalla chairman Greg Stel-tenpohl and president Stephen Williamson met with the parents themselves; they didn't just send their lawyers.

"You know, it was tough for Odwalla to face all of us," one father, Richard Dimock, said. "We got to talk across the table from them. . . . It was an emotional two days for everybody."

Another parent, Terry Beverly, after vividly describing the horrors of watching his two-year-old son so close to death, clearly one of the most dreadful things a parent could ever face, went on to share his impressions of the company. In his meetings with Greg and Stephen, he had a chance to see the people behind the company, and he became convinced of their sincerity. "They said they were very sorry. I know they were sincere about this. They have kids too."

Does Saying "I'm Sorry" Work?

So which company made the right choice? McDonald's, which was unrepentant even in the face of continued injuries? Or Odwalla, with their immediate response and overt remorse? On the face of it, McDonald's may actually have come out ahead. The cost of the suit and the previous claims together amounted to only a few million dollars, an insignificant amount for a company the size of McDonald's. Because of the way the suit was covered—as yet another example of the foolishness of the legal system—McDonald's managed to avoid the bad publicity that would normally have accompanied such a seemingly callous corporate response. I spoke with the chairman of a billion-dollar company about this case, and he felt that McDonald's had not acted at all incorrectly. After all, seven hundred burns when so many millions of cups of coffee are sold is statistically insignificant, and every company gets complaints.

But McDonald's took a chance. Had the press covered the story in greater depth or with a different "spin," the public would probably have reacted far differently. McDonald's can hardly afford to be seen as cavalier about their customers' well-being. The jury in the McDonald's case reflected a growing public sentiment: business has to care when it does something wrong.

On the other hand, Odwalla's response—the immediate recall and informing the public—was extremely costly, especially for such a small company. In the short run, Odwalla might have saved money by taking a slower, more private, less open approach.

But in the long run, Odwalla's response may have saved the company. Had word about the *E. coli* contamination leaked out slowly or had the company stonewalled, the public might have abandoned the company. Instead, trade partners jumped in to help Odwalla recover. Shortly after the recall, I walked into a Safeway and saw that the Odwalla cooler had been moved to the front of the store. Almost a year later, it was still in the highly desirable prime front location. I frequently notice Odwalla coolers in prominent locations in retail outlets, indicating a continued commitment by stores to Odwalla.

Even the press helped Odwalla recover. After their initial skewering of Odwalla, journalists who followed the company closely realized this was not just a big, uncaring company but a company truly trying to do the right thing. Throughout the year following the recall, Odwalla's activities received positive press coverage, and the company was able to successfully launch a number of new products.

But Odwalla had no way of anticipating how the public would respond; Greg didn't know his actions would turn out to be the *smart* thing to do, he just knew they were the *right* thing to do. Odwalla made their decisions based on their strong set of declared core values, including honesty, integrity, and taking responsibility. They did just what Mom would have wanted: understood the impact of their behavior, owned up to it, made changes, and tried to make amends, then said, "We're sorry."

8

Don't Judge a Book by Its Cover

Edward, the geeky-looking guy next door, has had a crush on you for years. It's taken until now, when you're a senior in high school, for him to get up the nerve to ask you out. He has two tickets to a Rolling Stones concert. You love the Rolling Stones. You're tempted, but . . .

He's just so nerdy. He's nice enough, sure. And funny. But he's short and wears thick glasses. He's always reading or doing math problems. He keeps a calculator in his top pocket. Geez, you can't imagine dating him. What if one of your friends saw you? But it's just about impossible to get Stones tickets.

Mom wasn't surprised when Edward asked you out. She'd been watching him watching you for years. Mom noticed when he drove across town to buy you the impossible-to-find book you needed for your English assignment, and she saw how patient and kind he was when he tutored you in algebra last year. She knows he didn't just stumble on those Stones tickets either but that he waited in line all night because he knew how much you wanted to see them. Mom's no dummy; she knows how some of these nerdy guys turn out.

Mom overhears you discussing the pros and cons of accepting Edward's offer—you really want to see the Stones, but what if someone sees you with him? When you've just about decided to turn Edward down, Mom interrupts and cautions you, "There's a whole lot more to this guy than meets the eye. Don't judge a book by its cover."

He's Taller When He Stands on His Wallet

I used to have a firm rule; I would never hire a woman job applicant who showed up for an interview wearing pants. No matter what the job, I expected a woman to be in a dress or skirted suit. It didn't matter how neat and pulled together she was; I just reasoned that wearing pants meant she didn't bring a professional attitude to the workplace. It wasn't until I interviewed Suzanne Fried that I was forced to abandon my usual practice. Suzanne informed me that she never wore dresses but convinced me she'd be a great addition to the office. She was well qualified and I really liked her, so I relented. Suzanne, of course, worked out great, and I had to reevaluate my preconceptions. Okay, so maybe just this once I was wrong. . . .

We all do it. We can't help it. We make up our minds from first impressions, outward appearances, superficial things. We attribute significance to clothing, hairstyle, body shape: "No one with any self-respect would go out in public like that."

And then we worry too much about what customers would think or say: "I can't hire a guy with a ponytail; my customers wouldn't like it." "This is a dental office; I can't have a receptionist with purple hair." Or we fail to give ourselves or our customers credit for being able to get used to something: "I just couldn't bear to look at that pierced lip every day." Okay, that one might be tough.

The former president of a very upscale department store recounted to me a story that happened there. One day, a wealthy local socialite came in, dressed very casually, possibly in jeans and a sweatshirt. The socialite, unrecognized, received rude service from the clerks, who were used to dealing with a posh clientele. As a result, she decided never to shop in that store again. And she was a woman who did a lot of shopping!

My friend Rachel came up with her own solution. Rachel's a true original; she's always dressed in her own unique style. She's impeccable but unconventional. One day Rachel showed up wearing a very impressive, hard-to-miss big diamond ring—very unlike her. But she explained that she had gotten tired of getting terrible service in stores and restaurants. She figured that a way to get attention was to wear something that let people know she could afford whatever they were selling. Not all of us want to—or can—adopt Rachel's solution.

Like the store clerks, most of us occasionally use superficial details to judge others, and if we stop and think, we may realize that these are not really reliable indicators. But we sum people up from other factors that we give more credence to: the amount of schooling they've had or where they went to college, the way they speak, what they do for a living, where they come from. Once we know one or two of these tidbits, we often mentally put people into categories, little boxes in our minds. We believe these indicators are reliable, critical, determinative. But mostly they just make things easier and faster for us: "She went to Harvard; she's smart. He dropped out of high school; he's stupid." Once we've found a box to fit someone into, we know how to relate to them, how to treat them. But once we've put someone in a box, it's pretty darn hard to ever get them out.

In life, this keeps us from dating some wonderful future doctors (Edward later became a world-renowned physician) or making some good friends. In business, this keeps us from hiring or promoting some wonderful employees. In sales, this keeps us from finding some wonderful new customers. As with books, judging people by their outward symbols—their "covers"—means we'll miss an awful lot.

First, Ask Me How Fast It Does Zero to Sixty

Jumping to conclusions can cost you. One of the most difficult challenges for employers is to train employees to treat customers well regardless of appearances.

"One way we try and talk about it to employees," said John Whitacre, chairman of Nordstrom, "is that you can be in a community where an individual might be working in their yard or whatever and just pop into the store, and they may be the wealthiest person in the whole community. Trying not to prejudge your fellow man or woman is very difficult. For one reason or another, human beings tend to want to try and judge each other. So at Nordstrom we fight real hard to create an open environment."

It's not just a matter of dress. There are many ways of categorizing people. Some people, unfortunately, base their assumptions on race or ethnicity. But there are also more subtle differences that influence us: cultural differences, gender differences, personal shopping styles. For instance, I once heard a professor say he had studied the way men and women shopped for computers. Men ask a lot of questions, spend a lot of time, come back to the store a few times. They may not be in the market at all, but they like to look, and if they get swept off their feet by a new gizmo, they buy. Women, on the other hand, tend to know what they want and buy quickly. They've done their research, so they ask few questions, or their questions may be very basic. The professor said that many male salesman will lose sales to female customers because they spend a lot of time with male "Lookie Lous," and don't understand women's direct style.

I experienced something similar myself the last time I bought a car. I knew the car I liked, telephoned the dealership, talked to a salesperson, Dean, and went down to the showroom with my checkbook. Dean never offered me a test drive; he didn't even give me a brochure. I told him the color and features I wanted, and we easily agreed on price. Dean said he'd have to get that particular car from another dealer; he'd call me the next day. I was there less than twenty minutes. I'm very busy, and it was days before I noticed that Dean never called back. A week later, I bought the exact same car elsewhere.

Later, an acquaintance, Kenneth, and I were discussing cars. Without any prompting, Kenneth told me he had test-driven the same kind of car I had just bought. Kenneth's a real car buff, and he went to the showroom just to look. A salesman approached and asked if he wanted to take a test drive. He replied honestly, "I'm just looking. I'm not in the market for this car." "No problem," the salesman replied. And off they went. The salesman, pulling on driving gloves, got behind the wheel; he wanted to show Kenneth how the car could perform. Then he turned the car over to Kenneth. Kenneth spent almost an hour with the salesman. I asked Kenneth which dealership this was since his experience was so different from mine. Surprise! It was the same one. And who was the salesman? You guessed it—Dean.

Clearly, Dean could relate to Kenneth. Kenneth's shopping style fit his expectations; mine didn't. I'm not sure Dean took me seriously. He jumped to conclusions about me from his own experience, not from my reality. It cost him a commission.

The newest wrinkle in the way companies categorize and pigeonhole customers is targeted marketing and membership programs—the "frequent flyer," "frequent buyer" approach. Now, I understand businesses making certain they pay particular attention to their best customers. I believe in the old 80/20 rule: you get 80 percent of your business from 20 percent of your customers, or some variation of that percentage. It's only reasonable to view some customers, some clients, as priorities. But all too often, this means neglecting those who don't make the top of the list.

I once interviewed a prominent marketing expert, who explained how this works: "Of forty thousand car renters, only eight hundred people rent twenty-five percent of all the cars. Traditionally, the car agency sees all forty thousand as customers; the new marketer sees only the eight hundred. The heck with the others." She thought this was desirable. I didn't. The fact is, all 40,000 *are* customers. Even Aunt Anita and Uncle Marvin, who rent a car only once every three years, deserve respectful treatment. As an old-fashioned salesman would have put it, "Their money is just as green." As I'd put it, "They're people too." And if Mom knew about these computerized tracking programs, I know she would have amended her warning: "Don't judge a book by its cover or a person by their bytes and bits."

Butcher? Baker? Candlestick Maker?

Imagine you're a career counselor. Your task is to evaluate a young man who's sitting before you. He's severely dyslexic. This learning disability makes it very difficult for him to read; in fact, he hates reading. As for mechanical ability, forget it. By his own admission, he can't even use a three-hole punch; don't even think of anything more challenging. He's been in trouble constantly since the second grade. He's been kicked out of schools, gotten into fights. He graduated eighth from the bottom in his high school class of 1,200. And though neither he nor his parents openly discuss it, the guy can't sit still.

Do you have a clear picture of this guy in your mind? Dyslexic, no mechanical ability, no great scholar, aggressive, possibly borderline attention deficit disorder. So what are you going to do with him? Suggest he become a janitor? A longshoreman? The guy who paints the stripe down the middle of the road? Clearly, this fellow's chances are limited.

Before you decide, let me give you a warning: Don't just keep an open mind about customers. You'd be wise to also keep an open mind about employees. And bosses.

It turns out, you see, that this guy is not a fictional character at all. He's a character, that's for sure, but not fictional. His name is Paul Orfalea. Paul, the man most singularly responsible for the greatest number of printed documents in America, hates to read; he's seriously dyslexic. Paul's company buys thousands of highly complicated machines every year, but he'd probably have a hard time operating anything other than the phone. Paul's the head of a company with tens of thousands of employees, but he has trouble sitting through a meeting.

But there's more to Paul than this. With his background and aptitudes (or lack thereof), Paul figured he'd never get a good job and had better start his own business. In 1970 he did. Paul thought his nickname, given him because of his curly red hair, would make a catchy name for his business; it did. He called it "Kinko's."

Don't judge a book by its cover.

"Happy Fingers Run Happy Cash Registers"

Like anyone really smart, Paul turned his limitations into advantages. He realized he couldn't run his own machines, couldn't read a lot of business documents, so he'd have to depend on his employees to run his business. This shaped a lot of Kinko's management philosophy. Paul knew he had to trust his employees, give them a lot of decision-making capability, and share and be fair with them.

"Do you think I've got the motto 'I can do it better than you can'?" asks Paul. "No, my motto is 'Anybody else can do it better.' I've had to rely on others . . . that's been the spirit of our company. It's other people's precious hands that build my business. Happy fingers run happy cash registers. You take care of them, they're going to take care of you."

Paul even uses the term "advantage" to describe his disability. "Now, because of my advantage in life, where I couldn't read and had no mechanical ability, I always defined my job in the business as one where things had to run *beautifully* without me." This kept Paul from falling into a pattern that is very common with entrepreneurs—having to micromanage everything, be involved in every decision. Kinko's started very small, as just a tiny shop with a copier, but from the beginning Paul delegated responsibility. "The very first day, I had a manager call me the CEO

What Paul Orfalea Learned from His Mother, Virginia Orfalea

There are so many things I learned from my mother. Everything. To save money. How to manage your day. How to keep a balance with your work life and your personal life. How to delegate.

When I was a kid and I'd get kicked out of school, my mother stuck by me. Believed in me. She got me tutors. She probably paid fifty dollars for every word I learned to read.

My mother taught me to save money. She'd always say, "How many hours a day can you work? But your savings work for you twenty-four hours a day, seven days a week."

My mom taught me to live a balanced life. She'd ask, "What difference is anything going to be if you have a heart attack at fifty?"

Paul's mother died in 1988, and he commissioned a private book of re-membrances about her. The comments below are from that book, Poker, Cooking, and Pearls of Wisdom.

> *I was expelled from junior high school and the vice principal said, "Maybe you could enter him in a good trade school, and he can learn how to lay carpet or something." My mother just went home and started crying and she kept saying, "I know he has more in him than laying carpet."*

> *Life's too short to be serious. I think business is very serious, but if I took it too seriously, I wouldn't sleep nights. I could not tell people I work with that I think it's a game: "Are you coming to work with me and play?" . . . But there are certain aspects of gamesmanship in business. . . . And I learned a lot about gamesmanship from my Mom."*

Paul had other sayings from his mother that he particularly liked:

"Why defend yourself? Your friends don't need to hear it and your enemies won't believe it anyway."
"We are poured from our own hands."
"Life is like a cash register. You get out of it what you put in."

of the business. . . . From the very first day, if I didn't show up for a month at a time, things ran beautifully without me.

"You asked me how I evolved as a leader. At first I was subordinate. The best definition of management I've ever heard came from my wife: 'Management is to remove obstacles.' The only reason for a boss is to make your life easier, not harder. So I've always subordinated myself to the person at the counter, looked to see what I could do to make their job easier."

Paul then expanded on how he builds the independent thinking and decision-making capabilities of people throughout the organization: "There are two concepts in how to manage a business, Theory X and Theory Y. Theory X is like running a military execution. You don't do a lot of independent thinking. This is a Theory Y business. Theory Y people think for themselves, have self-pride. I want to ask you a question: Your child comes home with a painting from school, what do you say?"

"It depends on what it is; probably 'Nice painting,' " I reply.

"That's absolutely the wrong thing to do, because what you do is, you instill in a child from very early in life a tendency just to please. What you should say is, 'Tell me about the painting and why.' In a Theory Y business, you let people figure it out for themselves."

When I interviewed Paul, he repeatedly stood up, went to his desk, paced. But Paul has even managed to turn the fact that he can't sit still into a business advantage. Since he hates meetings, he's become very decisive and allows others to be also. He gets out to the branches and spends an enormous amount of his time there rather than at corporate headquarters.

"Decisions are like garbage: the longer it takes to deal with them, the worse they smell," Paul says emphatically. "My thing is, make a decision; just make the decision. There's not one decision here that you're betting the farm on. Make the decision."

I Need This by Tomorrow Morning, or I'm Dead

Let me tell you how I decided to include Kinko's in this book.

For more than a decade, I've been a Kinko's customer. I've used Kinko's all over the country. At Kinko's I've produced slide shows, overhead transparencies, oversized color prints for presentations, brochures, and a whole lot of business plans. In more than ten years, I've almost never had a bad experience, and I've sometimes received incredible service. And I'm a tough customer. All of my work was important, mostly for clients. All of it, I'm sure, was last-minute, on a deadline. The fact that Kinko's could please me so consistently is nothing short of amazing.

I have a theory, which is almost always borne out, that one of the best ways to tell whether a company is well managed is to see how customers are treated over time. Unhappy employees don't give great service very long. So I was interested in finding out what Kinko's had or did to create such a positive track record. And when I learned how well compensated some of the employees at my local Kinko's were, I knew something was going on.

Besides, Kinko's is a tremendous business story. Because I write a nationally syndicated column on small business, I'd been following Kinko's for some time. Kinko's key target market is small businesses. But what really interested me was how this company had built one of the country's strongest brand names out of what could easily have been a commodity business. There used to be five-cent copy machines in every store and a raft of copy shops. There were few barriers to entry; it didn't take much to buy some copiers and compete. But Kinko's distinguished itself—big time.

All this with an ownership structure that was just plain kooky. Paul Orfalea started Kinko's, but he expanded by bringing in partners. Not for the company as a whole—in each geographic area Kinko's was owned by a separate partnership; Paul was a partner in all of them. Eventually, Kinko's had 128 partner/owners. Each partnership had a fair amount of autonomy, which is why Kinko's in different locations often looked different or the nature of services, hours of operation, and so on would vary. Nevertheless, my experience was that the service level was high just about everywhere. Something was going on, and I wanted to find out what it was.

Who Does She Think She's Dealing With?

You've probably been to a Kinko's. But if you're not a regular customer, you may think the person behind the counter running the copy machine makes minimum wage. That person's last job, you imagine, was probably flipping burgers.

Don't judge a coworker by the Kinko's apron. Kinko's coworkers are highly trained. They have to go through a whole battery of classes. Most

Kinko's coworkers are full-time, on a career path, with good benefits, a stock purchase plan, and profit sharing. And they can earn good money. Really good money. Each branch participates in its own profit-sharing plan, with branch managers particularly well compensated according to profits. Very entrepreneurial.

This training and compensation—along with Kinko's Philosophy—are what makes Kinko's so distinctive and separates it from other copy shops. Kinko's invests in their coworkers; they're not just running copy machines. They're people who understand how to use technology to achieve customers' communication needs. That's part of Kinko's Philosophy of using creativity and independent thinking: not to accept the obvious about a job. But customers aren't usually aware of these details, so they can jump to conclusions.

The manager at the Kinko's branch in Grapevine, Texas, recounted an episode: One woman came in to the branch, overdue on a project, really frustrated and anxious. She quickly became abusive to the coworker, yelling at her. Finally she shouted, in a voice loud enough for others to hear, "I don't need to take anything from you. You just run a copy machine. I make fifty thousand dollars a year!" as if to show how important she was. What she didn't know, according to the manager, was that the coworker waiting on her was making about twice that.

At that same branch, the courier arrived while I was there. The courier is a young guy in his early twenties who picks up and delivers customers' jobs. Most people might never notice him as he picks up their orders. But he doesn't just drive a van. Like all Kinko's workers, he goes through a full training program. He has full benefits. He's on a career track. The day we talked, he had just finished one of his courses, "The Theory of Digital Imaging." He could actually talk to customers about their jobs, answer questions, suggest alternative solutions. Think.

Mom would have been delighted. She always liked to hear that people were doing well.

The CEO Will Ring You Up

Kinko's has a very nice tradition. Each year, one Kinko's branch earns the distinction of being the "Branch of the Year." This isn't an easy honor to achieve. It's based on a combination of factors. The reward for being named Branch of the Year is unique: Kinko's board of directors—the chairman, president, board members, CFO, and so on—go out to that branch, spend the day with the coworkers there, have dinner with them, and then, the next day, run the branch while all the coworkers fly off to Disneyland or Disney World.

The Branch of the Year this time happened to be in Dallas. For this book, I was going to Southwest Airlines' headquarters in Dallas, and since I was going to be in the neighborhood, I decided to go visit them. I figured I'd see what made these folks so good, what motivated them. I reasoned that it would be a good opportunity to see some of the factors that contributed to excellence.

And to be perfectly honest, I thought I'd get some good quotes. I wanted to interview the coworkers to see how it felt to have the chairman of the company doing their job. Of course, I had my expectations—my preconceptions—of what they would say, the kinds of quotes I'd get. I figured the coworkers would think that having the top people in the company, the board members, take over their jobs would be *cool*. They'd tell me how honored they felt. Maybe they'd be a little intimidated.

I was wrong. I was projecting onto these coworkers what I thought they were like, what they would feel. Instead, I learned that Mom had clearly taught her lessons to the Dallas branch long before I arrived.

Much More Than Heavy Metal

The coworkers, of course, were honored to have made Branch of the Year. Delighted. And they did think it was a cool idea to have the board of directors come and work there, especially since it meant they got some new equipment before the big shots arrived. But how had they *felt*? I asked.

Universally, all of the coworkers had the same overriding reaction: "I was scared. Worried." Okay, so they were a little intimidated, afraid of the board. Right? Nope. What they were worried about was what would happen to their *customers*. They wanted to make certain their customers' jobs would be done properly and they wouldn't be at the mercy of these guys from Ventura or New York. Ahead of time, they warned any customers they knew might have difficult jobs and reassured them that coworkers from other branches would also be helping out. Phew!

Kinko's Philosophy

When I first met Paul Orfalea, founder and chairman of Kinko's, he was walking down a hallway at Kinko's Ventura, California, headquarters. When he was introduced to me and told what I was working on, he immediately and excitedly pulled a small plastic card from his wallet.

"This, this is what we're all about!" Paul said emphatically, tapping the card. "Right here. This is what Kinko's stands for, these are our values. This is what makes Kinko's work."

The card was printed on both sides. On the front was "Kinko's Philosophy," on the back "Kinko's Commitment to Communication."

Kinko's Philosophy is not treated like most corporate mission statements; it's more like the U.S. Constitution. Amending even one word requires a companywide debate and vote. During employee orientation, new coworkers (as Kinko's employees are called) stand up and recite the Philosophy out loud, together. Particular emphasis is placed on the line "We trust and care for each other." New employees are told that the worst thing you can say about someone at Kinko's is "He's not living the Philosophy."

In May 1998 Kinko's was considering a proposal to add the words "co-owner" and "community" to Kinko's Philosophy. This required a companywide discussion and vote. Here is Kinko's Philosophy with the proposed additions in italics:

> Our primary objective is to take care of our customer. We are proud of our ability to serve him or her in a timely and helpful manner, and to provide high quality at a reasonable price. We develop long-term relationships that promote growth and prosperity *for our customers, co-owners and community*. We value creativity, productivity and loyalty, and we encourage independent thinking and teamwork.
>
> Our coworkers *and co-owners* are the foundation of our success. We consider ourselves part of the Kinko's family. We trust and care for each other, and treat everyone with respect. We openly communicate our accomplishments and mistakes so we can learn from each other. We strive to live balanced lives in work, love, and play. We are confident of our future and point with pride to the way we run our business, care for our environment, and treat each other."

When I visited Dallas, the regional manager was about to put an employee on probation. The reason, his supervisor told me: "He's not living the Philosophy."

These Kinko's coworkers didn't get to be Branch of the Year thinking about the board of directors; they got there by thinking about their customers. They cared more about them than about Disney World. I had assumed these employees would think the way I imagined—concentrating on themselves. I should have known not to assume the obvious.

I found two factors that seemed to be the most important in creating such a motivated, entrepreneurial workforce at the downtown Dallas branch. It wasn't just the profit-sharing compensation structure. Nobody really mentioned money. Everybody mentioned Chris. Chris Jeanne is the manager of the branch, and boy, do his employees love him. And I mean *love*. That's the word they used over and over. His coworkers would just about lay down their lives for him. Why?

"It's a family," explained coworker Tina Marazon. "It's not a work environment. We talk to each other. If somebody gets upset, we'll talk it out and everything stays in that room. We celebrate birthdays, anniversaries. We always have snacks. We play music." But it's not just a festive atmosphere. It's that Chris will take a coworker aside, even in the busiest time, and if that person is stressed, he'll say, "Go take a break. Lie down. Go home." He watches out for them. He helps them with family problems. Chris's caring for coworkers translates into their caring more for Kinko's.

Michelle Williams, another coworker, explained the attitude: "Chris understands you have to take care of your customer, but you also have to take care of your employees."

But perhaps Patricia Wilson gave me the greatest insight into Kinko's, about what had enabled Kinko's to make a great brand name out of a commodity business; what made Kinko's work from both a customer's and an employee's perspective.

Patricia had been with Kinko's for a little more than two years. When she was hired by Kinko's, she had no technical background, but she relished the training. Patricia is African American, in her twenties. When I interviewed her, she was wearing a large red Mickey Mouse T-shirt. I asked Patricia to explain Kinko's Philosophy to me, to tell me what made Kinko's work. She summed it up in four words: "Never accept the obvious."

"We have these ten rules here: You don't talk about each other, coworkers. You don't judge one another on appearance. If someone walks in that door and they have on mismatched clothes, don't assume they're a bum off the street or something. They can be a lawyer walking in with a ten-thousand-dollar job for us, and that stuff's possible. Do not assume the obvious; there's potential in everything."

Patricia then told me a story about a guy who came in wearing a tank top and shorts, all sweaty, and pulled a disk out of a pouch. It was a fifteen-thousand-dollar job. "I wasn't expecting someone looking like that to come through the door and hand me a presentation like that. He just ran out like it was no big deal. It was in the middle of the winter, and he was running in shorts, but he was from New York; they're used to it. I was thinking, 'It's cold out there, why is this man in a pair of shorts like this?' So never assume the obvious."

The same is true with coworkers, she said: "Never assume the obvious. People will get kind of freaked out when they see people with tattoos and rings in their noses. They just assume they're a lost cause. It's not true. We have a lot of people here who have piercings. One of our managers at another store, he has tattoos over his body, but he is one of the best managers that we have. Never assume by appearances that they're unable to do something. That's a bad business thing to do.

"I've gone into places where they never look past the color of my skin and never look to find out if there's something good there. You know what I'm saying? It's not a racist thing. It's just so many people decide on looks. And that goes for weight as well. Look, if you're not thin, they think you're lazy. You're big; you've been sitting on the couch all day. They never look past this outer point, and to me, that causes a lot of businesses to fail, because they never look to see if there's something inside to make it work."

She summed it up: "It's, like, if you use a computer. You can't see all those chips, but they're a very crucial part of your job, a crucial part of your business. You don't know what the computer looks like on the inside; you just see a piece of metal. There's a lot more going on. Never assume the obvious."

Mom couldn't have said it any better.

Why Do We Do This?

Face it, it's easy. It saves a lot of time if you can take one look at people and decide, based on their age, race, clothing, hairstyle, and demeanor, what they're like, how they'll behave. The only problem is, you may be wrong.

I live in Silicon Valley. One day I had lunch with Jerry Yang, a co-founder of Yahoo. He was in his early twenties, wearing an imprinted T-shirt and jeans. Definitely looked like a student, but he was already worth millions. Never accept the obvious.

But even more than with clothes, we naturally choose to be around people with whom we are comfortable, and that usually translates into people *just like us.* Boy, is that a trap. We can easily miss opportunities and also deny opportunities to people who don't fit our expectations. Eugene Kleiner, the pioneering venture capitalist, once told me, "I don't need five reasons to turn down a business plan; I only need one." Now, Eugene is one of the finest, fairest men I've ever known. Eugene's the kind of man who would monitor his own reactions to screen out any kind of discrimination, no matter how subtle. But how many other investors have passed on great deals because the entrepreneur wasn't the age, the gender, the ethnic group they were comfortable with? How many employers have done the same thing?

This attitude works against us not only when we reject those who aren't like us but also when we blindly accept those who are. I know a situation where a fifty-three-year-old white man who had been fired from his last job was hired. After a few months, it was clear he wasn't really performing. But his supervisor let him pass probation anyway, saying, "You know, I understand him, and I think he needs the chance." As it happened, the supervisor was also a fifty-three-year-old white man who had been fired from a job. The company was stuck with an underperformer for years. Never accept the merely comfortable.

When we judge people by their cover, their superficial details, we lose sight of what's really there. I'm not saying you should overlook everything. Just ask yourself, what's a *real* requirement? I remember years ago hearing an announcer on a public address system in the Dallas airport with such a thick Texas accent that even I, who was living in Texas at the time, couldn't understand her. Speaking unaccented English might be a real requirement in that situation, whereas it might not be if she were interacting with passengers in person.

Working on this book, I discovered that one thing most of these companies had in common was that they didn't accept the obvious about people, they didn't judge a book by its cover. They were able to unleash the hidden talents, drive, and creativity of people others had overlooked or dismissed.

At Rachel's Bus Company in Chicago, Rachel Hubka has built a successful school bus company in the inner city. Some of her office staff members are people who might be categorized as former unwed teenage welfare moms. Rachel never saw them that way. She just saw people with talents and skills, with experience in understanding a complex bureaucratic system; people who had learned how to survive and were motivated to make the most of the situation they found themselves in. Rachel didn't assume the obvious.

At Zingerman's Deli, they regularly discover the hidden talents of their workforce, many of whom have a history of drug use, dropping out of school, getting into trouble with the law. Like Nic Schoonbeck. But Zingerman's doesn't assume the obvious.

These companies know that behind those pierced noses, dredlocks, tie-dyed torn shirts, the lack of ability to speak English, or the overweight exterior is a human being with intelligence, potential, feelings, and commitment—a wealth to contribute.

Jumping to conclusions may find us jumping over cliffs. Judging books by their covers can result in buying some pretty shallow tomes and leaving some terrific reads on the shelf. Mom knew this. She wanted us to look inside.

Paul Orfalea, by the way, still hates to read. When I told him I'd send him a copy of this book, he asked if I could send the audiotape version instead. Sure, Paul. No problem.

9

SHARE

Babies don't know how to share.

In infancy, even if we had a twin, we didn't think about how to divide up the milk. As toddlers, we wanted everything. No matter what it was, if it caught our eye, we wanted it.

It takes a little while to learn how to share, even though anthropologists say empathy and sharing are innate traits. Certainly we've all seen children spontaneously show signs of wanting to share. My friend Cathy has twins, and when they were about two years of age, they began sharing—Hallie would cry, and Ari would bring a toy to comfort her. But this innate desire to share is tempered by our own individual needs and desires. Ari and Hallie were just as likely to pull a toy out of each other's hands.

In bringing us up and helping us become healthy adults, Mom knew that one of her biggest jobs was teaching us to share—with siblings, classmates, other kids. Mom wanted us to share not only because it was "good manners" but because being willing to share made us better able to get along with others and better able to survive in the world.

Mom knew that sharing wasn't always easy. But as we grow, we have to learn how to balance our own wants with the needs of others. We have to learn how to sometimes give up things we want to make others happy, if only to keep the peace. And we have to learn what is *fair*—that sometimes giving to others isn't a matter of *giving* at all but of sharing what rightfully belongs to others as well as yourself.

When you really, really, really wanted the last chocolate chip cookie but you'd already had one and your brother Brendan hadn't had any, this could be a hard lesson to learn. But Mom knew you and Brendan wouldn't get along very well unless you learned to treat each other fairly and share.

Companies, too, are learning they can't get along very well unless they share. Increasingly, businesses share financial rewards throughout the company, with all employees. And I've seen a company that shares not only the monetary gains but also the management, decision making, responsibility—the *ownership*—of the company with everyone, even the most unlikely employee group of all.

And *Business Week*'s Planning a Cover Story

I help people develop business plans. That's my specialty as a management consultant. The majority of my clients come to me because they're seeking financing and they need a written business plan they can give to funding sources—investors, banks, venture capitalists—to explain their business in depth. Many of my clients are entrepreneurs with ideas for a new business.

Now, if you work with entrepreneurs for well over a decade as I have, you acquire a deep, abiding respect for the creativity, ambition, perseverance, and just plain hard work people bring to their businesses. They're amazing. And the range of ideas! I've seen everything from dream resorts on remote Australian islands to foot deodorizers to chocolate factories to a vast array of new technology.

Seeing both the ingenuity and the dedication of entrepreneurs is the most reassuring thing you can imagine. People will work long, hard, and lovingly—often without pay—to pursue their vision, follow their dream. My job is to help them clarify that dream into a plan, which they then use to find others who'll help make those dreams a reality—by giving them money.

Here in Silicon Valley, finding and funding new companies is a huge industry. Venture capitalists actively seek, court, wine and dine, and compete for promising entrepreneurs. They know that without those entrepreneurs and new ideas, there would be no way for them to make money. Investors can't survive without good investments.

This is a mutually beneficial relationship: entrepreneurs need venture capital; venture capitalists need entrepreneurs. The people with *ideas* need the people with *money;* the people with *money* need the people with *ideas.* So picture the following imaginary scenario:

Two entrepreneurs, Seth Slater and Kayley Connor, have been working on an idea for a new business, MicroWidget TechCom, for a couple of years. Seth and Kayley have done their research. They've identified their markets. They've created a prototype of their product. They've secured key strategic partnerships. They've lined up some initial customers who are eager to purchase MicroWidgets just as soon as production starts.

They present their business plan to one of Silicon Valley's most respected venture capital firms, Vulture Ventures. Vulture loves the plan and decides to fund the company. MicroWidgets are the hot new thing. (Kleiner, Perkins has already invested in a company in this space, and MicroWidgets got all the buzz at recent industry conferences.) Vulture offers Seth and Kayley the standard arrangement: Vulture will provide all the start-up money the company needs and, in return, own 100 percent of MicroWidget TechCom.

What do our two intrepid entrepreneurs receive? Good salaries, excellent benefits, nice job titles, and a possible bonus if the company does well. What don't they get? A piece of the ownership pie, a seat on the board of directors, input into the decisions of the company, equity.

Here's why this scenario has to be imaginary: *If it were real, Silicon Valley would dry up overnight.* People don't want to work that hard, sacrifice that much, give up their best ideas, just for others to own it all.

No, entrepreneurs need ownership. And no self-respecting venture capital firm would take 100 percent ownership of a company. Venture capitalists know that doing so would squelch the entrepreneurs' commitment to the company. Ownership is just too powerful a motivator, both financially and emotionally. The people who are most critical to the work of the company need to have a piece of the ownership pie.

Yet, every day, all across America, companies act out a version of this scenario with their own employees. Companies ask employees to come to work and give up their best ideas, their best efforts, their energy and commitment but don't give employees, in return, a share in the ownership, both financially and emotionally, of those ideas or that company.

If you want to unleash the power of ideas and creativity within an organization, you've got to allow people ownership of those ideas and the fruits of those ideas.

The way you do this is by *sharing*.

So When Do They Vest?

When people speak about business excesses today, the thing they usually point to first is the ever-increasing disparity in pay between those at the top of the corporate ladder and those at the bottom.

Just take a look at the salaries of chief executive officers compared to those of average workers. In 1965, CEOs were paid 44 times the average factory workers' pay. By 1997, that figure had ballooned to a CEO receiving 209 times what an average factory worker earned![1] Other figures also support the perception that some people are taking more than their fair share from the cookie jar: in 1996, executive pay (including stock options) increased 20 percent versus a 3 percent gain in workers' wages—while average business profits were 11 percent.[2]

Would this make Mom happy? Does this seem like a fair way to share?

One of the things that contributes to these wide disparities in income is the grant of stock options to key corporate executives. The use of stock options has received a lot of bad press, primarily due to excessive options granted to those at the very top of a company. But the theory behind stock options is sound: those who are critical to the success of a company should have a stake in its success.

But just who is critical to a company's success? Just the CEO? The top executives? The key managers? How about administrative support? How about the janitor?

In Silicon Valley, everybody talks about their stock options. I mean *everybody*. Terrific administrative assistants or receptionists apply only for jobs that offer stock options. It's nice, of course, to make a good salary, but the real potential, they know, is ownership. They're willing to work extra hard to help a company succeed, but they want to participate in that

---

1. Jennifer Reingold, "Executive Pay: Special Report," *Business Week,* April 21, 1997.
2. Ibid.

success. Silicon Valley's business culture is based on people knowing that if their company succeeds, they succeed.

Silicon Valley companies were among the first in the nation to offer stock options to a broad range of key employees. Over time, as they gained experience with employee stock ownership and saw the increased dedication such ownership brings, companies widened their stock option plans to include a broader and broader range of employees. Many companies now offer *all* employees some form of stock purchase or stock option plan.

But the trend toward employee ownership isn't limited to Silicon Valley. Throughout the country, companies have adopted stock purchase plans as a way of increasing employee dedication. The next time you buy a latte at a Starbucks, for instance, keep in mind that the *barrista* (the guy working that espresso machine) is almost certainly a stock owner. Through Starbuck's Bean Stock plan, all employees who work at least twenty hours a week are entitled to stock options, in addition to health insurance and other benefits. Owning a piece of the company makes it far more motivating to get your order right the first time.

Many companies have taken Mom's lesson to heart. Many have seen the benefits that come from sharing rewards throughout a company, not just at the top echelons of corporate leadership but all the way down the organizational ladder—even to the most unlikely group of employees of all.

The Old-fashioned Way

If you want to see the American dream at work, drive three hours west of Chicago through rolling farmland to Waterloo, Wisconsin, a town of 2,500.

Waterloo is a surprising place. Now, there's nothing surprising about the physical appearance of the town itself, which looks like any very small rural town in the Midwest: one main street with a few shops, one main intersection, an American Legion hall, and one fast-food restaurant. It's fairly unusual to find two pretty good-sized companies in a town this small: a printing company and Trek Bicycles. However, that's not what makes Waterloo surprising.

Waterloo is the home of McKay Nursery, a company that propagates, grows, and sells ornamental plants—not a particularly cutting-edge in-

But after a short while, the leadership at McKay became concerned. Their first worry was whether the workers were in the country legally. McKay staff also started to fear that some of the workers were of suspect character. They didn't like that.

But they became even more concerned about the way the workers were being treated. So Karl Junginger sent the company foreman to take a look at the housing and living conditions of the workers the recruiter was hiring. He was appalled by what he found. Junginger decided he couldn't allow his workers to be treated in such horrendous fashion. He felt it was totally inappropriate for McKay to be associated with such reprehensible behavior.

So McKay registered with all the appropriate authorities and sent people to Texas to recruit, directly hiring employees themselves and thus ensuring the quality of the people coming to work for them. McKay then built their own dormitories and housing for the migrant workers to make sure the facilities were adequate. It was a major commitment.

"Why did they go to all that trouble?" I asked Griff Mason, former president of McKay. "Why not just stick with recruiters?"

"Because it's just not right to treat people that way," he responded. "You have to do the right thing." He went further: "What if someone knew we were treating people that way? What would they think of us? . . . Our reputation is a source of pride."

Mom clearly taught the people at McKay to wear clean underwear.

What Are We Going to Do?

In 1984, McKay Nursery faced another turning point: Karl Junginger was in his seventies. The other senior managers, who, along with Karl, owned the majority of McKay Nursery, were all also well up in age. All had worked for the company for many decades. They wanted to get their money out of the company, liquidate their assets.

For more than a year, McKay's executives had sought alternatives. They had tried to find a buyer for the company. But every option meant that McKay would have to leave Waterloo. They would have to abandon the employees who had worked with them for a lifetime. They didn't want to do that. It didn't set well with Junginger's conservative values.

So they turned to a relatively little used way to sell a company: an employee stock ownership plan (ESOP). Through such a plan, employees take over the ownership of a company; they buy out the current share-holders, securing the purchase money through bank loans. This was a rare phenomenon then; at the time, there were only 2,500 ESOPs in the entire country.

But there was a hitch: McKay was a small company. The only way they could get the financing was if the ESOP were extended to include a broad range of employees and only if they chose to risk half the money in the employee pension plan. This was bold on everyone's part. It was bold on the part of management; by including everyone who worked at least 1,000 hours a year, it meant that the seasonal, migrant farmworkers would become owners of the company, too. And it was bold on the part of employees because they had to risk their pension funds.

They all had high hopes. "Owning ESOP shares allows us to have an ownership interest in the company we work for," explained the executives when they first proposed the ESOP. "To enjoy fair pay for our daily contribution to our company's success and have the opportunity to share in their profits if we all do our jobs well. We believe that's the very essence of the American Dream and are proud to participate in this growing realization of what is truly a uniquely American opportunity."

And that's exactly what happened. McKay made the American dream come true. Anyone who works at McKay year after year, who works hard and makes a contribution, can have a good and decent life with a comfortable retirement to look forward to. Any seasonal worker who works from March through Thanksgiving for twenty to twenty-five years can expect to retire with a six-figure distribution. Employees also get profit sharing while they work at McKay, so they can live decently, even on a minimum wage, and put their kids through college. Even if they work in the fields. Even if they don't speak English.

McKay's ESOP, unlike most, owns 100 percent of the company. So employees share not just the money but the responsibility and decision making. ESOP meetings are conducted in both Spanish and English. The company set up a financial counseling program for workers to help them understand and manage their profits and shares.

Almost everyone who touches a plant at McKay is an owner. Almost everyone who touches an invoice is an owner. Fifty percent of stock owners are migrants or former migrants. But McKay management goes out of its way to make sure people understand that this is about everyone, not just the migrants. Everyone's in it together. Everyone shares.

Not Just Filling Pots

Bernardo Garza is a supervisor out in the fields and McKay's third highest ranking production employee. But Bernardo began his career at McKay the same way as the young guys he now supervises: bending down and picking and moving plants. He was just another migrant worker looking for a job.

Born in Mexico, Bernardo was one of six children, only two of whom ever finished high school. Bernardo himself quit school at fifteen and then spent years as a migrant farm laborer in Texas, Ohio, and Montana, picking sugar beets and working in canning factories. In Texas, he used to get fifty cents an hour and work ten hours a day.

In 1969, Bernardo came to McKay, working part-time for $1.45 an hour, without any overtime pay. It was just another job—he didn't have any particular amibition or desire to stay in Wisconisn. But the people at McKay spotted something in Bernardo. "They wanted me to stick around. I always liked having responsibility. I decided to work full-time in 1971, because I got health insurance. And in 1968, they had introduced profit sharing."

Bernardo now oversees the production of about 200,000 containers of plants. His workers set these containers up, trim, weed the plants, and space them. He wants his workers to learn what they're doing and do it well. Otherwise the plants suffer.

Bernardo demands a lot of the men he supervises. And he wants them to grow—not just the plants but themselves. He's always urging them to learn more, to pay more attention, and to understand how their job fits into the whole picture.

"I don't want them to just be a worker," Bernardo explained, "just filling up pots. [I want employees] to know the names of the plants. To have a little more pride. We have all kinds of people who come here. We have nurserymen who know what they're doing who come here.

"How do you think those people would think of our company if they asked someone what they were doing and the worker turned around and

What William Hewlett and David Packard Learned from Their Mothers, Louise Hewlett and Ella Packard

Both William Hewlett and David Packard spoke repeatedly about the strong influence their mothers had had on their lives. Bill and Dave's fathers were both professionals, and both said their fathers were very busy while they were growing up, so their mothers had a profound influence on them.

Bill Hewlett told a story about being a child in the Depression. He just got a job that he really wanted: selling *The Saturday Evening Post* door-to-door. He was thrilled to get that job and earn some money.

But this was the Depression, and jobs were hard to come by. One day, his mother came to him and said, "Bill, you need to give up that job. There are people who need that job more than you do." Although he was absolutely crushed to give up his beloved job, it was a lesson he always remembered. His mother taught him about thinking of other people and their needs, not just putting his own needs and desires first.

Dave Packard talked frequently about his mother's influence. His mother supported and encouraged his radio experiments all through high school. While his father urged him to play sports, his mother taught him to be a gardener. Gardening was something Dave turned to throughout his life as a source of relaxation. He used the time he devoted to it to think things through. His legendary apricot orchard is a testament to his gardening prowess.

Ella Packard was even so supportive of her son and his experiments that she donated her kitchen oven to the development of the company's first product. Dave and Bill named the product the 200A because they wanted to make it seem like they had been around for a while. The reality was that they were working out of Dave's garage; in fact, the paint on that first product was baked in Packard's kitchen oven. David's mom, ever supportive of her son's endeavors, used to bring cookies out to the garage in the afternoons for everyone. But, after having the paint for the 200A baked in her oven, she complained (although in jest) that her cookies never tasted the same.

said, 'I don't know'? What do you think those people would think about our company? Instead, if the worker turns around and says, 'We're doing honeysuckle' or whatever, and they know what they're doing, you impress people. You want people [customers] to know you're doing your job, you're not only here to be a number. And you want somebody here to appreciate what you're doing and think of you as a good worker."

Bernardo lectures his young workers: "If you're going to work for me or for McKay Nursery, in my department, you're going to have to work. I tell the young guys, 'I don't want you to kill yourself working; just do your job, that's all. But . . . look here. If you spend ten years working here, do it for something, do it to learn. Don't spend ten, twenty years here, and then still not know what you're doing, what kind of plants you're using. Then you're just wasting your time and my time and everybody else's time. Because *what's not good for the company is not good for me*."

Working at McKay has enabled Bernardo, a former migrant field hand, to have a good life, to put his kids through college. He has three children: one daughter is working on her master's degree in fine arts, one is working toward a nursing degree, and his son works at a publishing company. His wife also worked full-time. They've worked hard, and their financial future is secure. Bernardo Garza has achieved all this because the people at McKay listened to Mom and were willing to share.

They're Not Alone

Many companies I looked at for this book were pioneers in sharing.

3M had profit sharing for key employees in 1916 and for almost all employees by 1937! They instituted unemployment insurance for their employees in 1932, one of the first companies in the nation. Before Social Security was established, 3M had pensions and sickness and disability insurance. And they currently offer stock options for some employees.

Kinko's has exceptional profit sharing. Branch managers act as entrepreneurs. They get a hefty percentage of the profit of their branch, so they run it like their own small business. But at Kinko's almost all employees—including *part-time* employees—participate in profit sharing. If the branch is particularly successful, Kinko's workers can earn really good money. I got to know the former computer department manager at a nearby Kinko's fairly well. He was terrific: solicitous, helpful, never lost his cool. While his hourly wage wasn't much, with profit sharing he made about $90,000 a year. So that's why all those people there are so-o-o nice, I thought.

Nordstrom also has generous profit sharing, which highly motivates employees to act like owners. One of the interesting benefits of profit sharing that I had never considered was pointed out to me by Susana Higuera Lerner, internal security manager at the San Francisco Nordstrom. In most retail businesses, theft by employees is high. With profit sharing, if an employee gets an idea that someone might be stealing, there's a general attitude, "That's my share of the profit that's walking out the door." It reduces internal theft tremendously.

Sharing More than Money

Sharing money and profits leads to all kinds of other sharing. First, you have to share information. And you want to.

To be seen as fair, management has to let employees know where the money they made went, which expenses reduced the amount of money they got to take home. If management hands out profit-sharing checks while keeping employees in the dark about expenses, they're going to look at that trip you took last month to New Orleans as just a boondoggle instead of the key sales trip of the year.

You need to share information. You want to get employees thinking about how they can not only save money but make more money. You want to get people thinking about what they can do to increase *profits*. That may mean being more careful with resources, or may mean being more conscientious about sales. You want employees to learn what costs money—and what creates it. The goal of profit sharing is to unleash potential and create a common bond, not common tension. Sharing information can help you do that.

Another Kind of "Ownership"

Patagonia presented me with an example of another kind of ownership. When I visited the company, I kept asking a question that never quite got answered.

Patagonia is owned 100 percent by Yvon and Malinda Chouinard. They're not handing out shares in their company to employees. Patagonia does have a profit-sharing program for employees, so there is a financial incentive for employees to feel a sense of ownership.

But Yvon Chouinard is physically away from Patagonia many months a year, engaging in adventure sports. He does not run Patagonia on any kind of day-to-day basis, even when he is there. Chouinard's vision and values set the direction of the company, but Patagonia is *run* by its employees, who do not *own* even one share. And the profit sharing doesn't appear to be exceptionally weighted to account for this fact. Yet I have never encountered a group of employees who exhibited a stronger sense of ownership than the people at Patagonia.

That was the question I kept asking: "What's the payoff that motivates you to work as though you own the place? What's up?"

The reason I never quite got an answer was that people would look at me, confused. It's like asking a parent, "What's the payoff for loving your children? The hope that they'll pick out a better nursing home for you one day?" Patagonia has such an overwhelming sense of shared values, of mission and purpose, that for employees the company is a cause, not a job. They share their passion. And that's the strongest thing you can share.

If I Give Them an Inch, Won't They Want a Mile?

So many times in life, we fail to give a little for fear others will want a lot. This is certainly true in our personal relationships. If I drive her to school one day, she'll come to expect it. If I tell her I love her on Saturday, she'll want to hear it every day. Give a little, they'll take more. So some people fear that Pandora's box. Okay.

But it's not. It's not okay. The world turns cold that way. Bitterness increases.

People understand fairness. And they understand limits. They're looking to be treated fairly. Their perception of fairness and yours may differ, but an honest attempt is usually recognized—as long as it's honest, not manipulative, not evasive. And it helps to communicate.

An entrepreneur once asked me, "My employees resent that I've just bought myself a new Jaguar and that I live in a really beautiful new house.

I've worked for many, many years, and I'm just starting to reach this level of success. I've sacrificed a lot, and I feel I deserve it, but they resent it. How do I handle this?"

Now, as someone who's started two businesses, I knew what she was talking about. She's the one who used up her life savings, took out loans, put herself on the line. She's the one who worked without income for years, eating spaghetti night after night because it was the only thing she could afford. Her employees don't see those years of sacrifice, don't know the risks she's taken. She's made a success of her company, and she's right—she *does* deserve the car and the house. In America, most of us don't begrudge entrepreneurs those kinds of rewards.

I suspected something else was going on as well, and it turned out there was. Her business focused on sales, and most of her employees were salespeople. Her company had had a really good year. That's why she bought the Jag. A good year meant her salespeople also made a lot of money, based on their commissions. But this entrepreneur had done nothing exceptional to share the rewards of an exceptional year with her employees. They received the same percentage commissions as usual. No special recognition. No bonuses. No profit sharing. She gave herself a bonus: a Jag. But she didn't give them one. We discussed ways she might do something exceptional for her employees: giving everyone a tangible bonus, perhaps throwing a party, maybe leasing a really nice car for the top-performing salesperson or two.

Sharing means sharing your successes, too.

We All Get a Slice

I'm a big fan of capitalism.

If you really want to become a big fan of capitalism, work for the government. My first professional job was working for a city government on a project funded by the federal government. Work for a government agency, where there is no profit motive, and you're almost willing to become an acolyte to Milton Friedman.

The program I worked with provided meals, programs, and social services for senior citizens. But food was the biggest part of the budget by far. The first year I worked in the program, our food purchaser was a government employee with no previous experience buying food. He did an okay job, nothing special.

But then we hired a man who had come from private industry to do the food purchasing. This guy knew what he was doing. He figured ways to do bulk purchasing, to purchase foods in season, various tricks of the trade. The result? Much better food bought at a lower price. This should have been great. It wasn't. It created a very real problem. November rolled around, and we had a big budget surplus. If we had money left over, our budget would be cut big time the following year. Even if we saved money, none of it ended up in our pockets. Thus there was no motivation to save.

Our immediately pressing issue was what to do with the large impending surplus. Our crackerjack food purchaser was told to go out and spend, spend, spend. Our manager directed him to use up his budget. This was not easy. He managed to do it, but it broke his heart, and dispirited the rest of the staff.

This was a ridiculous system. Not only were we *not* rewarded for saving, we were penalized. I was ready to have our program privatized.

Next, I spent years working for nonprofit agencies. I was fortunate to see many people who were very motivated by things other than money and who would work hard, creatively, doggedly. It didn't necessarily take money to motivate them. But when there was a loss of a shared sense of value, of purpose, then that motivation dropped precipitously. The less we shared, the less we cared.

I believe in capitalism. But capitalism that is based on greed, not profit, destroys the whole system. That's not capitalism. That's just greed. And it's bad for everyone.

People want to be treated fairly. What they want is equity. Whoa! Look at that word: equity. That's what we call company ownership—*equity*. And look at that other word: share. That's what we call stock—*shares* in the company.

Ownership is about sharing. It's about fairness. We understand that when we want to motivate people at the top of the corporate ladder. But they're not the only ones who make a difference. McKay Nursery has found that even a well-trained migrant worker who knows at a glance whether a plant has too much sun or too little water or is spaced too close to the next plant is a competitive advantage.

Fairness is what makes democracy work. It's what makes capitalism work. I make this point because, if they're new to you, reading about programs such as ESOPs or stock ownership or profit sharing for migrant workers may lead you to jump to the conclusion that these are liberal, do-good concepts. They're not.

Sharing is essential to making a capitalist society work. In fact, sharing is what makes capitalism work best. I'm not talking about charity. I'm talking about sharing with all those who contribute, but not just money: ideas, hard work, dedication, inspiration.

McKay Nursery embodies conservative, old-fashioned values. Hard work is honorable and should lead to a decent life. Everyone is entitled to respect, regardless of the work he or she does. People are entitled to dignity. It's the American ideal at work.

Sharing is exactly what Mom wanted. Mom and McKay make a good pair. After all, when you talk about something being truly American, you describe it as "American as Mom and apple pie." McKay Nursery can supply the apples.

10

IT'S NOT THE END OF THE WORLD

You finally got up enough courage to run for vice president of your senior class. Your two best friends helped you make campaign posters. Mom listened as you wrote and rewrote, practiced and repracticed your campaign speech. You handed out flyers after school every day for three weeks.

Then, after your opponent tore down all your signs one night, you became really determined to win. You just couldn't let him get away with that. And, anyway, getting elected would mean you'd be hanging out on the Student Council with the coolest kids in school, you'd get out of sixth period, and it would look terrific on your college applications. Being vice president would change your life. You just had to win. You just had to!

And then you lost. You were devastated, convinced you'd lost because the other kids didn't like you and thought you were ugly. Now you'd never get into college. And you'd have to take sixth-period horticulture with Ms. Compton. Your life was ruined.

In the midst of your tears and self-pity, Mom came to comfort you and put everything into perspective. She reassured you that you were popular and attractive, your grades were good enough to get you into college, and you could transfer out of Ms. Compton's class and take drama with Mr. Tracy instead. Your life had not, in fact, been destroyed forever by this terrible loss. Putting her arm around you, Mom pulled you close and said, "Honey, believe me, it's not the end of the world."

Success Is Just a Seven-Letter Word

Success! Success! Success! Business loves the word "success." Almost everything associated with business stresses "success." Seminars promote "Small Business Success!" Magazines run stories on "Secrets of Success." Even I'm guilty—my first book was titled *The Successful Business Plan*. But to make it in business (and in life), you have to learn to deal with another seven-letter word even more powerful than success: failure.

Failure is the "F-word" of business—it's not polite to mention it. As a result, we tend to treat failures as extraordinary events with earthshaking consequences. But all of us face disappointments and setbacks. When we either blow them all out of proportion to reality or push them into a dark recess of our mind, we are left ill equipped to deal with the failures we'll inevitably experience. Those who survive best, whether as an individual or as a company, are those who come to realize that failure is just part of life and then figure out how to live with and learn from their flops, fiascos, and faults.

Failure isn't necessarily bad, and it certainly isn't the end of the world. A few years ago, I had a major failure of my own. After working on a huge deal with a Fortune 500 company for many months, everything fell apart at the last minute. I was devastated. My future plans at the time all appeared to hinge on this deal. I remember exactly how I felt: as if someone had just kicked me in the stomach. I was depressed for weeks.

I was also lucky. Had the deal gone through, I would have spent years on a project that wasn't truly close to my heart or my talents. This "failure" forced me to take a closer look at how I wanted to direct my business life, and it opened me up to other opportunities that were far more rewarding and enriching.

Many failures are blessings in disguise. Most successful people (there's that word "success" again) will tell you that some of the most important events in their lives were things they viewed as "failures" at the time. But they used their failures to learn new attitudes and skills, to change direction, and to get a perspective on their lives and their businesses.

Some failures, of course, don't have much of a silver lining—losing a lot of money on a new business venture or a personal investment, for instance. But even there we tend to underestimate our capacity to change, adapt, and recover. And if we allow the idea of failure to paralyze us, we reduce our capacity to grow.

Call Me "Pioneer.com"

Traditionally, when someone failed at a major task or project, that person's career was tarnished forever. I remember a friend whose first job as an attorney was in a New York law firm. She was assigned as one of the many associates on a huge lawsuit, which lasted for a couple of years. And then the firm lost. Everyone involved—the partner in charge, the associates, I suspect even the secretaries—was tainted by the "failure."

There are also corporate "failures." A company takes a new approach, introduces a new product line, establishes a new division, and when it doesn't meet expectations, it "fails." I know of one company that was one of the earliest to advertise on the Internet. When they analyzed their marketing results at the end of the year, they determined that their Internet campaign had been a "failure," since it hadn't produced the kind of numbers the company had achieved in other advertising channels. They decided to limit their on-line activities.

Now, if in both these situations we change the way we look at and define "success" and "failure," the outcomes could have been far different.

Although her firm lost the lawsuit, my friend had acquired years of valuable experience working on complex legal issues during a very complicated trial that actually went to court. The other young attorneys who had started the same year as she were still shuffling papers, and most had never gone near a courtroom. She hadn't "failed"; she was getting experience that few other associates had been exposed to.

The corporation advertising on the Internet was a true pioneer. At the time, Internet advertising was in its infancy. This company was in a position to learn far more than its competitors and potentially "own" a big piece of the burgeoning Internet audience had its managers only stuck with an Internet commitment. If they had viewed their initial forays on the Web as experiments and learning opportunities rather than simply quantifying the results, I am certain the company would have been a major presence on the Web today.

Maybe We Should Branch Out

Some companies have learned how to use failure to grow in new directions. Kinko's, for instance, owes much of its current success to a major business failure.

Kinko's began near the University of California, Santa Barbara, and during the first decade of its corporate life, Kinko's main business was serving college communities. Kinko's big moneymaker, their cash cow, was copying selections from books and articles to put together into course packets for professors.

All that changed suddenly. In 1991, Kinko's lost a major lawsuit. Textbook publishers sued Kinko's for copyright infringement, and, besides having to pay a $1.9-million-dollar fine, Kinko's was prohibited from duplicating copyrighted material without first obtaining permission. There went their business. The cash cow had died. It was a major failure.

Except that Kinko's used this "failure" to reexamine their corporate direction. Looking around, Kinko's chairman, Paul Orfalea, and other Kinko's executives saw the growing number of small businesses. They aggressively refocused Kinko's corporate aims and products to serve that burgeoning market. Instead of being limited to the college environment, Kinko's brilliantly became "Your branch office."

If you don't let failure overwhelm you, sometimes what you learn is there are other, better ways to run your business. Ask the folks at Kinko's. They'll tell you that being forced to change direction was hardly the end of the world.

Just Stick with It

As I researched this book, I had many memorable and moving experiences. But without a doubt, a highlight was meeting the inventor of one of my all-time favorite products, Post-it Notes. True confession time: I am a Post-it junkie. I have Post-its in dozens (and I mean dozens) of different sizes, colors, and designs. I could be the Post-it poster girl.

Now, if you are under thirty, you probably don't remember a time when Post-its didn't exist, and I must sound as if I'm raving about the wonders of indoor plumbing. But Post-its are a relatively new invention, introduced only in 1980, and the inventor of Post-its, Art Fry, is still very much alive and well.

When I met Art at his home, he was in the midst of a small personal fiasco: his new recipe for chocolate chip cookies was turning out to be a disaster. The cookies were simultaneously runny and burnt. Offering both the cookies and his apologies, Art didn't seem the least bit fazed. But then again, Art Fry knows how to handle failure. The story of Post-its is a tale of failure after failure, defeat after defeat.

If Art Fry was the kind of guy who melted in the face of failure, then I wouldn't have a neon green Post-it stuck on my computer at this very moment reminding me of a call I have to make tomorrow and bright purple Post-it flags marking changes on drafts of this book's manuscript. No, Art is the kind of guy who, once he starts on something, sticks with it.

Considering how big a role failure would play in his life, Art Fry certainly chose the right company to work for. At 3M, failure is not only accepted, it is celebrated. 3M executives like to boast about how many times they personally "killed" Post-its. At 3M, getting things wrong is a badge of distinction.

Art, my Post-its, and his chocolate chip cookies are all evidence that failure is not the end of the world.

Hey, Buddy, Want to Buy a Mine?

There's no nice way to put this: the people who founded 3M were lousy businessmen. Few companies have had less auspicious beginnings. In 1902, five businessmen formed the Minnesota Mining and Manufacturing Company (MMM), bought a mine, and started mining for a high-quality abrasive, corundum. What were they thinking? The mine didn't contain corundum, and an artificial substitute had already been invented anyway. They failed.

Next, outside investors took control of MMM and decided that as the company had a mine full of sand, 3M would make sandpaper. Like many of today's venture capitalists, they had grand strategic visions but no grasp of how to actually run a company. They couldn't manage either quality control or cash flow. They were failing.

For the first fourteen years of its life, 3M was in trouble deeper than its mine. It wasn't until a bookkeeper turned salesman, William McKnight, took over as general manager that 3M pulled out of trouble.

Now, what's great about this tale is not just that there's a long history of failure at 3M, it's that virtually every 3M employee knows this story. It's told at new-employee orientation, and it's repeated frequently throughout the company. 3M doesn't idealize any larger-than-life inventor/founder/creator; there's no Thomas Edison, David Packard, Estée Lauder, Steve Jobs, just a bunch of regular people who kept stumbling around until they made a go of things. 3M's corporate culture embraces failure as the very cornerstone of the company.

"Don't You Do What Your Bosses Tell You?"

3M might have stayed only a sandpaper company if it hadn't been for their original problem employee, Richard "Dick" Drew. Drew also failed, but what he failed at was taking direction from his supervisors. Thank goodness! It was Drew's disobedience that not only paved the way for today's 3M but resulted in two products so common that they are in just about every household in America, if not the world. I bet you've got at least one of them in your home or office now.

Dick Drew was a lab technician, testing sandpaper. Part of his job was taking sandpaper samples to auto body shops. Auto shops used sandpaper to prepare cars for painting. On a routine trip to an auto shop in 1925, Dick overheard some of the workers complaining. One of the new fads in auto painting was two-toned cars. Pretty snazzy. But to separate one color from another, the workers had to mask off one section as they painted the other color. To do this, they glued newspapers, using library paste, to the parts they didn't want painted. This was a messy, ineffective procedure. When Drew arrived at the shop, the workers were swearing openly at the results.

Drew decided to go back to the 3M lab and see what he could come up with. He was only a technician in a sandpaper company, but he was curious, and he wanted to satisfy 3M's customers. When his immediate boss found out what he was doing, Drew was told to quit; it wasn't his job. Moreover, 3M had already been burned trying to diversify into other areas besides sandpaper. Just the year before, they had tried to add auto

---

What Art Fry Learned from His Mother, Nevada Fry

There are two lessons I most associate with my mother: to try a lot of things and to be able to do things for yourself.

When it came to food, my mother would say, "Eat a little bit; you might like it." She did that with all sorts of things. She wanted me to be as broad in my experiences as I could. I got to try a lot of things and find out they weren't as different as I imagined. She thought it was also important to find out what you don't like.

My mother also taught me that you can't expect somebody else to do everything for you. You have to be willing to do the things no one else will do.

My mother taught me how to cook, sew, take care of myself. When I was about eight years old, she wanted me to darn my socks, and I balked. "This is girl's work," I said.

My mother responded, "You do what has to be done. How do you think the cowboys did it? The cowboys darn their own socks."

---

wax and polish, also responding to the needs of auto body shops. Those had both failed. 3M had learned a lesson from that failure: Stick to sandpaper and abrasives.

Fortunately, Drew didn't listen. He kept on experimenting with masking tape. He was so determined that his boss finally relented and committed resources to the project. Eventually, Drew invented what would be called "Scotch" brand masking tape.

It failed.

The stiff paper backing of the tape didn't allow it to conform to the curves of the cars. The quality was lousy. William McKnight, 3M's chief, took it off the market; he was worried it would ruin 3M's reputation. He directed that 3M's masking tape efforts be ended, and Drew got a letter from his boss emphatically directing him to stop working on it. He was once again assigned to work on sandpaper.

He failed to listen.

One day, McKnight walked into the lab and caught Drew still working on masking tape. Drew had discovered a roll of crepe toweling paper, much like a rough paper towel we'd have today, and he was experimenting with that as a backing for the masking tape. The uneven surface of the crepe made it possible for the tape to conform to the cars' shape.

"Didn't you get the letter from your boss instructing you not to spend your time on this anymore?" McKnight asked Drew.

"Yes."

"Don't you do what your bosses tell you?"

"Well, Mr. McKnight, listen to me." McKnight listened, liked what he heard, and allowed Drew to continue. Drew soon improved his product, and masking tape became a necessity in manufacturing and consumer life.

Five years later, Drew invented another product destined to become a household staple. Du Pont had recently introduced a new material that was moisture-proof and transparent: cellophane. It caught on quickly as a packaging material, but there was nothing appropriate to seal it with. Drew experimented with various adhesives until he came up with one that could be applied directly to the cellophane. Voila! Cellophane tape. Or what we would all come to know as Scotch tape. Scotch tape was difficult to handle, however. It wasn't until a 3M salesman invented an easy-to-use dispenser that Scotch tape became indispensable.

Drew's inventions saved 3M. Scotch tape was introduced just as the Great Depression hit. Scotch tape was a perfect product for bad times. Financially strapped consumers turned to Scotch tape to mend things they could no longer afford to replace. They used Scotch tape to fix lamp shades and sheet music, books and baby dolls, picture frames and family Bibles, even to hold cracked eggs together. Income from masking tape and Scotch tape provided the cash flow 3M needed to survive the Depression. In essence, 3M itself was held together by Scotch tape. That's a pretty darn good adhesive.

Mistakes Will Be Made

Many companies might have viewed all this as a fluke; just one disobedient employee who turned out to be a creative genius. But 3M's chief, McKnight, was smarter than that. Drawing an important lesson from Drew's disobedience, McKnight realized that employees would see opportunities and solutions that management never would. If 3M was to make the greatest use of the creative talents of its employees, he'd have to get out of their way. He'd have to give them room to use their initiative, and he'd have to make it safe for them to fail. McKnight pioneered what today we would call employee empowerment and initiated one of the most innovative corporate policies in existence in any business.

To this day, 3M employees are allowed, indeed encouraged, to use 15 percent of their time on projects of their own choosing or devising. The 15% Rule is probably more responsible for 3M's success than any other policy. Employees get to tinker, to experiment, to go where their curiosity leads them.

And they're allowed to fail. McKnight knew that if you don't allow failures, you can't achieve successes. To guard against failure, you'd have to adopt stringent rules, but such rules also keep people from doing their best work. One of the most important things a manager could do, he felt, was allow employees to do their best work.

He ran 3M by those principles, which he set down in writing in 1948. To this day, these "McKnight Principles" form the foundation of 3M's management philosophy. They are written everywhere—and I mean *everywhere*—around the company. They are framed on walls of managers' offices; they are reprinted in corporate literature; and I have on my desk the mouse pad given to every new 3M employee, on which is printed McKnight's dictum:

As our business grows, it becomes increasingly necessary to delegate responsibility and to encourage men and women to exercise their initiative. This requires considerable tolerance. Those men and women to whom we delegate authority and responsibility, if they are good people, are going to want to do their jobs in their own way.

Mistakes will be made. But if a person is essentially right, the mistakes he or she makes are not as serious in the long run as the mistakes management will make if it undertakes to tell those in authority exactly how they must do their jobs.

Management that is destructively critical when mistakes are made kills initiative. And it's essential that we have many people with initiative if we are to continue to grow.

The 15% Rule frees employees to pursue anything that interests them. Regardless of their regular job assignment. Regardless of what their manager says. Regardless of the mistakes they make. If they want to stick with something, even after it keeps failing, they can. Thank goodness. Or I wouldn't have my Post-its. Which would feel like the end of the world.

"The Adhesive That Fails"

In 1974, Art Fry was working diligently on a high-priority corporate research project: shelf-arranging tape. 3M had identified libraries as an important and growing market, and one problem plaguing libraries was how to keep books in place. 3M's solution? Shelf-arranging tape.

Art also sang in his church choir. Choir members marked their places in the hymnbooks with small pieces of paper they used as bookmarks. These, of course, would keep fluttering out, sometimes at most inopportune moments during the service. The unruly bits of paper irritated Art. During what he describes as a particularly boring sermon one Sunday morning, Art kept thinking about the problem of the bookmarks.

Now, 3M's 15% Rule allows individuals to work on projects they find interesting, but if they need more money to pursue their work, they often have to "shop" their ideas around to different departments to find a sponsor. One guy who had been unsuccessfully looking for a sponsor for his work was Spence Silver.

Working on another adhesive, Spence had come up with an adhesive that didn't quite stick properly. It stuck, but it didn't. They called it "the adhesive that fails." It was really different. "This was just too big not to be good for something," Art recalled. "We know its weaknesses; what are its strengths?" (By the way, that's not a bad question to ask about yourself or your employees from time to time, too.)

Sitting in church that Sunday, Art thought about Spence's nonsticking adhesive. He'd heard about it when Spence had come looking for a sponsor. It seemed like the perfect solution for his bookmarks. If Art used Spence's adhesive, he could have a bookmark that would stick when he wanted it to stick and come off when he wanted it to come off. Neat.

No one had had any idea what to do with Spence's "adhesive that fails." Then Art Fry came along. Spence's adhesive and Art's bookmarks were the perfect match.

"The Solvents Have Finally Gotten to You"

Now this is where I'm supposed to write, "The rest, as they say, is history." Only it wasn't.

Art's boss was particularly unsupportive of his invention. As Art recalls, his supervisor was a real "don't rock the boat" kind of guy who was focused on getting current products out the door. And shelf-arranging tape was a high priority. He didn't need Art goofing off with some lousy adhesive. He made Art's life pretty miserable and then tried to get him transferred. Fortunately, Art took cover in the 15% Rule.

Then Art started distributing his little bookmarks around the company. People liked them well enough, but no one came back and asked for any more. Why? They'd keep using the same sticky bookmark over and over, and how many bookmarks do you really need anyway? Art's pet project looked as if it had failed.

How about knocking off your project now, Art?

Nope. After a while, one guy Art had given the bookmarks to came back and asked for more. And more. And more. Why? Art wanted to know. It turned out he was *writing* on the sticky bookmarks. Eureka! Let's make the bookmarks bigger and turn them into "self-attaching notes"—no need for paper clips.

At this point, Art became, by his own description, "the whole world's supplier of Post-it Notes." He made up a bunch of pads and gave them to secretaries and executives and administrative assistants. But there was a catch.

"If you wanted a sample, you had to get it from me," Art told me. "I would give you one pad. . . . I would say, 'When you finish one pack, I'll give you another one, but you've got to come yourself.' So we had vice presidents going through the snow to get their pads. That was how I measured use rates. I figured it showed a bell curve with use rates from seven to twenty pads per year per person within 3M. If you compare that with Magic Tape, which was our cash cow for this division—it was one roll of Magic Tape per year. I said, 'This is going to be bigger than Magic Tape.' And they said, 'Art, the solvents have finally gotten to you over there.' "

Art understood the power of secretaries. When he was turned down for a pilot project grant, he stopped giving the executives' secretaries any more pads. He told them it was because his grant had been rejected.

Why Are Post-its Yellow?

I have Post-its in just about every color of the rainbow and a lot of colors that aren't in the rainbow, but the original Post-it Notes were a three-by-three-inch square pale yellow pad. The color we still most associate with Post-its is yellow.

There is some controversy within 3M as to how Post-its got to be yellow. But Art Fry, the inventor of Post-its, provides the definitive explanation.

The adhesive in Post-its is actually fairly sophisticated science. Before Post-its, there were other paper tapes, such as masking tape. All previous adhesives were stronger than regular paper, and the paper had to be reinforced internally to keep it from pulling apart when you pulled on the tape.

One of the great things about the adhesive in Post-its is that you could use any paper, right off the shelf, no special reinforcement needed. You could use any color paper.

Unfortunately, distributors thought Post-its wouldn't sell very well. Post-its, at the time, cost many times the price of plain notepads. Office supply stores wouldn't give them much shelf space and would take only one color.

Art tested various colors on the then-new photocopying machines. Only a few pale colors didn't copy as gray. Yellow copied as clean white.

Yellow was also easy on the retina; it took no effort to focus on. Both black and blue ink were completely legible against the yellow paper. Besides, Art felt yellow was a "cheerful color."

But one of the most important factors—and this comes from Art himself—was that yellow was not seen as either masculine or feminine. At that time the feminist movement was at its height. Everything was controversial. "There was a strong interest in women's issues," Art said. "We didn't want to step on any land mines."

Frustrated, they, in turn, told their bosses, "If you had approved the project, I'd have more of those notes." He got his money.

3M management finally took note of the potential of Art's creation and did what any self-respecting corporation would do: they paid a big national consulting firm a lot of money to do a formal market research study.

I asked a lot of people at 3M if they could find me a copy of this study. No one had any idea where it might be. "Perhaps it was lost when we moved our archives." I asked if anyone remembered which company had conducted the study. No. "One of the big management consulting firms, but we just can't remember which one." Apparently, this is as close as 3M gets to a cover-up. And here's why: the study reached the following conclusion: "This product has, at most, the potential for perhaps a three-quarter of a million dollar total business. There is no market for self-attaching notes." Yeah, right.

Guess how fast 3M pulled the plug on Art after that? Failure yet again. It looked like the end of the world.

"How Do You Describe the Flavor of an Artichoke?"

Art, of course, stuck to his nonsticking notes.

"You're not in marketing," Art was told. "These people know what they're doing." It helps to be the kind of guy who doesn't listen. Like Dick Drew. And it certainly helps to be in a company that lets you keep failing.

Art persuaded his division vice president, Joe Ramey, to let him keep trying. Ramey was pretty convinced himself that these notes would sell, regardless of the market research study. And 3M's stated policy, dating back to the 1920s, is to allow products to start small and build a market, to give something a chance. So he let Art go out and sell them.

3M test-marketed the self-attaching notes in four cities. Four communities in America got Post-its before any one else. They had a chance to embrace these wonderful little pieces of paper that could stick to a letter so you could make a comment without ruining the original, or you could stick them on your mirror to remind you to take the dog to the groomer, or you could attach them to your college textbook to scribble notes without lowering the book's resale value at the end of the semester. Citizens of these four towns got to be the "early adapters," who later could say they had used Post-its before anyone else. And what did they do?

Nothing. Art's self-attaching notes failed once again. Yikes!

Art got one more chance. In the next, and what might have been final, test market, Boise, Idaho, Art just gave Post-its away. He gave hundreds and hundreds of pads away as samples. He knew he had to get people actually using and interacting with Post-its because no one had any idea what to do with them when they just saw them in the store.

"How do you describe something that hasn't existed before?" Art asked. "It's very hard to do. How do you describe the flavor of a new food? How do you describe the flavor of an artichoke?" Customers had to use Post-its, interact with them, play with them, before they could fall in love with them. 3M later gave away millions of samples of Post-its nationwide to get customers used to them.

The rest, as they say, is history. Post-its now are one of the top ten best-selling office supply products. 3M's division that produces Post-its would by itself be a Fortune 500 company.

Oh yes, the shelf-arranging tape sold great for about a year.

Tell Me Again, What Do I Do with Her Hair?

Many years after Post-its had become an everyday product, Art Fry sat next to an executive from Mattel on a plane. "Why did it take you so long to invent Post-its?" the man from Mattel asked after he learned Art's background.

"When you marketed the first Barbie doll," Art responded, "did you have to first go out and invent plastic? Then did you have to invent the extrusion technique to manufacture Barbie dolls? And what if, after all that, you then had to teach little girls what to do with them?"

The problem with truly great new things is that they are truly *new*. That makes them hard to deal with. It was six years between the time Art Fry thought about using Spence Silver's adhesive-that-failed as a bookmark and the introduction of Post-its to the market. Six years!

I once heard someone say that being ahead of your time is indistinguishable from failure. A friend of mine, venture capitalist Eugene Kleiner, lost money investing in automatic teller machines a decade before consumers were ready to accept them. Eugene's investment failed.

But being ahead of your time is *not* failure. Automatic teller machines didn't fail. Post-its didn't fail. They just needed time.

In today's world, we rarely give an inventor or an entrepreneur the time to prove a market. I can't imagine any venture capital firm giving a company fourteen years to get out of debt, the time it took 3M to get established. Many wouldn't give a company fourteen months. Companies likewise pull the plug on internal developments in increasingly short time frames. They do an analysis of the cost of money and show they can't get a sufficiently high return on investment in a sufficiently short period of time.

Yes, the rate of change has increased. But people are still human, and we need time to adjust to new developments, time to figure out what to do with sticky paper. If we want great new things, we've got to let the Art Frys of the world make mistakes. We've got to have patience with our employees, our companies, and our investments. Or we won't come up with tomorrow's Post-its or ATMs or cures for cancer. That would indeed be the end of the world.

"You've Got to Work for Years to Be an Overnight Success"

Learning to accept, anticipate, and even applaud failure isn't only for situations where we're inventing or creating something new. It's how we need to approach all of business.

Most of what we do in life, we have to practice. This is easiest to see in sports. All sports teams schedule practice sessions. In individual sports, too, we practice. I ice-skate, and I certainly don't make any progress unless I practice what I learn in a lesson.

But we never think about "practicing" business. Sure, some business school students may have internships while in school, or our first job or two might be considered an associate, apprentice position. But business itself is never considered practice.

That concept changed for me when I interviewed Bill Walsh, the former coach of the San Francisco 49ers. Walsh told me that he viewed even games themselves as learning situations, "practices," so to speak, and that it's what you learn in the process of losing that determines whether you'll eventually win.

An executive at 3M told me, only half facetiously, "We don't have failures, we have learning experiences." That's how a sandpaper company came to make Post-its. 3M may no longer have open mines, but they have thousands of open minds.

When anyone starts throwing around the words "success" and "failure," watch out! These terms tend to overwhelm the activity and become the thing itself. They're like the terms "win" and "lose": "How was your softball game?" "We lost." No discussion about the amazing catch you made in the third inning or that you're finally improving your swing. *Success* and *failure* stress results rather than process, short-term outcomes rather than long-term development. These words treat each event in isolation. But almost everything we do, whether in business or in life, contributes to a continuing journey. We tend to put too much emphasis on where we are at any given point instead of what we're learning along the way.

I'm not suggesting that every failure holds the seeds of a potential Post-it Notes. Nor am I naively saying that every time life gives you lemons you can make lemonade. (Or that even when life gives you sand, you can make sandpaper.) Some things just don't work. Some things do fail. But you can squeeze a lesson out of even life's sourest moments.

When things don't turn out the way you planned, ask yourself: What have I learned? What do I need to know to change this in the future? Do I need to give this more time? Has this gotten me further down the road on my journey?

And don't let failure overwhelm you, discourage you. Remember one of Rhonda's Rules: "You've got to work for years to be an overnight success."

"So how was your softball game?"
"It was a learning experience."
"Oh, well, it's not the end of the world."

11

Remember Where You Came From

You're back home for the summer after your freshman year at college. You've changed. Your hair's now long, a French cigarette—unlit—constantly dangles at the edge of your mouth. Every day you wear the same outfit: black turtleneck, black jeans, black boots. Even though it's July. You don't care how hot it is. You're cool. Hip. Sophisticated. You could use a bath.

Mr. Schwed, who's known you since you were a baby, generously gives you a summer job at his pet shop. One day, he mentions to Mom that your demeanor sometimes frightens the pets.

Mom's not surprised. After all, you play Edith Piaf songs till two A.M., read and reread Kafka, and constantly jabber on about deconstructionism. You're not exactly a ray of sunshine. But Mom's patient with you—until the Fourth of July. At your neighbor's barbecue, while everyone happily munches on their hot dogs and burgers, you launch into a diatribe about the immorality of eating beef, the horrors of bovine growth hormone, and the destruction of the South American rain forest.

"You've got to stop this," Mom warns. "Be polite. Especially to Mr. Schwed."

"But I can't stand it!" you shout. "It's so unbelievably bourgeois to be stuck here among the bourgeoisie. Cretins! The other day when I told him he should only sell dog food that's made from tofu and be truly avant-garde, he thought avant-garde was a deodorant spray!"

Mom's had enough. "The people in this town are your friends, the folks who were there for you when you were growing up. These are the people you could turn to, count on. Who tutored, coached, and cheered you. Don't think you're suddenly so much better than them just because you're in college. These people helped get you there." Mom then paused, snatched the Gauloise out of your mouth, and said, "Don't forget the people who were with you from the start. Don't be such a big shot. Remember where you came from."

Parental Discretion Advised

Before I go any further, I have to warn you that this chapter contains language that may be hazardous to the health of management consultants. I've included a graphic description of a man who, eschewing "businesslike" behavior, has made decisions straight from the heart. In open defiance of contemporary management theory, this man has not only refused to "downsize" or "rightsize" his company, he has intentionally "wrongsized" his business. He has still prospered. It's earned him, from me at least, the title of "The Sweetest Man on Earth." Those with cold hearts and MBAs may want to leave now.

Nice Work If You Can Get It

We read about it every month in the press: another company closes a plant, moves its headquarters, relocates overseas. Looking for cheaper labor and special tax treatment, companies pick up and go as quickly as a single man hearing his girlfriend use the word "commitment."

The result, however, is far more serious. For the city or state the company leaves behind, the impact is a loss of jobs, sometimes a loss of a whole community. Abandonment of a community by a company can be devastating.

Jobs create a ripple effect. When a new employer comes to town, the town gets more than just those few hundred or few thousand jobs the company directly creates. That company and those employees also benefit other businesses and create additional jobs. That company's employees buy lunch, have their clothes cleaned, remodel their kitchens. Restaurants, dry cleaners, and contractors all benefit. The company itself needs janitors, office supplies, security guards, and caterers for their holiday party. Those businesses and workers benefit.

Jobs do more than just bring money to individuals; they help keep a community together. Parents who go off to work are positive role models for their children—children learn what work is like from seeing their parents get up and go to work every day. Those children grow up with a stronger work ethic: they're more employable. Jobs bring structure to family life. And generally, it's the people who go to work who build the institutions of a community: the schools, churches, synagogues, and mosques, the community centers, the soccer leagues. Jobs serve as the mortar holding communities together.

When jobs leave, a lot of that mortar erodes.

City councils and state legislatures know this. That's why they fight hard to keep from losing jobs and are eager to bring new jobs in. Corporations know this. Some use this knowledge to pit community against community, state against state, in a bidding war to see how much they can get just for staying or for relocating there.

Often it's a game, but for a community it can be a costly one. I had a client who was a major real estate developer. They were building a national headquarters for a high-prestige employer. The employer knew they wanted to stay in their present location, but to squeeze tax concessions out of the local community, they solicited proposals from a number of other states to use as leverage in local negotiations. Of course it worked. The city excused the company's property taxes for a number of years.

I understand this. If I were a voter, I would have wanted my elected officials to do everything they could to keep that employer there. If I were on the city council, I'd probably have voted for those tax cuts. But I'd feel like having Mom come by to remind the company, "These are the people who helped you get where you are. This is where you grew. Remember where you came from."

A Story As Warm As My Parka

In 1995, all of America was touched by the moving story of Malden Mills. Malden manufactures textiles; they're the creator of the Polarfleece and Polartec fabrics. That year, a fire nearly destroyed Malden's entire manufacturing plant in Lawrence, Massachusetts.

Malden was one of the few textile manufacturers remaining in New England; most others had moved their jobs either to nonunion states or overseas long before. With the fire, most people naturally assumed that Malden would take the insurance money, close what was left of the factory, and move too. Instead, Malden's owner, Aaron Feuerstein, not only decided to rebuild right in the same location and keep the three thousand jobs in the community, he continued to pay employees while the factory was shut down—for months. He stayed, and he paid.

"I consider our workers an asset, not an expense," Feuerstein said in an interview with *Parade* magazine. "I have a responsibility to the worker. . . . I have an equal responsibility to the community. It would have been unconscionable to put three thousand people on the streets and deliver a death blow to the cities of Lawrence and Methuen."

The story received national coverage, and Feuerstein was celebrated nationwide. In 1996, President Clinton invited him to sit next to the first lady during the State of the Union Address, and the president acknowledged Feuerstein's actions in his speech.

Mom would have loved Aaron Feuerstein. His commitment to the community where his company grew up and to those who helped build that company was an outstanding example of remembering where you come from.

But the attention rightfully showered on Feuerstein might lead you to believe that he is the only businessperson who would take such an action. Such a belief might be comforting to a number-crunching financial analyst, but it would not be accurate. There are many others who understand the importance of the relationship between a company's success and its community.

Of course, not all do.

How Do You Say "Stingray" in Chinese?

Growing up, you and your bike were inseparable. Your bike gave you freedom; it was a way to see your friends, extend your territory, and get away from your parents. You loved your bike. And the bike you always wanted was a Schwinn. Schwinns were the best. A Schwinn bicycle was a symbol of American freedom.

The Schwinn Bicycle Company was founded in Chicago in the 1890s, just as the country's bicycle craze began. Schwinn always concentrated on

---

What Marv Eisenstat Learned from His Mother, Betty Eisenstat

My mother had four children, but there's lots of space between us, so it's practically like she raised us separately. My mother is very smart. She loves to read. My parents were very poor, but they couldn't do enough to help others.

My mother never wanted us to worry, to have troubles. There was a *Star Trek* episode where some alien took on all the pain of others. My mother was like that; she'd take on all the pain for everyone else so we wouldn't have to worry.

My mother is tremendously loyal. She still lives in the same neighborhood where I grew up. No matter the changes. When we've asked if she wanted a new house, she just said, "Why move out?"

My mother has always treated people very, very well. There was not an ounce of prejudice in her, and she taught me the same thing. She taught me how to treat people. She told me the best of life is in helping others. My mother taught me you've got to be productive with your heart.

My mother has a joke she likes to tell:

A pig and a dog are arguing, discussing who is more valuable to humankind. The dog says, "I'm more valuable. I provide companionship. I guard people's homes. I can guide blind people. I can round up sheep. I'm man's best friend."

The pig says, "Hah! I can top that. Look at me; I give everything for mankind. My bones they use for gelatin, my skin for football, my flesh for meat; they even eat my snout!"

At that, the dog says, "You're right, you're useful, Mr. Pig, but at least I don't have to be dead to be appreciated."

---

quality. The quality workmanship, from Schwinn's own factory in Chicago, and their company's long-term relationship with dealers, enabled Schwinn to survive the Depression. And by the 1950s, more than one out of every four bikes sold in America was a Schwinn. Schwinns were the best.

Then the best got even better: in 1963, Schwinn introduced the groundbreaking, heart-stopping Stingray, the coolest bike any kid ever saw, with its long handlebars and amazing banana seat. It was like a Corvette for kids. My brother, Arnie, had a Stingray, and I imagine I can trace my own continuing desire for sports cars to the jealousy I felt over Arnie with that bike. It was a beauty. Zoom!

Over time, however, Schwinn's management neglected the people and the community that had been key contributors to the company's success. Focusing more on their bottom line than business basics, they looked for the quick fix, especially in the form of cheap labor.

Ignoring Mom's advice to remember where they came from, the Schwinn Bicycle Company turned its back on its roots.

According to authors Judith Crown and Glenn Coleman in their history of Schwinn, *No Hands,* Schwinn's executives saw the company's increasing problems as stemming primarily from foreign competition; they completely overlooked their own failure to innovate. Constantly searching for cheap labor and ignoring the well-being of those who had been part of Schwinn's history, Schwinn's management ironically sped the company's decline. They made a series of disastrous decisions, each of which took Schwinn farther and farther away from Chicago.

Schwinn turned to a manufacturer in China to outsource production; the Chinese supplier then became one of Schwinn's major competitors. Schwinn invested in a plant in Hungary; they lost money. And when Schwinn eventually closed their own plant in Chicago, instead of rebuilding locally with their experienced labor force, Schwinn relocated to Mississippi to avoid having to pay union wages. But once there, Schwinn could no longer secure the talent or transportation needed.

Schwinn's quality, market share, and brand image plummeted. By the 1980s, a "Schwinn" bike might really have been a bike made in China, Taiwan, or Hungary. Schwinn's market share dropped from more than 25 percent in 1950 to 12 percent by 1979 to 5 percent in 1992. In 1992, the Schwinn Bicycle Company filed for bankruptcy.

The Schwinn family lost their company after nearly one hundred years. This sad fate might have been avoided if only they had listened to Mom and remembered where they came from.

Okay, So I Couldn't Resist

It is tempting, indeed, to describe Marvin Eisenstadt as a "sweet" man, but not only would that be too obvious, it might lead you to conclude that Marv is "artificially sweet." Marv, you see, is the president and co-owner of Cumberland Packing, the company that makes Sweet'N Low, an artificial sweetener.

Marv, however, is the genuine article. There is nothing artificial about him. His character is one of unadulterated sweetness, more like one of the company's other products, Sugar in the Raw.

Although you can find those little pink packets of Sweet'N Low in virtually every restaurant in America, you may be surprised to learn that Cumberland Packing remains an independent, family-owned business to this day. It's a small company with about four hundred employees. And it's still located exactly where the Eisenstadt family started it: inner-city Brooklyn, New York. Although the years have been good to Cumberland and not so good to Brooklyn, Marv Eisenstadt remains firmly committed to the place where his family's business grew. He has never forgotten where he came from.

More than just staying committed to the *place,* Marv is committed to the *people,* the *community* where the company began. As company after company fled as the neighborhood started to decay, Marv and others at Cumberland felt they owed an obligation to the community that had helped them get their start. It would have been easy, understandable, an apparently rational business decision to move Cumberland's plant to the suburbs or out of state. Instead, Marv gave Brooklyn what every community needs: jobs.

And Marv does this not merely by staying where Cumberland started but by purposefully, intentionally, adamantly *wrongsizing* his company.

Marv Eisenstadt could cut his workforce in half tomorrow. He could easily eliminate about two hundred jobs with no perceived negative effect on his business and a healthy boost to his bottom line. Marv doesn't need a management consultant to tell him how to do it. He knows how to eliminate jobs; so does everyone else in Cumberland's management.

After all, Marv deliberately designs his manufacturing process to keep *extra* people on the payroll. Marv refuses to purchase new equipment that would eliminate jobs. This isn't a matter of money—he actually has *new* equipment adapted so it requires *more* workers, not fewer. Marv has nothing against technology; his head computer guy told me that Marv encourages him to continually update the management information systems. It's just that Marv won't allow any new development that elimi-

Jobs for Real People

Jacqueline Serrano dressed up especially to meet me. I was flattered.

Jacqueline works in one of the administrative offices at Cumberland Packing and she had heard I was coming. She wanted to make a good impression. Jacqueline was wearing a very nice dress; I've got a photograph. She wanted the company to look good; she wanted to look good. She did.

At Cumberland, where many people work for twenty, thirty, even forty years, Jacqueline's considered almost a new employee—she was hired in 1989.

Jacqueline had heard about Cumberland, and, like many people in the neighborhood, she had wanted to work there for years.

Jacqueline was nervous about my visit. What if I stopped and asked her some questions? What would she say? So she asked Isabel Siegel, who handles human resources, what kinds of questions I might ask her.

"She might ask what you do here," said Isabel. Jacqueline was comfortable with that.

"And how long you've been here," said Isabel. Jacqueline was comfortable with that, too.

"And what you did before you came to Cumberland." At this, Isabel realized that she didn't know what Jacqueline had done before. After all, at Cumberland, a person's background doesn't make much difference in getting a job, and one's past doesn't matter.

But now that they were talking about it, Isabel asked, purely out of curiosity, "What was your job before you came here, Jacqueline?"

"Numbers runner." Whoops! A numbers runner is someone who takes bets for a bookie—not exactly a sterling qualification.

Isabel looked at Jacqueline, so nervous and eager, then smiled and said, "We'll just tell Rhonda 'self-employed.'" They both laughed.

Jacqueline started as a factory worker, putting little pink packets in boxes. But she was a great employee. Responsible. Ambitious. She wanted to work her way up to a desk job. She studied and went to night school. She was smart and capable. Eventually, Isabel felt Jacqueline was ready to move up.

Isabel hit on a solution: Jacqueline now works in the office, on the accounts. As Isabel explained, "She's great with numbers."

nates even one job from the factory floor. Not one. He was even willing to put it in the contract with the union.

Don't say I didn't warn you: Marv Eisenstadt is terrifying—that is if you're a "corporate reengineering" expert. "Chain Saw" Al Dunlap, beware!

Howdy, Sailor, New in Town?

During World War II, Benjamin and Betty Eisenstadt ran a cafeteria directly across the street from the Brooklyn Navy Yard. It was called the Cumberland Cafeteria. Throughout the war, Cumberland Cafeteria's business boomed. All those workers from the Navy Yard filled the restaurant twenty-four hours a day. And the adjacent bar as well.

Then—peace. Work at the Navy Yard stopped. Cumberland Cafeteria's business stopped with it. The Eisenstadts faced a dismal future. One day, Betty Eisenstadt, looking at a sugar bowl in a restaurant, came up with the idea of putting sugar into little bags instead. (Just like a woman— Betty thought this would be so much cleaner.) Using a tea-bag-making machine, the Eisenstadts started bagging sugar in packets. They took the idea to a nearby sugar manufacturer, which liked the idea but figured it could buy their own tea bag machine instead of hiring the Eisenstadts. Betty and Ben started bagging soy sauce and ketchup instead.

One day, a man approached them with an idea for a sugar substitute in packets. The Eisenstadts' son, Marvin, had a chemical engineering degree, so he set about devising a formula. The man changed his mind, but Marv thought the sugar substitute was still a good idea, and he pursued it. Marv decided to make the color of the packets pink to stand out from sugar packets in a sugar bowl and because he didn't think blue was a color naturally associated with food. The family named their product after a poem by Alfred, Lord Tennyson, "Sweet and Low." That was in 1957.

Good timing. The first diet soft drink was widely introduced just about the same time. Public demand for sugar substitutes in all forms climbed. People were used to using saccharine in little pills, but Sweet'N Low provided a more versatile powdered version. What the public wanted, they got. The supermarket chain A&P called Cumberland and asked them to supply all their stores. Sweet'N Low was on their shelves and on its way!

Sweet Dreams

The two events that most boosted Sweet'N Low's brand recognition were the banning of cyclamates in 1969 and the oil embargo in 1973. In each of these, Marv's actions brought him extensive national publicity—for free.

Sweet'N Low contains saccharine. But the earlier formula, like those of most artificial sweeteners at the time, contained cyclamates. Don't forget, Marv was the creator of Sweet'N Low; he's a chemist. He had been following the literature and had seen the possibility of a ban on cyclamates about a year before the government took action.

So Marv borrowed $1 million from a bank to reformulate Sweet'N Low and to replace every box in the country. When the ban was announced, Marv was ready: All of the national newscasts showed Marv burying a huge pile of the old Sweet'N Low. The new formula was already on supermarket shelves. This gave Sweet'N Low nearly a year's jump on its competitors and made Sweet'N Low a household name.

The next major national publicity shot for Sweet'N Low came in 1973. During the Arab oil embargo, the price of sugar soared. As a result, the demand for artificial sweeteners skyrocketed. Marv could have easily raised the price of Sweet'N Low; he didn't. Once again, this brought the company good national publicity.

Marv's refusal to raise prices in a tight market wasn't calculated to get such a response. It's just the way he does business. Marv can't stand to cheat anyone. He really can't. That's why there are about 102 packets of Sweet'N Low in every box marked "100." If you stand and watch the boxes being filled, you'll see that machines automatically load 100 packets into every box. But Marv couldn't bear to have a customer only get 99. So by hand, just to make sure, a worker adds one or two packs to each box.

"Marv," I asked, "haven't you ever figured out how many extra packs this means you have to make in a year? What does this cost you?"

"This way I know I'm not cheating anyone," Marv replied. "I sleep well at night."

Without Equal Among His Peers

The potentially biggest threat to Cumberland, however, came in a little blue packet—aspartame, marketed under the brand names NutraSweet and

Equal. If it hadn't been for Marv's insistence on staying in the old 'hood, however, those little blue packets might have been called Sweet'N Low.

Recognizing the value of the Sweet'N Low brand, Searle, the original makers of aspartame, approached Marv before they introduced their new product, NutraSweet. (Monsanto now owns NutraSweet.) Searle wanted to buy Cumberland to acquire the name. But Marv was committed to the company, committed to creating jobs for people. That's what Marv's about. He loves jobs. And he feels an obligation to the community where Cumberland grew up. He refused Searle's offer.

The result? The massive advertising campaign for NutraSweet vastly and dramatically expanded the market for artificial sweeteners. Even the demand for Sweet'N Low exploded! Sure, they lost market share. But Sweet'N Low went from an 80 percent share of a relatively small market to a 50 percent share of a much, much larger market. Currently, Cumberland makes about $100 million in sales annually. Thank you, NutraSweet.

Now, in retrospect, this looks as though Marv made a brilliant business decision. But put the tape in reverse for a moment and think about the decision Marv actually faced at the time. Searle did not have to tell Marv, "Sell to us or be crushed by us." Any first-year business student could see the threat a huge competitor like Searle presented to a tiny company like Cumberland. The smart *business* decision, as seen at the time, would probably have been to sell out.

Fortunately, Marv thinks from his heart.

"You have to understand," he explains, "when we first started out with Sweet'N Low, we needed these people. We needed them. The machine wasn't evolved the way it is today, and they really were my success. They were the reason for my success, these people. Some of them have been here from the beginning. I just can't abandon that. I really feel that it was their efforts that made this company. I just can't forget it, and I won't. I have to live with myself, and I wouldn't be able to if I did that.

"This neighborhood is where the cafeteria was. We don't have to stay in this neighborhood; we can open up a modern factory elsewhere. But most of these people live up in the projects. They just walk down here. It's a good area for shipping. We have space in the Navy Yard. It's a mixed bag. But this is where it all started."

Mom would be proud: Marv remembers where he came from.

Ponce de León, I've Got the Answer

Employees work at Cumberland forever—or just about. I kept meeting people who had worked there thirty, thirty-five, forty years. After a while I began to notice that everyone looked young, remarkably young considering the number of years they'd been working. Men who looked forty had been working at Cumberland thirty-five years. I was starting to wonder if the chemicals in Sweet'N Low served as some kind of youth enhancer, a human preservative.

No, I was assured. It's because working at Cumberland is low stress, high satisfaction.

Employees are paid well. Factory workers get higher wages than the average prevailing wage, good benefits, and excellent vacation and sick leave. Even better, for many, is that the work shift is timed so the factory workers, who are mostly women, can be home when their kids get off from school.

And Marv didn't need the federal government to mandate family leave time. Employees have always been able to take off to take care of sick children, family emergencies, court dates.

Court dates? Almost all of Cumberland's employees are fine, upstanding citizens. Many may not have high school diplomas or speak English, but few have actually ever been in trouble with the law. That wouldn't present a barrier to being hired, however. Marv believes in creating jobs for people who would have a hard time finding a job elsewhere because of education, language, or background. Marv hires from the heart.

"I try to give people a second chance. We all want second chances. We've all done those things in our life that maybe a second chance would have helped. I have a guy here who was out of work, he came out of prison. I had another guy with me who had been here for twenty years, he committed a murder. Or at least he was in jail for a murder, which he said he didn't commit."

A few times, Marv's trust of and love for his employees have backfired on him, most notably when his former comptroller and the comptroller's brother, who had been head of purchasing, stole money from the company. They were later tried and convicted of tax evasion and are now in jail. But this put Marv in jeopardy with the IRS. (Marv has cooperated with the government and testified during the trial.)

And over the years, Marv's lent a lot of money to people that he's never gotten back. That hasn't changed his outlook. He still views his employees as his most important asset.

Marv walks through the factory every day, stopping and talking to workers. He asks about their children. He says *"¡Hola!"* and shakes hands with those who don't speak English. Every day. Marv wants to let his employees know how important they are to him.

Cumberland has one of the most ethnically and racially diverse workforces I've ever seen, both in the administrative offices and on the factory floor. There are men and women, black, white, Hispanic. The plant manager, Jesus Ferriero, doesn't even speak English. That presents some minor difficulties, but he's a good plant manager, and that's why Marv promoted him. Employees sometimes work on college or advanced degrees that would enable them to leave Cumberland. One or two do leave from time to time, but often they return to Cumberland to work there again.

As I went through Cumberland's offices and factories, employees would literally stop me and pull me aside to tell me how much they love Marv, how much he did for them and their families. How he had helped them buy a home or get out of a debt. One man, Ernie Serrano, physically intercepted me, took me by the arm, sat me down at his desk to tell me that if it weren't for Marv, he, a single father, couldn't have raised his sons.

People kept starting to cry. "Everything I have, I owe to this man. My house. My food. My kids' schooling. Everything. Everything," one man told me, his voice choked with emotion. "I would give him anything."

Marv turned away, embarrassed. "I got more from him," Marv said. "Everything I have, I got from him and the others here."

And There's No Corporate Jet

Not all companies could do what Marv is doing. I don't know if a company with very fierce competitive pressures could afford to keep the extra jobs. Southwest Airlines competes heavily on price, and still employees receive excellent pay, benefits, and profit sharing. But Southwest certainly doesn't keep extra job slots.

Sweet'N Low is in a unique market position. It faces one very well funded, very strong competitor: Monsanto, the maker of NutraSweet.

But, as so often happens, Cumberland's competitor actually expanded the market for its product.

Marv's success, however, is not solely the result of the unique characteristics of his competitive environment. It also springs from his own intelligence, guts, and integrity. The way he responded to the cyclamate ban and the oil embargo made Sweet'N Low a household name.

That strong brand recognition and loyalty keep customers coming back. Cumberland does a miniscule amount of advertising in comparison to the ad budget for NutraSweet. Yet more than 30 million people use Sweet'N Low every day. And it's not just name recognition. Most of those customers prefer the product itself to NutraSweet.

Cumberland owns their own buildings. This puts them in a position where they are not constantly facing increased rents. (Lest you think that's the only reason Cumberland stayed in the neighborhood, please note that Cumberland has, over the years, purchased and leased additional factory space across from their original site.)

And Marv pointed out another factor that makes it possible to compete.

"Marv, how can you afford to keep two hundred extra people on your payroll?" I asked.

"I don't pay myself forty-two million dollars." This was Marv's one and only jab at his competitor, Monsanto. In 1997, Monsanto's CEO, Robert Shapiro, received a total compensation package of $51.2 million.

Marv's right: you can buy an awful lot of jobs for $51 million.

Is This Good Business?

For weeks after visiting Cumberland, I was haunted by the same nagging question, "Is this good business?" Marv's story is heartwarming. There's no doubt he is making an immense contribution to the community. Marv's clearly a good person. But is this good *business?*

Maybe Marv should reorganize Cumberland into a nonprofit organization, I thought to myself. Except . . . it's not nonprofit. Cumberland *is* profitable. Marv likes making money. Cumberland Packing has a definite, strong profit orientation. Moreover, if Cumberland were truly in financial jeopardy, Marv would do the things he needed to do to save the company, including, I'm certain, eliminate jobs.

It's just that he and the others there have been able to keep the company profitable while keeping jobs. Marv believes that if others help you succeed, they shouldn't be penalized by the loss of their jobs.

Well, how about eliminating jobs through attrition? Marv wouldn't have to ever lay off any particular individual. The job would just get cut after someone retired or quit. How about if we just did that, Marv?

No! Marv sees his responsibility as being to the community, not just to individuals. He is very aware of the effect of jobs and job loss on a community, and he wants to meet his duty to Brooklyn. He knows the most important thing he can contribute is not a big check to a local charity but jobs.

In the short term, Marv's philosophy may not seem like good business. But taking a longer perspective, I see that Marv's commitment to the community, to those jobs, probably turned out to be the wisest *business* decision after all. Remember, a number of companies have wanted to purchase Cumberland over the years. Each time Marv's commitment to the community, and to his family, wouldn't allow him to sell. Had he sold Cumberland back when he was approached by Searle, the amount would have been paltry in comparison to the company's value today. So it was a very smart *business* decision.

But You Don't Get to Put on a Tuxedo and Eat Rubber Chicken

Marv is the first person I've ever met who proves that money *can* buy happiness. Marv has used his money to buy him happiness. Marv loves jobs, and he's bought about two hundred jobs a year.

Guys like Marv typically start and build a business, make a lot of money, sell their business, and then make money off their investments. They golf. They write big checks for charities and have black-tie banquets held in their honor. Then they go home to their big empty houses with their plaques naming them "Man of the Year."

Marv goes to work every day. He works with his brother, Ira. His wife, Barbara, and some of his children work by his side—not because they have to, but because they want to. Marv has challenges, successes, a company filled with friends who've worked with him for decades, a plant full of people who know the effect he's had on their lives.

Over the years many other companies have tried to buy Cumberland.

Marv has steadfastly refused. "Alberto Culver, years ago, tried to buy us out, and they just could not understand why I wouldn't sell. Another big company offered us so much money that I had to speak to Jeff [Marv's oldest son] and my wife about it. The other companies couldn't understand, either. I tried to explain to them why—that there's more important things than always thinking about the bottom line. What am I going to do with all this money? They said, 'Well, it's power.' I said, 'I don't want power.' And I could see from their attitude that they just did not understand.

"I wake up in the morning, I'm looking forward to going to work. This is something that I've created over the years. I still look for Sweet'N Low packets wherever I go. Life is more than just the bottom line. I wanted to have something for my children. It's a legacy that I want to carry on."

Isn't that better than a banquet and a tee time at the country club?

Okay, So Let Me Be Your Consultant, Jeff

Jeff Eisenstadt, Marv's oldest son, works at Cumberland. Steven, his youngest son, also works there. As does his brother, his wife, Barbara, and his son-in-law, Michael Drinkard. In fact, it is Barbara, a graphic artist, who was largely responsible for developing the Sweet'N Low packaging as you see it today.

I'm sure the Eisenstadt children will face decisions about what to do with Cumberland in the future: whether to sell, whether to move out of Brooklyn. I hope they keep some perspective as they make their management decisions. I hope they learn from Marv's example, and from the examples of their grandparents Benjamin and Betty, that sometimes the very best *business* decision is the one that's made from the heart and not from the calculator.

I'm not saying that Cumberland should necessarily stay in Brooklyn forever. Or even stay in the Eisenstadt family's hands forever. But the love and loyalty, the strength of character that Cumberland gets from staying in touch with its roots, are a tremendously valuable corporate resource. It's shortsighted to overlook these factors just because they don't show up on a balance sheet.

Which brings us back to Schwinn.

After the bankruptcy in 1992, Schwinn was bought by folks from Chicago, Schwinn's birthplace. The Zell/Chilmark Fund and Scott Sports Group Inc. purchased Schwinn, with a desire to rebuild the brand.

Unfortunately, the management talent they wanted and needed wouldn't relocate to Chicago, so Schwinn was reborn in Boulder, Colorado, a hotbed of cycling enthusiasm, where the company could find a workforce that lived the sport.

Schwinn has prospered in the hands of people who love the brand. Schwinn's new owners beefed up the product development and design staff and budget. They adopted a management system that empowers employees, giving them the opportunity to take initiative, to innovate.

The result? At the time of the bankruptcy in 1992, Schwinn sold around 300,000 bikes. By 1995, Scott/Schwinn sold an estimated 640,000 bikes, three quarters of which were Schwinns. In 1997, Schwinn was subsequently sold to an investor group, Questor.

Schwinn's owners are committed to making Schwinn the American icon it once was. To that end, Schwinn's top-of-the-line bicycle division is named Homegrown. These bikes are made in America with as many American-made components as possible. When the next great heart-stopping bicycle successor to the Stingray comes along, it's likely to carry a Schwinn name and be made right there in the neighborhood.

Meanwhile, Edward Schwinn, Jr., the last Schwinn to run the company, had a far different fate. After the bankruptcy, the Schwinn family lost the right to use the name Schwinn on any bicycle. According to the authors of *No Hands*, Edward Schwinn, Jr., moved to Lake Geneva, Wisconsin, where he and a partner ran a gift shop selling jams, jellies, pickled vegetables, and cheese in the shape of cows.

The Sweetest Man on Earth

One of the things Marv said to me a few times was "I sleep well at night." I bet he does. He deserves to sleep soundly.

I have to tell you, quite frankly, Marv Eisenstadt got to me. Cumberland was one of the last companies I visited for this book, and by then I had seen many truly wonderful people, truly wonderful companies. I'd been moved to tears a few times in the previous months, touched by the stories, by the sheer decency of so many people in business.

Partly it's because Marv is just so uncomplicated. Marv doesn't work any angles. It's so easy to be cynical these days—we see a company doing something good, and we think they just want the positive publicity. Not Marv. Marv is not a publicity-hungry man, and Cumberland is not a publicity-hungry company. I had put together binders with background information on each company in this book; Cumberland's was by far the thinnest. To get an interview, I had to just about go and camp out on their front step.

Partly it's because Marv doesn't decide on his management policies or style by figuring out the economic benefits. He just manages from his heart. This frustrates other, younger managers in the company, who often want to protect him from himself. But Marv manages like his parents. He takes care of business. He expands markets and extends the brand name, but when it comes to employee matters, he does what he thinks is the right thing, the human thing.

Part of the reason I was so moved by Marv was because the love Marv's employees feel for him is so palpable, so apparent. Many of Marv's employees told me they'd work for him for free. If Marv were in financial trouble, his employees would probably bail him out. Because he's family. Cumberland's home.

Is Marv a good businessman? I still shake my head and wonder. But think about this when you pick up that little pink packet: two hundred extra people have jobs that would be almost impossible to replace. Probably well over two hundred children have parents who come home from a job, a good job, instead of from a welfare line. Two hundred extra people have jobs in a neighborhood that desperately needs jobs. Two hundred extra people spend money in that neighborhood. Go to church. Play soccer. Help keep the neighborhood together. And everyone at Cumberland is treated with dignity and respect. All of them can be proud of the company they work for.

Is this good business? Someone at Patagonia told me that the traditional goal of a business is *increasing value for the shareholders.* So in these terms, Marv's been a magnificent businessman.

Marv has the love and respect of those who work with him, his large extended family. He has the satisfaction of knowing he runs his company honestly and fairly. Marv is loyal to those who've been with him along the way, and so people look up to him not because of power or prestige but because of his heart. How much would you *value* that?

Marv has the day-to-day companionship, affection, and respect of his own family, who see a decent, fair, and nice man living a life and running a business with integrity. A man who makes choices based on what is the right thing to do, on what helps people, not on how it will affect his bank account. How much would you *value* having your children and grand-children think of you that way?

Marv Eisenstadt sleeps soundly at night because, while he may not rec-ognize it, he has, for a certainty, made a huge difference in the lives of others, has left the world a better place for his being here. How many people can say that? What is the *value* you could place on that?

Marv's rewards are so obvious, so real, so much more important than just a big bank account. They just don't happen to be the kind of rewards that are measured on Wall Street. Their value is not in terms of power or money but in terms of personal satisfaction, honor, decency, integrity, making a real difference. *Increasing value to the shareholders.* There's a lot more to value than just money. Mom always knew that.

An old folk legend has it that, scattered throughout the earth, there are twenty-eight people on whom the future of the world depends. These twenty-eight people do not know who they are—you could be one. But their actions determine whether the world will continue or not. If the leg-end is true, I'm hoping Marv Eisenstadt is one of these twenty-eight. Then we'll all have a safe and sweet future.

12

QUIT PICKING ON EACH OTHER

You and your sister fought all the time. You couldn't help it. She just annoyed you. You pinched her when she kept playing with your Barbie clothes after you told her not to touch them three hundred million times. She socked you when you used her hairbrush—again—and left it—oh, somewhere. She called you a baby; you called her stuck-up. You shoved her when she crowded you in the backseat of the car; she shoved back. It was constant conflict.

Mom would try to bring peace: "Why can't you two just get along? You're sisters. You should be nice to each other; you should help each other out." That, of course, had no effect. Mom would just lose patience: "All right, enough already. I've had it with you two. Quit picking on each other."

We keep picking on each other in business, too. One of the things I've noticed in my work is how many people go around with an "us versus them," "me versus you" attitude. Some treat business as warfare: competitors are the "enemy," the marketplace is a battlefield, and the objective is to win market share. But all too often, this enemy orientation spills over to other aspects of business life. We find ourselves thinking of every interaction as a competition, even when dealing with those who are on our own side: our employees, our suppliers, sometimes even our customers.

This attitude treats business as a series of adversarial relationships. First it's us against our competitors: Let's take market share. Then it's us ver-

sus our suppliers: How little can we get this to cost? After that it's us versus our customers: What's the most we can charge? Finally, it's even me
versus my employees: What's the least I can pay? This may seem like just
plain good business sense. It's not. And when taken to extremes, this adversarial orientation can lead to ridiculous situations.

I know a business owner—but he is hardly alone—who hates, *hates*
writing out large commission checks to his salespeople. As soon as a salesperson becomes really successful and the checks get *too* big (in this business owner's estimation), he cuts the commission or makes life miserable
until the salesperson quits. Now, this is totally irrational: the more this
salesperson makes, the more the business owner makes. *They are both on
the same side.* In the business owner's mind, however, the salesperson is
just getting *too much.* It feels as if the salesperson is *winning.* This business owner sees every interaction as having a winner and a loser.

There's a term for this approach to life: it's called a "zero-sum game."
In this way of viewing the world, the pie (of income, of the market, of rewards, of power) is finite; there are only so many pieces to go around. You
get one more, I get one less. Every time you win, I lose. Every time you
lose, I win. We are, in all things, competing for limited resources. We are
all constantly picking on each other. We'd drive Mom right out of her
mind, and I can just hear her say, "You're on the same side. You should
help each other out. Quit picking on each other."

We'll Make More

A friend of mine caught me off guard a few months ago. A few of us were
talking, and as part of the discussion he commented about something, "To
use Rhonda's favorite expression, 'Let's make this a win-win situation.' "

"Do I really say that a lot?" I asked, surprised.

"You use the term 'win-win' all the time," he answered. The others all
quickly agreed.

I puffed up with pride. I could hardly have received a nicer compli-
ment. As anyone who knows me well can attest, I'm a competitive individual. I used to do lap swimming for exercise; if a faster swimmer was in
the next lane (and everyone in the entire universe is a faster swimmer), I'd
start swimming faster. Now, this usually threw my entire pace off, with
the result that I'd poop out sooner, thus getting less exercise and defeat-

ing my goal. This was silly, of course; I wasn't trying to win any swimming championships, but subconsciously I just hated seeing that swimmer pass me on every lap. I'm easily distracted by competition.

It takes a lot for me to rein in my competitive instincts. But over the years, I've come to realize, both philosophically and practically, that the important thing is to concentrate on how well I myself am doing, not whether I'm "beating" a competitor. I've learned that the key to success is focusing on what's good for me and my business, having my own internal goals, not being driven by competitors' actions. This isn't merely a matter of being a nice guy or listening to Mom; it's been shown through studies of businesses over time that those companies that focus on their own goals, instead of on "winning" or "beating the competition," are the companies that succeed and survive.

I've come to understand that it doesn't matter if your competitors "win," your customers "win," or your suppliers or employees "win." What matters is how you're doing at your own game. And often, the best way for you to win is to find ways for others also to win. There doesn't always have to be a loser; all sides can win. You can have, to use one of Rhonda's favorite expressions, a "win-win situation."

We can easily see a win-win situation in the case of the business owner and his sales force: when they get bigger checks, he gets more income. And vice versa. They win; he wins. They're both on the same side. But this is often also true in situations with less immediately apparent confluence of interest: making sure your customer has a good deal, giving your supplier a fair profit, providing your employees with good pay and benefits, even dealing with your competitors decently and fairly. Mom knew what she was talking about when she told you to "quit picking on each other."

This Seems Nuts

In my very earliest years in business, I had a friend who was also starting a business. She was making bottled peanut sauce, the kind of peanut sauce you'd find in Thai food, to sell to grocery stores. She mentioned to me that the people who were giving her the most help in getting started, telling her about suppliers, where to rent a commercial kitchen, sources for bottles and labels, and so on, were her *competitors*—other companies that were making and already selling peanut sauce. I was flabbergasted!

This went against everything I had ever learned about business. Why would they do this?

Certainly she and her competitors were competing for very limited shelf space. Shelf space in supermarkets is very valuable. Much of it, I'm sorry to say, is usually "sold" to products, through the payment of "slotting" fees, so it's difficult for products from small companies to get onto the shelves. Peanut sauce was a relatively new product at the time; if grocers were going to experiment with selling peanut sauce, most would likely only choose one brand. If a grocer stocked my friend's brand, it's probable the grocer would not also stock her competitors'.

Fortunately, her competitors understood the concept of enlightened self-interest. They rightfully recognized the need to build a market, not just capture a portion of the teeny market that existed. They figured, rightfully, that the more companies that sold peanut sauce, making both grocers and consumers aware of it, the more demand there would eventually be. All boats would rise.

Cumberland Packing, makers of Sweet'N Low, experienced exactly that phenomenon when NutraSweet entered the market. Sweet'N Low could theoretically have been squashed by such a huge competitor. Instead, NutraSweet's advertising made consumers more aware of sugar substitutes as a category, and Sweet'N Low's sales increased significantly. The total market for artificial sweeteners expanded. NutraSweet didn't just take a piece of Sweet'N Low's low-calorie pie, it actually made the pie bigger. Not all competitions, it turns out, are "zero-sum games."

When Someone Says "Market Share," Watch Out

Business is based on competition. But there are different ways of approaching competition.

Take sports. When we talk about business, we frequently use sports as a metaphor. Competition is at the heart of sports, and competition appears to be at the heart of business.

In sports, which mind-set works best: "I'm going to beat the pants off the other guy" or "I'm going out there to do my best?" When fans cheer, is it better for them to yell, "Kill the Dodgers" or "Go, Giants?"

This is more than just a sports question, it's also a business question. How do we approach competition: as a race to win or as an impetus to do our best? Are we better off with a competitor orientation or an internal orientation?

While I can't say what works in sports, I can tell you what studies show about business.

While Olympic athletes compete for gold medals, companies compete for "market share"—how much of a total market a company controls. If the Coca-Cola Company wants to know how it is doing in comparison to Pepsico, it evaluates what percentage of soft drink buyers purchase Coke rather than Pepsi—what share of the total market Coke controls. All those commercials you see on TV, all those ads in magazines and on buses, all those cute jingles, by both Coke and Pepsi, are designed to keep or gain market share. Even one or two percentage points of market share are seen as being important.

Traditional business strategy places great emphasis on increasing market share. The theory is that large market share enables you to better ward off competitors over time, control market conditions, and set prices. If you have the dominant market share, goes the theory, you can eventually weaken your competition and drive many competitors out of the market. Only a few companies will be left standing after a market share war; you had better make sure one of them is yours.

But what happens when you're worried primarily about market share? Two professors, J. Scott Armstrong of the Wharton School of Economics and Fred Collopy of Case Western Reserve University, conducted a study to see how important "beating" the competition was to managers and what effect it might have on the bottom line.[1]

Armstrong and Collopy gave managers two pricing options for a new product:

1. A low price with *low profits,* but their company would make more than the competition, (a "beat the competition" approach).
2. A high price with *double the profits,* but the competition would make more (a "concentrate on our own performance" approach).

Surprisingly, a whopping *60 percent* chose to reduce their own profits by half in order to "beat" the competition. They did this even when the

1. J. Scott Armstrong and Fred Collopy, "Competitor Orientation: Effects of Objectives and Information on Managerial Decisions and Profitability," *Journal of Marketing Research,* May 1996, pp. 188–199.

professors indicated that reducing the competition's market share would not reduce its ability to stay in the market over time. These managers just wanted to win for winning's sake, not to increase their company's bottom line or make their company more competitive.

It turns out, however, that concentrating *primarily* on winning, on beating the competition, turns out to be a fairly poor strategy in the real world of business. In addition to the theoretical pricing question the professors posed, they also reviewed the performance of twenty large American companies over fifty years to see the impact of being oriented primarily towards increasing market share—beating the competition—rather than being oriented toward their own profitability and well-being. They found that those companies that concentrated primarily on increasing market share were *less* profitable and *less* likely to survive than those companies that focused primarily on increasing profits.

In fact, the two professors not only recommended that companies not use market share as an objective, they specifically advised companies to "avoid using sports and military analogies, because they foster a competitor orientation."

A similar conclusion was reached by James Collins and Jerry Porras in my very favorite business book, *Built to Last: Successful Habits of Visionary Companies*. Collins and Porras compared eighteen "visionary" companies—the "premier institutions" in their industries—with eighteen other leading companies in the same industries. They were seeking to determine which factors enabled a company to endure, to prosper over a long period of time while surviving changes in leadership and remaining widely admired.

One of Collins and Porras's findings was that "Visionary companies focus primarily on beating themselves. Success and beating competitors comes . . . not so much as the end goal but as a residual *result* [emphasis theirs] of relentlessly asking the question 'How can we improve ourselves to do better tomorrow than we did today?' "[2]

It turns out that putting a company's energy first into increasing profits—improving internal performance—produces healthier results than concentrating primarily on beating the competition.

---

2. James C. Collins and Jerry I. Porras, *Built to Last: Successful Habits of Visionary Companies* (New York: HarperBusiness), 1997, p. 10.

What Ben and Jerry Learned from Their Mothers

What Ben Cohen Learned from His Mother and Grandmother

It was mostly my grandmother Ray [Rachel Abrams] who taught me lessons that have helped me in business.

I remember three quotes from her that I think about all the time:

1. Honesty is the best policy.
2. Good, better, best. Never let it rest till the good is better and the better is best.
3. *"A brokheh oyf dein kepeleh."* (Translated from the Yiddish: "A blessing on your head.")

And what my mother, Frances Cohen, told me? "Don't you ever, ever, ever do that again." So I rebelled, and I love to make mistakes.

What Jerry Greenfield Learned from His Mother

I guess what I got from my mother, Mildred Greenfield, was the Golden Rule: "Treat others as you would want to be treated yourself."

Remembering this saying helps me a lot when I am dealing with staff. It was particularly helpful in the early days. I wanted to create an atmosphere where people knew we cared about them. People knew if they had a problem, I'd come through for them. And when I had a problem, they'd come through for me.

This doesn't mean you should ignore your competitors, of course. It just means that being willing to reduce your own profits to undermine a competitor turns out to be a foolish long-term strategy. Picking on each other, as Mom could have told you, doesn't get you anywhere—it doesn't do *you* any good. Thanks, professors, for proving that Mom was right again.

Whose Side Are You On?

When we develop a strong competitive orientation, it's hard to rein it in. All too often, it spills over to the treatment of others in our business lives, even those on our own side.

I've worked with a few employers who are outright antagonistic to their employees. They would be dismayed to hear me describe their behavior as hostile or oppositional, yet they engage in a tug-of-war with employees over every item: pay, benefits, authority, power. This establishes an "us versus them" atmosphere, and nothing is as dispiriting to an employee as knowing your boss is against you. These employers are surprised when employees then aren't motivated, don't take initiative, or, in the worst cases, steal, never realizing that they themselves have set up the terms of the interaction. They just view their own behavior as being normal, good business: getting the most work out of employees for the least amount of money. Described that way, it can *seem* sensible.

Sometimes this oppositional behavior, amazingly, even extends to the treatment of customers.

Take Fry's Electronics. Here in Silicon Valley, almost everyone has a story about Fry's. Fry's is an electronics emporium extravaganza. Fry's huge stores, each in a different theme (western, space, Egyptian tombs), are crammed with everything a prototypical computer nerd could ever need: electronic components, hardware, software, cables, accessories, plus the other vital necessities of a nerd's life: potato chips, Coke, candy, video games, and lots of magazines, including those with centerfolds.

But the stories people tell about Fry's are not only about the wonderful gadgets or hard-to-find components—no, mention Fry's, and frequently people jump in to tell their own Fry's story of being treated like the enemy. Try returning something at Fry's; even with a receipt and an unopened box bought just the day before, you have to jump through hoops, seeing at least four different employees.

The treatment at Fry's is so bad, it's legendary. Web sites have sprung up devoted solely to sharing Fry's horror stories. People are sometimes so amazed at the lousy service, they just have to tell someone. Like my friend who eagerly—and repeatedly—tells me of the time she wanted to buy a big-screen TV. Now, this was a splurge, costing nearly $3,000. You expect some kind of service. Not at Fry's. After she desperately searched the store trying to pin down a salesperson, one employee grudgingly said, "I'll sell it to you, but don't ask any questions."

Or this story off the Web: "I once wanted to buy a compiler. . . . I couldn't tell from the box if it had certain documentation or not. A clerk was walking by, and I asked if they had an open box I could look through.

No. Taking a long shot, I asked if I could open the box and look inside. A little too much to ask? Compare that to his response: "You want to open the box?" He turned to another customer, who was looking at a different package: "Hey, you want to open that up and take a look? Why not? Let's just let everyone open up the software and play with the stuff inside."[3]

One could easily chalk up a certain amount of criticism of Fry's to the fact that people who spend their time interacting primarily with computers can sometimes be less than artful in human interaction themselves. Even so, Fry's has an unusually bad track record. It doesn't take much to see why: it's a war between Fry's and their customers and Fry's and their employees.

"The family is convinced to its core that everyone in every store . . . has but one goal—to steal the Fry family blind," according to an employee quoted in an in-depth story in the *San Jose Mercury News.*[4]

"They are very militaristic in how they handle employees," said a former employee, Arthur Dressel. "Their attitude is 'We need to run a tight enough organization to make it impossible for our employees to become dishonest.' "[5]

Dressel later outlined for me some of the steps Fry's takes to keep a vigilant eye on their employees, including camera surveillance, locking trash and removing it to a central location, and searching employees when they leave. Other former employees mention that the company's computers have no floppy drives so employees can't copy records.

"Every minute of every day is recorded on VCRs," said Dressel. "Most people who are there feel oppressed."

Nevertheless, Dressel defends Fry's management practices "given the class of employees they have to deal with. . . . They have a lack of education and lack initiative." Dressel reported a conversation with a hiring manager, giving a glimpse of how Fry's views their relationship with employees: "They have constant turnover. They are constantly trying to hire new people. Of twenty-five applications, the first thing they do, they send for a drug test. Now we're down to five. Twenty either don't pass or don't take it because they know they won't pass. Of the five, we run a background check.

3. From Web site, http://www.crl.com/~jnelson/nauseam/verbage/seven.htm.

4. Larry Slonaker and Mike Langberg, "Expansion into New Markets Will Test Fry's Spotty Record on Customer Service," *San Jose Mercury News,* August 24, 1997, p. 13A.

5. Mike Langberg and Larry Slonaker, "Workers Kept on Tight Leash, But Some Praise the Practices," *San Jose Mercury News,* August 24, 1997, p. 12A.

Check for felonies, misdemeanors. Then you're down to one. You got to take him as an employee, whether he speaks good English or not."

Fry's continually sends employees the message that they are not trusted. It's a battle, and both customers and employees are treated like the opposition.

Believing in Strangers

For a retail experience at the opposite end of the spectrum, visit a Nordstrom store. Look around. There are no armed guards by the doors. There are no sensors or alarms. There are no security tags that explode red ink. And Nordstrom's liberal return policy makes it a snap to get a refund on merchandise, even without a receipt. Nordstrom is a trusting place.

Nordstrom begins their trust of employees with their employee handbook, which consists of just one sentence: "Use good judgment in all situations." (See Chapter 4, "I Don't Care Who Made this Mess, Just Clean It Up.") They allow their employees wide latitude in their decisions on behalf of customers. Most stores would view such a policy as an invitation to theft.

Nordstrom continues to show trust in both their employees and customers in the atmosphere they create within the store, an atmosphere that appears to have virtually no restraints.

Of course, Nordstrom takes steps for security; it's just their philosophy to not penalize the overwhelmingly large percentage of honest customers for the behavior of the few crooks. They don't want to turn Nordstrom stores into war zones, and they don't view the people in their stores as the enemy.

"Our responsibility is to protect the company but also to protect those who are honest," said Nordstrom's chairman, John Whitacre. "Only one out of a hundred thousand [customers] abuses the return policy. . . . We want to create an open environment. That's the backwardness of our society right now. Someone does something wrong, and then rules are made that take away all of our freedom. We're trying to protect the freedom of those who aren't doing anything wrong."

But they're not fools. Nordstrom knows their liberal return policies and their open environment make them a target for thieves. They just know it's their job to work harder, and smarter, to prevent theft. They do this by making their security systems subtle, unobtrusive. Yes, there are security cameras, but you've probably never noticed them. There are detectives in every store, and Nordstrom aggressively tracks and prosecutes both shoplifters and internal theft by employees, much more aggressively than other department stores.

"We have great loss prevention departments in every store," said Susana Higuera Lerner, internal investigator at the San Francisco Centre Nordstrom. Susana should know; she's been with Nordstrom since she was sixteen years old, eventually leading to her choice of major in college, criminal justice, and her attending the Federal Law Enforcement Training Center in Atlanta, training side by side with FBI agents.

At seventeen, Susana started as an undercover detective in Nordstrom: a sweet, sightly schoolgirl seemingly shopping for sweaters while secretly snooping for shoplifters. No one but a thief would have been bothered by Susana's presence.

Unlike most department stores, Nordstrom will prosecute shoplifters fully. Many department stores catch shoplifters but then don't bother to follow through with the entire legal prosecution. Nordstrom does. Part of the reason is that they train their security personnel more thoroughly, and when they prosecute, they have stronger evidence.

"Any case that can be prosecuted will be," said Susana. "It's very frustrating work, really hard work. It can be frustrating if you have to let someone walk because you don't have all the elements [necessary for a good prosecution]. We train our security personnel that we're not after how many cases you close in a month—worry about the quality of the cases. At other companies it's more about numbers.

"Some other companies were known for getting in a lot of lawsuits because they stopped people they didn't have any business stopping, perhaps because of their color. You can lose your job if you use bad judgment.

"Nordstrom looks out for the company by training the loss prevention team properly and empowering the employees to use good judgment," Susana explained. "We spend a lot of time and money on sensitivity training, making sure we know what to look for, what the real indicators are, and they're nothing to do with age, race, poor or rich. You have to know the indicators, and that's all you look for. And they're careful in hiring to make certain they're getting people who are fair. . . . Nordstrom spends a lot of money making sure they have good employees in loss prevention.

"Our attitude here is, a few crooks get away with it, but you don't want to offend an honest customer," Susana continued. "If I owned my own company, I'd want to run it like Nordstrom. If you treat your customers right, well, they're going to keep coming back to you, they're going to be loyal. With all the competition out there, that's important. . . . You may get two hundred customers from one very happy, satisfied customer, and you can lose two thousand customers from one bad scene."

Whitacre tells me another story of how "generally good people are." When he was store manager at the Nordstrom in Walnut Creek, California, a salesperson came to him, saying a customer told her a hundred-dollar bill was missing from the pants he had left in the fitting room. What should she do? He asked her what she thought; she'd been working with the customer, did he seem honest? The salesperson said she thought the customer was telling the truth. So she went and gave him $100. The customer, of course, was grateful. A few moments later, the customer came back. As he was leaving the store, another man came up to him; he had found his hundred-dollar bill. The customer came back to John and gave him back the $100. He not only praised the salesperson but promised he'd be a Nordstrom customer for life.

All this requires a lot of faith in people. It means you have to stop picking on your customers and employees and start trusting them. You have to believe that by treating people well, decently, with respect, they will return that respect. If you quit picking on them, they'll quit picking on you.

That's not easy in today's world, where we keep our guard up, believing everyone is out to take us for all we're worth. It's hard to imagine that if we stop being adversarial in our interactions, if we stop protecting ourselves first at every turn but look for ways for everyone to benefit, we won't get taken. But some people, some companies have found that it's worth taking that chance.

It has paid off for Nordstrom. Nordstrom has one of the strongest brand names and company reputations in the world. And if there's a Nordstrom in your area, check your local newspaper. You'll find dozens of full-page ads and full-color Sunday inserts from other local department stores every week, sometimes every day. Not from Nordstrom. The exceptional loyalty of their customers makes it possible for Nordstrom to spend only a fraction on advertising compared to other retailers.

"When you compare the dollars we could spend advertising with what we get back by trusting people," said John, ". . . we're far better off in this company, we're far better off in this country. We're fighting like mad for our vision of the world."

And what is Nordstrom's vision of the world? "Our whole ethic is based on goodwill towards each other. Goodwill towards each other is so important. We want to be people that believe in strangers and trust them.

"I don't want you to get the wrong impression that we're just an idealistic company, that we're just here to be good and trust people," he continued. "I want the whole thing. *I want to win on all levels.* I want to play the game, and I love to compete. But I also like the way we are as a company."

John Whitacre wants to win. And he wants his customers and employees and strangers who walk through Nordstrom's doors to win. To use one of Rhonda's favorite expressions, he wants a *win-win situation.* Or, as Mom would have said, he wants everyone to just "quit picking on each other."

What Battle Do You Want to Fight?

Right, I can hear you saying, but Fry's is a discount store and Nordstrom is an upscale department store. Fry's runs on tiny margins; Nordstrom can afford the greater losses.

Well, first let's make it clear that those statements may not be entirely correct. Fry's doesn't necessarily fit the description of *discount.* Their prices are in the moderate range for electronics stores. What brings people to Fry's is the wide selection, not the prices, except for a few promotional items. And Nordstrom sells a large selection of moderately priced clothes. But even if these statements were true, Nordstrom reports no higher-than-average pilferage and losses.

Fry's and Nordstrom just achieve their results in different ways. Nordstrom concentrates on making the shopping experience the best it can be, encouraging customers to return time after time and give Nordstrom their loyalty. Nordstrom's profit sharing also reduces employee theft because employees are motivated to watch for loss, brought about by both customers and other employees. Fry's spends their energies, and a lot of money, making theft as difficult as it can be, and if customer service and employee loyalty flag as a result, so be it. Nordstrom concentrates on its own game. Fry's concentrates on their "opponent."

What Colleen Barrett, Executive Vice President of Southwest Airlines,
Learned From Her Mother, Barbara Crotty

Everything I am today I learned from my mother.

I'm from a very poor family. I really mean *poor*. We were from north-east Vermont. And even though we were very poor, from early on, my mother's message to me was:

- there's nothing you can't do;
- we will always have room for an extra person;
- never think you're better than someone else.

We lived in a tiny, tiny house. I had two brothers. One night, some people showed up just at dinnertime, and my mother asked me to set two more plates. I remember thinking, "How are we going to feed them? There isn't enough." But she always found enough.

In later years, I constantly gave my mother's phone number to people from Southwest if they were traveling near her. That person would not only be welcomed, they would be invited to stay overnight.

My mother was totally nonjudgmental. She was a loving, humble person. I want to be the same. My mother gave her heart to people. We tend to do what we've seen those around us do. So, if I have a giving heart, I got it from her, from my mother.

But both companies are still in business, and both, it seems, do very well. Fry's stores are packed; try to find a parking space. They're not about to change. It's not that you can't win the game, at least for the short run, by picking on one another. It's just, what kind of world do you want to create? And if the studies are right, I believe Nordstrom, a company that is already a hundred years old, has the better chance to survive in the long run. I know Mom is pulling for them.

How Do You Know If You Won?

So if you're not focused on beating the competition, how do you know if you're successful? That may seem like a silly question with an obvious answer: I'll be successful when I'm making enough money. But how much is "enough"?

The truth is, external numbers have a great deal of power over us. If I say, "I'll be successful when my stock hits eighty," does that mean I'm not successful at seventy-eight? Does it mean success at eighty, even though I'm not profitable?

If you don't have a competitor, when do you know you're successful? Success seems an elusive target. Take one of my clients, who was building a beachfront property. For a full ten years he had to fight the planning authorities for permits. I was with him the day he received final permission. "You should feel really proud of yourself for accomplishing this," I said. "No time to think about it; I'm already worried about the next problem," he replied.

He's not alone. In my own business, I find myself always looking over the next hill, not the one I've just climbed. And while that trait may be necessary for achievement, it also contributes to a constant sense that success lies somewhere in the future and what's been accomplished so far doesn't count for much.

So we need to set our own goals, establish our own standards, and keep challenging those. That's what makes us a success in the long run. And we can do it while others are doing well, also.

We can even, surprisingly, take a lesson from sports.

Like many people, I loved watching the 1998 home run race, seeing Mark McGwire and Sammy Sosa compete for title of "home run king." Each man showed enormous drive and determination, yet each also respected and admired the other.

These two gentlemen—and it's clear that they are gentlemen—showed us the ideal way to compete: you go out and do *your best;* you see the other guy also doing *his best.* That, in turn, spurs you to do better than your best. Both of you.

Would Mark McGwire have hit seventy homers without Sammy Sosa? I doubt it. Competition spurred him on. Was Sammy a "loser" because he got "only" sixty-six home runs? Not in my book, not in the record books. McGwire may have come out on top, but they were both winners.

But each focused on his own performance, not on the other guy's. Part of it was that they didn't just focus on the numbers. Sosa said, "If it would be easy, I'd have a hundred home runs right now. I'm just going up there to do the best I can."

We can do the same in business. Take my sister, Janice. She's been in sales for almost twenty years. In all that time, she's never made a negative comment about a competitor to a customer. Never *once,* although a few engage in some pretty underhanded practices. Instead, my sister concentrates on getting out there and doing her best. When she sees a competitor doing something dirty, she responds by being more creative, more responsive, *better* than that competitor. The result? She's won the respect and loyalty of her customers—and won the district sales rep of the year award from her company time after time.

In our own business lives, we may have come to view competition as winning at any cost. The goal is to destroy the competitor, even if we destroy our customers and employees at the same time.

Mark and Sammy serve as a reminder of how we can compete with integrity and dignity, and bring sportsmanship to our own business lives. I go out and do *my best.* My competitor goes out and does *her best.* Watching each other, we both do even better.

We follow the lesson from Mom and quit picking on each other, so we have the energy to excel. And we make Mom happy.

13

Eat Your Vegetables, or You Don't Get Dessert

Remember the feeling? There you were, sitting forlornly in front of a plate of green beans while eyeing the chocolate chip cookies on the counter. You sat there stubbornly, refusing to eat the now-cold, rubbery beans. Mom was just as stubborn. She might let you get away with leaving some of the Tater Tots, but she was absolutely firm when it came to those beans: "Eat your vegetables, or you don't get dessert."

As usual, Mom turned out to know her stuff. Study after study now shows that vegetables are just about the best things you can eat. They're the basic nutrients that help us grow and guard us against disease. No matter how much we love our chocolate chip cookies, we had still better eat our green beans and broccoli. Good health requires starting with the basics. Dessert stays dessert.

The same is true in business. I write a column about small business. A question I often get is "What's the biggest problem facing a small business?" People expect me to offer one of the traditional answers, one of the ones that come up in market research: paperwork, regulation, under-capitalization, getting good help. My answer always surprises people: "Focus."

People in small companies have to handle a lot of things at the same time. Some of it is inevitable. There aren't really enough hands to go around. One self-employed artist told me that throughout the day, she mentally switches from thinking about herself as "artist" to "marketing director" to "chief operating officer."

But regardless of the size of the business, we invite trouble when we fail to eat our vegetables—fail to recognize what ingredients make our business healthy and focus on those first. Like kids, we get tempted by tasty treats: a new marketing campaign, a new business development opportunity, redesigning our logo. None of these are just fluff—empty calories—but we can easily fill up on them and neglect the activities that contain our company's fundamental nutrients. When faced with goodies tantalizing us away from our core business, we had better heed Mom's warning: "Eat your vegetables, or you don't get dessert."

This Is No Mickey Mouse Business

This truth came home to me on a visit to Disneyland in 1992.

From childhood, I've been a frequent visitor to Disneyland. It's one of my favorite places to go. Growing up in Southern California, we went to Disneyland every time a relative visited from out of town. I have a lot of relatives. One year I kept count: fifteen trips to the Magic Kingdom! So I have very vivid images of Disneyland: Sleeping Beauty and Tinker Bell. Tom Sawyer's Island. I even remember the flying saucers. The first time I ever saw a microwave oven was at the House of Tomorrow in Disneyland. In fact, every time my travel agent tells me I have an "E ticket" for my next flight, I figure I'm in for a great ride.

On that trip in 1992, however, I noticed something unusual, something that totally surprised me. Mickey Mouse was everywhere. Mickey greeted guests at the gate; Mickey starred in the nighttime parade; Mickey rescued the damsel in distress during the glittering multimedia presentation. Now, it would seem there should be nothing remarkable about Mickey Mouse being omnipresent at the theme park built on income from the world's most famous rodent, but in years immediately past, I couldn't recall Mickey playing such a prominent role.

Mickey's resurrection represented, to me, that the Walt Disney Company was once again getting around to eating its vegetables. Mickey was a lively symbol of Disney's revival of animation, and the famed mouse himself was friskier, healthier, and more alive than he'd been in years.

And Donald Too

It's hard now to imagine that animation was pretty much a dead medium in 1984. There was no *Simpsons* or *Beavis and Butt-head* on television. No Dreamworks. And no Blockbuster or Hollywood Video stores from which to rent armloads of old animated features. Animation basically consisted of Disney dusting off a classic from its vault once or twice a year for a rerelease at Christmas or during the summer.

Even Disney, the name synonymous with animation, had let the art languish as they turned to other enterprises. Before Walt died, according to his nephew Roy Disney, Walt himself had been tempted away by the tantalizing idea of building a "city of tomorrow" in Orlando, Florida, anchored by a new Disney theme park and another Magic Kingdom.

"Walt's thrust," Roy told me, "got to be the parks. Building the 'city of tomorrow.' Walt was such a hands-on guy that nothing happened if Walt didn't touch it. . . . Walt was too overextended." Walt's lack of personal attention meant a loss of satisfaction to Disney's corps of leading animators: "We lost a lot of people in the animation department when Walt lost interest."

After Walt died in 1966, Disney's neglect of animation became more pronounced. The staff shrank from 650 artists to 200. Financial support of the animation department dropped.

More important, the company started making rote, formulaic "Disney" animated films; the animators weren't given leeway to use their creativity, to innovate. Key animators, including Tim Burton and Don Bluth, left, complaining about the lack of creative freedom. It seemed you couldn't just follow some formula of what made an animated Disney film work; you needed vision and a degree of daring. The animation department's motto, however, seemed to be "We may bore you, but we will never shock you."

Meanwhile, Disney's film division turned increasingly toward adult-oriented movies, and their children's fare consisted of such memorable offerings as *The Love Bug*. But the world didn't need just another indistinguishable movie studio, and profits dropped, along with the company's reputation. By 1984, Disney's filmed entertainment profits were a mere $2.2 million. Disney stock plummeted.

Like many companies, Disney at this point was driven more by formulas, rather than by the things that made the company unique, how its customers related to it, what internal strengths gave it character. When Disney executives thought about what new directions they wanted to take, the controlling thought was "What would Walt have wanted us to do?" But soon the concept of "Walt Disney" became stultifying. Disney management had lost sight of the reality that Walt Disney the person had been a visionary, a pusher of boundaries, a man who had treated his work as an artistic expression, not merely as a commercial venture. And that ever since Walt Disney's first animated short, "Plane Crazy," three generations had grown up thinking of Disney, Mickey Mouse, and animation as a set. Disney was badly neglecting Mickey.

So they allowed their animation department to wither, and they lost direction.

Enough!

Roy Disney loves animation. He should; he was exposed to animation while still in the womb—literally. While pregnant with Roy, his mother, Walt's sister-in-law, worked at the Disney studios inking cartoons. He had animation in his blood.

Sitting with Roy Disney, you're struck by the remarkable physical resemblance he bears to his uncle Walt. Roy's father cofounded the company with Walt, and Roy is a major Disney shareholder. When the company was in trouble, it wasn't only his money, it was also his heritage that was being devalued throughout those years.

By 1977, Roy Disney couldn't take it any longer, and he resigned as an employee from the company he had grown up in. "The creative atmosphere for which the company has so long been famous and on which it prides itself has, in my opinion, become stagnant," Roy said in his resignation letter. In 1983, having become even more disgusted, he even resigned from the board of directors.

Roy could see that the company had drifted away from its focus—not just from animation, not just from family fare, but from Disney's long-time commitment to quality and creativity. In a valiant effort to save the company from being taken over by corporate raiders and broken up into

---

What Michael Eisner Learned from His Mother, Margaret Dammann Eisner

Everything you are is a result of your background. Everything. You have a piece of both your parents that you carry with you.

I don't want to demean what I've learned from my mother by saying something like "My mother said have only the open pillow facing the door or whatever." No, I can't give you any one thing. It's a myriad of attitudes and directions and don'ts and do's. A sense of ethics, a sense of hard work, fair play.

From Eisner's autobiography, *Work in Progress*, another way he mentioned his mother influenced him: "From my mother, I discovered how to establish goals, set my own rules, and then cajole and charm people into going along with me."

Eisner also reported that he inherited from his mother the temptation to push boundaries: "She was fundamentally honest and decent, but she was definitely willing to cajole and rearrange in order to get what she wanted. My mother was also much more ambitious and goal oriented than my father." Eisner recalled being told that his mother "could have run General Motors if she had grown up in a different time."

---

small pieces, Roy masterminded a move to take over Disney, bringing in Michael Eisner to run it.

The day Michael Eisner was named Disney's CEO, he made what may have been one of the best moves of his brilliant career. Michael took Roy aside and asked for his advice: What should Michael do to revive Disney? And what part would Roy like to play in the company?

Roy knew what needed to be done: "Animation!" He wanted to rebuild animation, reinvest in the company's heart and soul. Having grown up at the Disney table, Roy Disney knew what constituted that company's "vegetables": animation, creativity, innovation. Between Walt's death in 1966 and Michael's arrival in 1984, Roy had seen what can happen when a company neglects its basic needs. He saw how its health had suffered, how it had lost its vitality. The Walt Disney Company, ignoring its vegetables, became more a still life than an animated feature.

Vitamins from Under the Sea

Eisner showed great foresight in turning to Roy Disney to help lead the rebuilding of animation. And he showed great courage in taking the financial risks associated with that rebuilding. Making a commitment to animation meant that Disney would now start pouring millions into that division. They would hire new artists, build a new studio, and invest millions in computer equipment alone.

The result was a series of moneymaking hits. It takes about four years to develop a Disney animated film, and in 1989, Disney released *The Little Mermaid,* which reawakened the audience for animated feature-length movies. Suddenly, movie theaters were packed. And something else was happening: children were clamoring for dolls, lunch boxes, and clothes emblazoned with Ariel, Ursula, and Sebastian.

And not just children. Roy Disney, along with the two other men running the animation division, Jeffrey Katzenberg and Peter Schneider, remembered that Walt had never meant animation to be just a medium for children's movies and had never intended his animated features for an audience solely of kids. *The Little Mermaid* had a hip, contemporary sensibility. Ursula the sea witch was a lot more hard-edged than anything seen in a Disney film for a long time.

Animation was once again Disney's cash cow. Disney would soon have almost one thousand employees working full-time on animation, spending millions on each new movie (official estimate for *Aladdin:* $25 million). But Disney reaps the rewards. According to company executives, each new animated feature brings the company more than $1 billion in movie revenues, video sales, product licensing, song royalties, and theme park tie-ins.

Those vegetables contain some pretty strong vitamins.

How Belle Got to Broadway

Now, when Mom said, "Eat your vegetables," she didn't want or expect you to eat *only* vegetables. And she didn't want you gobbling down the vegetables and then moving straight to dessert. You have to have a well-balanced meal.

The same is true in business. Your "vegetables" are your heart and soul, what your company is all about. And you've got to start with the questions: "What is my company really about? How do my customers think of me? What is it that drives me? What is my passion, our company's passion?" Those questions are essential.

Venture capitalist Eugene Kleiner told me that most companies fail because they don't know what business they are in. I have certainly discovered that to be true in my work with businesses. Business managers and owners can often tell me what they *do* but not what business they are *in*: "We sell advertising" instead of "We help our clients attract customers." This may not seem an important distinction, but the first definition may keep a company locked into activities that are too narrow. More important, it switches your focus to *what* you do rather than *why* you do it. The second, of course, involves a risk that you may become too broadly spread. The key is to keep your activities closely aligned and to take care of the first part, "We sell advertising," first, while understanding why and what the broader context is.

Take Disney theme parks, for instance. Walt became entranced with theme parks; but not just theme parks, the idea of building a whole new "city of tomorrow." That was certainly not one of Disney's vegetables, and it took too much of Walt's attention away from more fundamental things.

Michael Eisner views the theme parks differently—as "an extension of our animation. Our theme parks—they are not really theme parks," Michael told me. "That's what other people have called them. They are really animated environments, and we take you inside of them. Therefore, our core business really is animation in the broader sense of the word, moving images that evoke emotion."

The company's animated films lead to many of its other activities, most becoming the building blocks of the company's success in other areas, such as Broadway shows based on *The Lion King* and *Beauty and the Beast*.

"We got into Disney's America through *Pocahontas*," said Michael, referring to the theme park the company had planned to build in Williamsburg, Virginia, before it was stopped by those who wanted to protect the historical areas. "We were doing our core business. We were talking about doing a movie about Pocahontas, and we were walking around Jamestown, Williamsburg, and all of a sudden the extension of that was a whole project based on America."

The connection to Disney's animated features is obvious at the theme parks, where many of the rides are based on characters from its animated films and Disney animated characters walk around the park interacting with visitors: Sleeping Beauty, Peter Pan, Snow White, and of course, the star of stars, Mickey Mouse.

Beginning, Middle, and End

Okay, so you have to eat your vegetables, but how do you make them taste good? One of the reasons many entrepreneurs get bored with their core business is that after a while they've stopped being challenged by it and they no longer put their best efforts in that direction. The vegetables start growing cold. That was certainly what happened to animation in the interim between Walt and Michael.

"Walt was an instinctive storyteller," explained Roy. Without him, the animated features became more consciously constructed, more of a product to meet market demands and to fit some stale concept of what made a "Disney" film, rather than to suit the artistic standards of the animators themselves.

With Walt, the basics were "good story, happy ending, some moral value," said Roy, "but the moral aspect wasn't so conscious." After Walt died, the idea was to make "moral" animated features—it didn't matter if the kids fell asleep and the parents refused to go.

Roy and Michael, however, understood that the most important component of a movie, whether animated or not, was a really good story. "We start by making a picture we'd like," commented Roy.

"Emotions aren't contemporary. Emotions are emotions," Michael added. Eisner had grown up exposed to Broadway theater and fine literature rather than movies, and he has a strong sensibility for what makes a story work. He understands that the key to success is telling a story that grips the audience, that people care about.

The public forgets that Walt Disney made animated features in a literary tradition, not merely from a commercial entertainment point of view—and that you can underestimate an audience.

Look at Shakespeare. At age sixteen, my nephew Aaron went with a number of friends to see the movie *William Shakespeare's Romeo + Juliet*, starring Leonardo DiCaprio and Clare Danes. They all loved it, and they all sobbed. What was interesting was that every word was exactly the same as Shakespeare wrote it; the producers had not pandered to the audience. The stage set was contemporary, and some wonderful visual puns were made to render some of the anachronistic words understandable, but the producers didn't "dumb it down" to make it palatable.

Now, here was a group of sixteen-year-olds watching characters exactly their age facing tragedy of grand proportions. We later realized that this might have been the first movie Aaron and his friends had ever seen with an *unhappy* ending. But it was real, it was moving, and it was wonderful. The quality of Shakespeare comes through every generation, and you don't have to worry about whether market research shows that consumers won't go to a play or movie in which the hero and heroine die in the end.

Walt Disney, too, had been willing to include unhappy and uncomfortable stories in his movies—stories that today would probably make him the target of a boycott by some group, perhaps the Happy, Well-adjusted Childhood Association. Imagine if *Bambi* were released for the first time today. Wouldn't that be considered just awful for kids? And how about *The Lion King,* in which the cub's father is murdered? Is this the kind of movie parents can take their kids to?

"I think you have a better chance of having a healthy childhood if you are at a Disney movie with both parents," Michael commented, "experiencing *Bambi,* which is devastating. What more devastating can anything be than saying, 'Your mother will not be around anymore,' after hearing a gunshot? . . . I don't think I have the courage to do that. But I'd rather have that in a film, with you sitting with your parents, dealing with it, than being dropped off at a mall for some vapid piece of mindless morality. The key for our movies is for an adult to want to be there with their kids and to deal with some of the things. Children are very resilient. Children are very strong if they get the support of family."

More Than Clean Streets

I was a weird kid. Even as a child, I was interested in "business," though I didn't think of it that way. I remember being in a department store when I was about twelve years old, wondering whether they placed certain items near the elevators, where more customers would see them, be-

Maslow's Hierarchy of Needs

Abraham Maslow was a psychologist in the 1950s and 1960s who became well known for postulating his "Hierarchy of Needs."

Humans, according to Maslow, have certain basic needs. As each of these basic needs is satisfied, a person can move toward satisfying higher needs. Maslow felt it was impossible to take care of higher needs until the fundamental needs were taken care of.

At base, people must fulfill their own personal physiological needs: for food, shelter, air, sleep, sex. The next need level is for safety: to feel secure in one's surroundings, in one's home, with one's family and community. If our safety needs are unmet, we cannot move on to other needs that are more purely "psychological" in nature.

After that comes our need for love, according to Maslow: love and belongingness. After our physical and safety needs are met, only then can we turn to our need for love and belongingness. Once we feel loved, we can move to the next level in the hierarchy, our need for esteem. This, Maslow postulated, is of two kinds: self-esteem, the ability to feel capable in our own lives, and the esteem that comes from the recognition and appreciation of others.

Finally, and only after all those other needs are partly met—even if they are not fully satisfied—can we move to the highest level in the hierarchy, the need for "self-actualization." This need is to become more of who we truly are inside, to recognize our true self, seek peace with others, express ourselves artistically, and find creative fulfillment.

Although best known for his Hierarchy of Needs, Maslow also studied the workings of a company in 1962 to see how a business organization that had broken work down into teams functioned. From this study, he wrote a book with the dreadful name of *Eupsychian Management: A Journal.* In his study, far ahead of his time, Maslow showed that employees who were able to see the final results of their work and who were able to work with others in a spirit of teamwork, trust, and recognition were the most productive and satisfied. "Generosity can increase wealth rather than decrease it," according to Maslow. "The more influence and power you give to someone else in the team situation, the more you have yourself."

cause the store made more money on those items. I had never heard the phrases "traffic flow" or "profit margins," but that's what I thought about. What an irritating kid!

Given that, it wasn't so unusual that I once sat on a bench on Main Street, Disneyland, musing about what made it such a great place to go, time after time.

Most of it, of course, was that Disneyland was just plain fun. You had a good time. The rides were great. But it was also because the whole experience was smart and clever. Most other *amusement* parks were just silly diversions, rides that went up and down or round and round. You got scared or you got thrilled or your got dizzy and threw up. Disneyland was more than just a series of rides; it was a series of concepts, ideas: Tomorrowland, Fantasyland, Adventureland. They were aspects of what we needed in our lives: fantasy, adventure, a sense of the future. We were invited to live our lives a different way, not just be amused. Nothing else came close.

But as I sat on that bench on Main Street waiting for my family to emerge from the gift shop (I must have exceeded my souvenir limits), I realized one other thing that made Disneyland so appealing—it was perfect. There was not one piece of trash on the ground. Everyone was friendly. The grounds were perfectly maintained. The horses in front of the horse-drawn carriages didn't mess the streets. Everything was as it should be.

Even the people. Rumors had circulated that only blondes got hired to work on Main Street and that African Americans could work only on the Jungle Ride and in Aunt Jemima's Kitchen. In college, I had a roommate who worked at Disneyland during the summers, and with her long dark hair and her dark skin, she was "themed in" to work in the Indian Village. This may have made for a better picture, but it limited opportunities for many.

As a result of these rumors, I held the notion that Disney was an exclusionary employer until 1985. The brother of my then assistant, Suzanne Fried, worked for Disney as director of their home video division. Richard was Jewish; he was gay; he was dying of AIDS. Suzanne regularly sang the praises of how well Disney treated her brother, how compassionate and accommodating they were—not because her brother was suffering from AIDS but in spite of it. Suzanne said it made a terrible time in her life easier, and when her brother died, Disney donated an entire collection of their home videos to the AIDS ward in the hospital in his memory.

During recent years, Disney has ended up being criticized for policies just like that. The Texas School Board divested itself of Disney stock, even though the stock performance had been outstanding, and the Southern Baptist Convention boycotted Disney, in part for extending health care benefits to partners of gay employees. Disney's public comment at the time was frank and without apology: "We question any group that demands we deprive people of health benefits."

The revitalized Disney has reenergized another concept that Walt wanted to achieve: he wanted to show an idealized view of America. Disney still does, but it's one in which all people are included and freedom of expression is treated as an essential American value.

Fresh Vegetables

If you're going to eat your vegetables, they had better be fresh. You can't just let them sit there getting moldy. From time to time, you have to find ways to reinvigorate your core, to keep you, your customers, and your employees interested.

"What I've been interested in doing from 1984 on was to reinvent the brand," Michael explained. "The first reinvention was basically going back to understanding what our core business was.

"I think employees are very happy that we are not a museum, that we are not just dealing with a video of *Bambi*," he continued. "I think they are very happy that we are reinventing, that we are continuing, that we are not a company that is in a dry period."

Eisner emphasizes that no matter what else he does, he stays closely involved in animation—perhaps he has learned from Walt's example of what can happen when you allow yourself to get distracted.

That will be an even bigger challenge now that Disney has acquired Capital Cities/ABC and Eisner has many more activities that appear to be far from the Walt Disney Company's core activities, its "vegetables." As he develops a corporate entertainment empire that includes properties such as ABC, ESPN, Lifetime, and many, many more, he'd be wise to put up a little reminder from Mom never to neglect Mickey and to eat his vegetables *before* dessert.

Can Sleepy Hold Up His End?

"Eating your vegetables" reminds us to take care of our core business first. It's easy to get distracted. There are so many tempting business opportunities, so many tempting new activities. We all want the cookies first. But that leads to growth through girth rather than growth through health.

Eating your vegetables is about understanding your core business, your core values. It's about "character." Some companies, like 3M, appear to be totally scattered, not minding their vegetables much at all. But 3M's character is about innovation.

In his book, *Work in Progress,* Eisner further explained, "The underlying qualities that made the company special lived on [during the time after Walt's death], just the way a person's *character* [emphasis mine] endures. Our job wasn't to create something new, but to bring back the magic, to dress Disney up in more stylish clothes and expand its reach, to remind people why they loved the company in the first place."

"Take a look at our headquarters building," Michael said to me while we were sitting in a fantastic building in Burbank, with seven huge dwarfs seemingly holding the building up. "People think we put the seven dwarves in front because it was silly and fun and all that, but that is not at all the reason. The company went broke when they were making *Snow White* . . . and the picture wasn't finished." Back in the 1930s, it looked as if Disney was going to go under. No one would refinance until Walt got a banker at the Bank of America to look at the film in progress.

"He said, 'This is a fabulous thing—the first full-length animated movie,' " said Michael. Walt got the money to finish, and *Snow White and the Seven Dwarfs* became an enormous hit, winning an Academy Award and rescuing the company financially. "So look at the front of our building—I asked Michael Graves [an architect] to have Dopey hold up the roof of our building and have the other six dwarfs hold up the building. . . . This company is being held up by those seven dwarfs. . . . It's a metaphor for what animation means to this company."

What holds your business up? Who are your seven dwarfs? What are your vegetables?

Well, What About Mickey?

Walt Disney, Michael Eisner, and Roy Disney are three strong personalities who have built and rebuilt the Disney company, but there's one personality that the company simply cannot do without: Mickey Mouse. And it's good that they have reinvigorated, breathed new life into, the world's favorite rodent. Mickey is now the star at theme parks and of some new animated short subjects, and will star in the remake of *Fantasia*. But even more is planned.

"I'm interested in—this is almost sacrilege—but Mickey has gotten a little too nice. . . . You go back and look at the early Mickeys, he was a little feistier," Eisner commented. "He used that twinkle of Walt's, because he was Walt's character. He took some risks, he got himself in trouble. I don't want to end up with Mickey as some sort of corporate symbol. He is not totally Mr. Good Guy."

Mickey is clearly the key character of the company. Eighty to 90 percent of Disney's consumer products bear the image of Mickey Mouse. "Every age group you ask, 'How old is Mickey?' " says Eisner, "they say he's their age."

Mickey Mouse is on the company's stationery, fax paper, paychecks, stock certificates, and executive dining room plates. And all new employees, of any Disney division, go through an orientation program during which they are shown a videotape of Walt Disney. At the end of it, Walt looks straight at the camera and reminds each and every one of them, "Never forget, it all started with a mouse."

I'm Waiting for Morty

One new development planned at Disney that goes back to the company's very roots has particular meaning for me: the company plans to introduce a new/old character, Mortimer Mouse.

I was introduced to the art of Disney animation by my father. He loved to draw, he loved animation, and he loved Disney. He had been fascinated with Disney and Mickey Mouse from the time he was a kid.

When I was a child, my father somehow managed to arrange a tour for us of the Disney animation studio in Burbank. I saw the animators working on the drawings for *The Sleeping Beauty*. I was particularly struck by the evil queen. It was a memorable experience and a memorable day with my father.

As an adult, my father changed his name to Alexander, but his given name was Mortimer. He once told me that Mickey Mouse's original name had been Mortimer, too. Doing research for this book, I discovered that was indeed true. Walt had wanted to call his mouse Mortimer, but his wife had liked the name Mickey.

Michael Eisner says Disney will soon introduce a new character, Mickey's mischievous cousin—Mortimer. I'm looking forward to meeting him. Maybe Morty and I will go grab a chocolate chip cookie.

14

WEAR CLEAN UNDERWEAR; WHAT IF YOU GET INTO AN ACCIDENT AND SOMEBODY SEES IT?

When I started working on this book, I went around asking people to tell me the sayings they remembered from their Mom. Without a doubt, the one saying that was repeated most frequently was "Wear clean underwear; what if you get in an accident and somebody sees it?" I heard this from people from several different cultures. I can't guarantee that it's universal, but an awful lot of mothers seem to have repeated this phrase or one fairly similar.

Why? All these moms can't really be worried about ambulance drivers checking out your BVDs. Well, maybe just a little. Mom certainly didn't want the doctor to think she was a bad mother.

No, the real message Mom was trying to teach you was that you need to behave, to be clean, to do the right thing, just because it's the right thing to do—even when no one else will notice. Mom's admonition to "wear clean underwear; what if you get into an accident and somebody sees it?" was meant to encourage you to behave in ways you wouldn't mind other people seeing. It was about learning to live up to your own standards and values. To be able to be proud of what you do, so you'd never have to be embarrassed or ashamed.

Mom was talking about substance, not image. We live in a world obsessed with images: of beauty, health, good corporate citizenship.

One day recently I had lunch with a man whose partner serves on the board of directors of a Fortune 500 company that had been getting a ton of bad press. My friend said the board was very worried about how the company was being *perceived*. I chuckled. "Perhaps," I suggested, "they should be worried about how they *behave*." This was a company, I knew, in desperate need of clean underwear.

There's a television commercial that says, "Image is everything." Companies constantly seek to control their image—crafting, shaping, spinning. But image isn't everything. Indeed, image, by its very nature, is *no thing* at all. Image is not substance; it's not real.

That's not what Mom was talking about. Mom was talking about how we really behave; what we're really like. All the way down to our underwear.

Let's Start by Unbuttoning Our Shirts

Integrity—that's what this book is all about. Integrity and character. That's what constitutes our moral and ethical underwear: the values we have at our core, underneath the outer layers we consciously show to the world.

Over and over again, as I visited the companies in this book, I saw examples of companies that did the right thing just because it was the right thing. Not as an advertising ploy or to get publicity. Repeatedly, I got to see examples of companies wearing clean underwear in a myriad of little and big ways that showed their integrity but that no one will ever notice. So let me share a few with you, give you a glimpse of some of these companies' underwear.

Let's start with buttons. I first wrote about Patagonia in 1994. At that time, I interviewed an apparel industry analyst who was highly critical of Patagonia and of Yvon Chouinard, its chairman. "Yvon doesn't understand the apparel industry," this analyst said. "Take buttons. Chouinard believes you have to make shirts so the buttons never fall off. That's ridiculous. It's way too expensive."

I had never forgotten that remark, so I wanted to track down the truth behind it. Yvon is indeed obsessed with buttons. If you recall, Yvon wants Patagonia clothes to be built the way he'd build any outdoor equipment—to last even through hard use. So he doesn't want Patagonia buttons to come off. Ever.

Now, the way most buttons are sewn on commercially is with button machines that use a chain stitch. Chain stitching is much, much cheaper than lockstitching. With lockstitching, the sewing machines have two bobbins, and each stitch is knotted, or "locked." So if one thread comes loose, the next stitch is still locked: the button stays on. With a chain stitch, the first loose thread pulls out all the remaining stitches.

Patagonia, however, is a small though prestigious customer. It didn't make financial sense for a commercial sewer to buy an expensive lockstitch machine for the small amount of work they got from Patagonia. So Patagonia bought the machines themselves, $7,000 per machine to supply sewers who might produce only ten thousand shirts. Ridiculous! Very few customers, after all, would ever notice. You certainly never notice a button that *doesn't* come off. But Yvon noticed. And cared. Yvon had his standards, his sense of how to behave. He would wear clean underwear, even though no one will ever catch a glimpse of it due to a button falling off. Mom would approve; she hated having to sew buttons back on.

It Takes a Licking and Keeps on Sticking

Next, let's take a peek at 3M's clean underwear. I don't think I actually heard any one use the word "integrity" while I was at 3M, but it permeates the place. Instead, the word I heard over and over was "honest."

3M emphasizes innovation in everything they do; in fact, it's the company's one-word guiding principle. But 3M products have to be more than *new*. They have to be truly useful, real improvements. They must meet a real need of the customer. The company stresses innovation with integrity.

When I bought a new laptop computer, it came with a new version of my word-processing software. Now, I don't have any particular need for an update. My previous version suited me just fine. But the upgrade drives me crazy. I can't imagine 3M producing an upgrade every year just to resell to customers.

Ah, I hear you saying, but it's far easier to make Scotch tape than software. So let's take a look at how 3M developed a software "Post-it Note" for computers. Customers had started asking about a simulated Post-it for their desktop computer. 3M thought it was a great idea. They then spent two years watching how people interacted with "real" Post-its, seeing what features of Post-its could be translated to software with *integrity,* two years before the engineers wrote even one single line of code.

204 ≡ Wear Clean Underwear

In the meantime, of course, other companies introduced virtual sticky notes. But 3M wanted to make certain they maintained the *integrity* of the original Post-its. They didn't just jump on a market opportunity because it was there; They wanted the product to be right.

And don't be so quick to dismiss the complexities of Scotch tape.

I asked someone at 3M, "Why do people keep buying Scotch brand adhesive tape?" After all, the patent on the original Scotch tape ran out years ago, so why does 3M's Scotch tape still sell so well when there are cheap knockoffs available?

It turns out that 3M is constantly improving Scotch tape. They keep changing the adhesive. It's now totally biodegradable, for instance. And 3M took what they learned from their medical tapes division, and the adhesive on Scotch tape now won't irritate your skin. They've improved the manufacturing process to vastly reduce waste. This has made it possible for 3M to keep costs competitive with the knockoffs while offering a superior product.

Cheesecake, Anyone?

I got another tasty example of integrity when I attended a class at Zingerman's called "The Art of Selling Great Pastry." Zingerman's is not just a deli, it's also a bakery. They make their own breads and pastries.

Zingerman's runs a huge training operation for its employees to help them better understand the food industry, their company, and how to improve their own skills, including sales skills.

Now remember, the name of this particular class is "The Art of *Selling* Great Pastry," not "The Art of *Making* Great Pastry."

The class lasted about one and a half hours. It began, interestingly enough, with each person describing the types of pastry they had eaten when they were growing up. The average age of the attendees was probably in the early twenties. So it wasn't surprising that the kinds of "pastries" most had eaten were Duncan Hines cake mix, toaster pop-ups (not even the brand-name ones) and other packaged baked goods. Ari Weinzweig, co-owner of Zingerman's, put everyone at ease, however, when he confessed that the pastry he remembered most from childhood was Twinkies.

For the next hour and fifteen minutes, we all went through an education on how Zingerman's makes their pastry great. We had tastings of its butter (European) as opposed to the shortening in most baked goods. Compared the taste of expensive imported spices to the spices usually used commercially. Learned about the difference in the taste of freshly cracked eggs from that of preprepared eggs. And kept tasting and tasting.

Yet nothing, nothing, was said about sales.

What became clear was that this was really a class about what makes pastry great. Zingerman's had enough faith in its salespeople, and even more faith in its product, that the only thing necessary to sell it was a belief in the quality of and an understanding of the differences in their pastry.

I realized that the message that these employees were receiving along with the only cheesecake I've ever liked was that Zingerman's doesn't cut corners. They make their pastries with integrity.

Business Wisdom

When I set out to write this book, I looked at the values I thought were important in business and then set about finding great companies that exemplified those values. What I found was that these companies shared most of the same values. They had learned not just one or two lessons from Mom, but had taken much of Mom's wisdom to heart. They had *character* in the old-fashioned sense. We talk a lot about personality in our society, but personality is only a little more substantive than image. It's character that drives our actions. Character, values, and integrity define who we are, how we behave.

Here are some of the traits, the lessons I found to be most prevalent and most important at these companies.

Be Yourself

Here's where I lose the business school market. Remember, one of the reasons I started writing this book was that I had clients who wanted to do things differently but felt it wasn't "businesslike."

We can get too smart for our own good. We think we have to be "businesslike," follow the standard practices, see what the industry averages are and follow those guidelines. But what does it mean to be "businesslike"?

No one in his right mind would organize 3M's new-product development the way 3M does. It results in an amazing array of seemingly unrelated products. It's not "businesslike." Other major R and D companies don't work that way.

Marv Eisenstat sure isn't "businesslike" in how he runs Cumberland Packing. But he runs a good *business* that *does* good too. Marv cared about the neighborhood regardless of whether other companies stayed or went. And he refused to sell his company, which makes Sweet'N Low, to Searle, then the maker of NutraSweet, when it certainly looked like the prudent, "businesslike" thing to do. He did far better by sticking to his values rather than the conventional business practices.

Southwest not only defied the hub-and-spoke system but also brought "love" to the workplace.

Patagonia refused to get outside financing to expand their markets, which would have been the traditional approach to their financial situation. These companies were themselves.

John Whitacre of Nordstrom said that there's an art and science to retailing. It seems that there's an art and science to *all* of business. Science is what gets the nitty-gritty taken care of. It's the kind of stuff that every business needs—a company's "vegetables." But it's the art of business that makes a company extraordinary—the art and the heart of business. And you can only achieve art by being yourself.

Respect Employees and Treat Them Fairly

Even ordinary companies should treat people with respect, whether employees or customers. But *extraordinary* companies recognize the potential in all their employees. They don't judge people on their backgrounds, their language skills, their education, let alone their race, gender, religion, or age. They get more *from* their employees because they recognize that there is much more *in* their employees.

The companies I visited for this book recognize the value of their employees to their success. They treat people with dignity. They give them opportunities. They show respect for them and their potential.

Take, for example, Guillermo "Memo" Castillo, McKay Nursery's assistant propagator. Memo is only in his twenties, and he started at McKay as a migrant farmworker. His English is still very limited. He works with Dan Moore, McKay's lead propagator, on developing and tending to the new young plants. Memo says it's "like taking care of babies." But what he really

---

We're Here to Save the World

In their book *Organizing Genius*, Warren Bennis and Patricia Ward Bie-derman vividly describe the difference that feeling a sense of passion and purpose in your work can have.

The Manhattan Project was brought together to develop the atomic bomb, to stop Hitler and literally save the world. But only a few of the scientists knew the true purpose of the work. The leaders, of course, were aware of the goals, but there was a whole staff of engineers and others to do the routine calculations and the tedious scientific jobs, and they were kept in the dark.

They were also lousy employees. After all, they just had to show up, do the work. The result was a highly unmotivated staff. They worked slowly and poorly.

The physicist supervising these technicians, Richard Feynman, was dismayed. Finally he secured permission to tell the technicians the nature of the work and to share the magnitude of what was at stake.

"Complete transformation," Feynman recalled. "They worked at night. They didn't need supervising in the night; they didn't need anything. They understood everything." They worked ten times faster.

Not every company has a world to save, but every company has some purpose at its core. People want a reason for getting up and going to work every morning, a reason more than just making money: making a difference.

---

likes is that Dan asks his opinion "all the time": "The bosses here do for me, so I try to do all that I can for my bosses. Dan comes to me, asking me my opinions. And when I suggest something good, he'll come to me and say, all happy, 'Good job.' It's one of those times when you feel good. I like it. I like it. I feel more energy to do better and better."

And at Zingerman's everyone gets respect. Every suggestion is listened to. Zingerman's, after all, has, as one of its guiding principles, "We give great service to each other." Nic Schoonbeck, a former drug addict, blossomed there. But there are hundreds of other stories at Zingerman's. And that's because, as Nathan Oswald, a former dishwasher, remarked, "Here everyone treats you with respect. Nobody throws plates at you."

They Tolerate Failure, Applaud Success

One comment I heard repeatedly at the companies I visited was "This company allows me to do my best."

It's amazing how many companies get in the way of employees doing their best. I've seen a lot of them personally. They become more interested in maintaining control or filing the paperwork. More interested in sticking to procedures than in allowing employees to think, take the initiative, and act.

Of course, the opposite example here is 3M, a company that recognizes that failure is a necessary component of innovation. Many of 3M's great products failed when first invented: masking tape failed technically, and Post-its failed in marketing. But acceptance and celebration of failure are a welcome part of life at 3M.

As William McKnight, the late president of 3M, said, "Mistakes will be made, but if a person is essentially right, the mistakes he or she makes are not as serious, in the long run, as the mistakes management will make if it's dictatorial and undertakes to tell those under its authority exactly how they must do their job."

Another company that depends on experimentation—and thus failure—is Hewlett-Packard, which has a sterling reputation as a great place to work with outstanding core values they have lived by for decades. They, too, recognize that you have to give employees a lot of room to do their own good jobs. As William Hewlett said, "Men and women want to do a good job, a creative job, and if they are provided the proper environment they will do so."

But it's not just companies that depend on innovation that have to learn to get out of employees' ways so they can do their own good jobs. Kinko's recognizes that there are literally trillions of different products that can be produced at a Kinko's location. Kinko's coworkers have to think for themselves, make their own decisions. They're taught never to accept the obvious. But if they don't accept the obvious, they have to be allowed to do jobs their own way.

Nordstrom's one-line employee handbook implicitly authorizes employees to do their best. The company just wants them to "Use good judgment in all situations." That's it. Nordstrom knows their employees are capable of thinking for themselves and recognizes that different situations may require different responses. Sometimes they'll make mistakes, make choices their manager wouldn't make. But if they use good judgment, employees are supported and encouraged to keep making their own decisions.

I like to tell people who work for me, "Bring your brains to work." By that I mean they get to think, they're allowed to use their own common sense, their own intelligence. And I hope they know I won't pounce on them if they sometimes make mistakes.

The important thing is to let people know the standard, the quality of the outcome you are seeking—not every step you want them to take to achieve that, nor the exact specifics of the outcome. There may be better solutions to your problems than you can think up alone. Remember, Babe Ruth *was* the home run king and he was also the *strike-out* king. If you want people to succeed, you have to sometimes let them fail.

Love and Family

The companies I visited are *family* businesses. The first picture that comes to mind when we speak of a "family business" is a "mom-and-pop" corner store or perhaps a small manufacturer. A small company with maybe a few dozen or a few hundred employees, where the owners and managers are blood relatives (or in-laws) of the founders. We use the word "family" to describe the nature of the *ownership* structure.

In this book, there are only a couple of companies that are actually owned or run by a family: Cumberland (Sweet'N Low), where the third generation is now entering management; Nordstrom, with six cousins serving as copresidents. There are also some whose original founder still runs or owns the company: Kinko's and Patagonia.

But there's another way to think of a business as being a *family* business, and that's by the nature of the corporate culture, how people inside that company treat one another.

Only two companies I visited overtly used the word "love" to describe their management style. Most companies are uncomfortable with that word. Instead, many of these companies used the term "family" to describe their corporate culture, to convey the sense that people are cared for as people. But ideally, a family is a loving relationship dedicated to the well-being of all its members and a long commitment over time.

The current American workforce spans generations who grew up watching television shows in which coworkers served as surrogate families (e.g., *The Mary Tyler Moore Show, Murphy Brown, Suddenly Susan*), and they look to their work environment to provide some of the same support. Indeed, many people today look to their work life as well as their home life for personal growth and support. They seek a "familylike" feeling at work. In *Time Bind*, Arlie Russell Hochshield shows that for many women, work has now taken on the aspects of home and vice versa.

"People want to be loved," says Southwest Airline's Colleen Barrett. Even at work. Love, caring, treating employees as "family" can happen in a business of any size, even a company with as many as 26,000 employees. Possibly even 75,000!

Profits Not Greed

All right, let's talk about making money. That's what business is about, isn't it? Every one of the companies in this book focuses on profits. They all care about profits, understand the importance of profits, and look for ways to continue to be profitable and to increase their profitability. But being profit-oriented is not the same thing as being *greedy*.

It is not true what that movie about the 1980s said, that greed is good. In fact, greed is unhealthy. You see it in people; it's also true in companies. Greed leads to very bad business decisions, choices that sacrifice tomorrow's health and well-being for today's bottom line or the current quarterly report. Greed gives you a *short-term orientation*.

Extraordinary companies keep their eye on the long term. Greed today takes what you might need tomorrow. Greed keeps you from sharing fairly. Greed may give you great near-term quarterly returns and get your stock price high enough that you can exercise your stock options, but it sacrifices the health and well-being of your company. Greed also leads you to a belief that there's only so much to go around, that life is a zero-sum game and you had better grab the biggest slice of pie you can.

The companies I've seen instead have an *abundance mentality*. They know that if they share, if they invest in growth, if they support one another, not only will there be enough pie to go around now, the pie will just get bigger.

Greed is not the same as profits. All companies, of course, want to be profitable—they need to! If you don't worry about the bottom line, you won't stay in business very long. But the bottom line is just that: the bottom. Some companies aim higher. You can build a very profitable business that's ordinary, or you can build a very profitable business that's extraordinary—one whose employees enjoy coming to work, whose customers feel they are taken care of, and whose community views as a good and responsible neighbor.

"More and more people are coming to realize that you can do two things with a business at the same time," explained Kevin Sweeney of Patagonia. "You can make money and do good. You can do great things. And people want to do great things with their lives."

Being focused solely on the bottom line—making as much money as possible—is like being focused solely on eating as much as you can. We need to eat to stay alive, but if that were all we did, it wouldn't be much of a life. We'd be bloated, immobile. Like people, companies need purpose in their lives. They need a reason for being. A purpose that motivates, energizes, enlivens.

But is there still a payoff? My employees will be happy. My community will be better off. My customers will like me. But what will happen to my bottom line?

According to *Fortune* magazine, in 1998, of the one hundred best places to work in America, sixty-one are publicly traded. From a stock market point of view, they did much better than average, returning 27.5 percent versus 17.3 percent for the Russell 3000, an index of representative firms. Over ten years, these companies made 23.4 percent versus 14.8 percent for the Russell Index.

If you had invested $1,000 in an average company, concluded *Fortune,* you would have made $3,976 in a decade. But if you had instead received the average return of the one hundred best places to work, you would have gained more than twice that, or $8,188.

The companies in this book are all profitable, some extraordinarily so. Zingerman's performs in the top 1 percent of their industry. Southwest has managed to be profitable at times when no other airline was. Nordstrom has the highest returns per square foot of almost any department store.

There's value in values.

"If you do the right thing, you'll make more money," said Hal Thomson of Patagonia. I can't guarantee you'll make more money. I can guarantee that you won't necessarily make any less. Being good is *not* bad business.

What do you want to achieve with your business, with your life? You can achieve profits with a business that's ordinary, or you can achieve profits with a business that's extraordinary. It costs no more to be good than to be mean. And it gives you a lot better chance of staying in business longer.

And, as Marvin Eisenstadt would tell you, you'll sleep better at night.

Passion and Pride

People want to be proud of what they do every day. Is that so hard to understand? They want to know that what they do has meaning, that they make a contribution to the world, if only to make a shirt that lasts for years, a cheesecake that makes a great dessert for a family get-together, or Scotch tape that really sticks.

They want to feel they can do their jobs and still hold their head high. If an employer asks an employee to lie a little, to squeeze a customer too hard, to put a damaged product back out on the shelf, to cut corners and sell inferior products or services, it takes away employees' pride. They don't feel good about themselves or their companies.

There's pride in doing what we used to call *good, honest hard work*. If the work has purpose, if it's *good* and has integrity—if it's *honest*—we don't mind working hard.

Even helping someone make a copy. "The work we do, our workers can relate to," explained Paul Orfalea, chairman of Kinko's. "There was a lost little girl in Spokane, Washington. What do parents and neighbors do? First, they call the police. And second, they call us, wanting us to do the posters. It's helping somebody do a résumé so they can get a job. It's helping somebody do a project to get funding for sickle-cell anemia or AIDS. Schoolchildren getting a better project grade. Our employees see it every day. So they can see their relationship to the society and know that they're contributing. Also, our business caters to the highest needs of a human being, self-actualization. You think of Maslow's Hierarchy of

Needs. I can't think of a business in the community that caters more to an individual's creative process than us. And that has been what's built our business."

We need passion and purpose. An executive from Ben & Jerry's, Alan Parker, once commented, "If business is the most powerful force in a society, how come a Bach cantata can move us to tears but a healthy balance sheet cannot?"

What If You Get into an Accident and Somebody Sees It?

Wearing clean underwear—maintaining integrity at the core—may be a company's greatest resource. It's what makes employees proud, loyal, and willing to make sacrifices. Integrity you can sense is real is what makes customers stick with you through your difficult times. Integrity at the core—honesty—is what makes a company secure. When you have integrity and honesty, you don't have to manufacture lies or develop cover-ups, and you don't have to spend time, energy, and money getting employees to go along. Integrity and honesty just make things easier.

"There's no magic formula," explained Colleen Barrett, executive vice president at Southwest Airlines. "It's really very simple. People keep looking for our secret. It's just basically, practice the Golden Rule and treat people the way you want to be treated. We try to do all that with a little bit of fun. . . . Life is too short, our people work very hard, so it helps that we enjoy each other."

We underestimate the importance to employees of working for an honest, decent company. A while back, while interviewing for a new assistant, I was bowled over by the quality of the people who applied for the job, including a number of people who had worked in very high executive-level positions. Why leave those types of jobs to work in this kind of role? There were different reasons: one wanted to be a writer, one had personal reasons. But two applicants surprised me; they were tired of having to lie for their companies. They hated going to work.

Tom Vaaler, a former executive at 3M, once asked a manager why he had never left 3M, even though he had had to move his family many times. He responded, "The company never asked me to do something I had to be embarrassed about. They have integrity, honesty. There aren't any clever agendas. You can have a good time selling sandpaper and Scotch tape."

Odwalla didn't have a crisis management program set up before the *E. coli* incident. And they didn't need one to figure out how to behave. When the crisis occurred, company management called the top people together. Within two hours they had a decision. Why were they able to make such a fast decision when so much of the company's future was in the balance? Why did they not have to consult with their attorneys and a public relations firm first? Because they focused on the sole important question: What is the right thing to do? What do our company's stated values and our values as people and as parents tell us we should do? When you make that kind of decision, you can look at yourself in the mirror for the rest of your life.

When you're in an accident, the fact that you are wearing clean underwear certainly makes life simpler. In a business, it makes communication policies simpler because employees can just tell the truth. This proved true when Southwest Airlines had an emergency. Now, Southwest has had little experience dealing with emergencies; it has an outstanding safety record. But one time a plane's landing gear was stuck and wasn't lowering. The plane couldn't land. The local news media found out about it while the plane was still up in the air and drove out to cover the story live, peppering Southwest staff with questions.

Southwest employees knew how to respond: they just told the truth. They didn't have to check everything with the national office, looking as if they were stonewalling. And after the plane landed safely and no one was hurt, Southwest didn't have to call a bunch of meetings to evaluate how they handled the media.

Here's a question to ask yourself about your company: In the midst of a crisis—a crisis so extreme that some people would view you as "baby killers"—would your employees voluntarily choose, on their days off, to go out of their way to put *on* your company's T-shirt—as Odwalla employees did in the midst of the *E. coli* crisis? Would they be able to say to themselves, "I see how this company operates, I know what we do. I know our standards and how we treat people and how we make our product. And now, when my company needs me, I want to show the world that I'm proud to be associated with this company. I know we have nothing to hide. I know we wear clean underwear, so I'm pulling out my T-shirt. Just like the company I work for, I wear clean underwear, too."

When a crisis occurs, just doing the right thing frees you from obsessing about lawsuits, your image, or your stock price. You only have to think of two things: What's the right thing to do? And what if Mom saw me now?

There's no secret formula to running an extraordinary company, no exact right percentage spent on marketing versus product support, no exact right employee benefits package, no secret strategies. People keep looking for *the answer:* the key to success. But you already have the keys to success. You know what to do; you learned it from Mom. Just remember what she taught you and wear clean underwear.

15

What I Learned from My Mother, Susan Abrams

While working on this book, I naturally thought a lot about my mother and all she taught me, the values she gave me, values I use both in my life and in my business, every day.

My mother died in 1985, suddenly and unexpectedly.

I guess you never realize what parents give you until you've lost them. Until then, the trivial details of a life usually get in the way of fully appreciating your parents as human beings and role models. The arrangements for a visit, the petty disputes, the little habits that either annoy them or annoy you often became the focus of your interactions, keeping you from seeing what parents give you and how they help mold you into a caring, loving person.

My mother was born "Sarah Rebeccah." But after my father died, she reinvented herself as "Susan." And that's one of the first things I learned from my mother: resiliency and adaptability. My mother was a survivor.

I learned about fairness and decency from both my mother and my father, Alex Abrams. My mother treated all people as equals; more than that, as possible friends. She didn't care how much money someone earned, what kind of car they drove, or the color of their skin. But she cared deeply if they were good and generous and compassionate. Those are fine ways to judge people, and I'm glad my mother taught me how.

My mother never read Martin Buber, but she shared the same philosophy of how you should treat human beings: always as people, never as things. When my sister, Janice, and I cleaned out her apartment after she died, there were so many things we didn't want to let go of. But we remembered another thing Mom had taught us: "Love people and use things; never the other way around." Mother lived her life that way, and it's a goal I strive for too.

My mother understood love. I remember being in psychology class and hearing, for the first time, the term "unconditional love." I knew immediately what it meant. My mother loved people that way. People my mother loved could do nothing to ever lose that love. We could make mistakes, and she'd gladly tell us when she thought we did, but our essential worthiness was never questioned.

And my mother certainly taught me, and everyone around her, how to laugh. My mother was the original dyed-in-the-wool optimist. There was nothing in life, she felt, that you couldn't laugh about. There was always laughter when she was around. She was fun, and she was funny. I think she knew she could laugh at anything because she trusted life and she trusted God.

My mother had her favorite sayings, of course. The one she said most often was "The grass is always greenest on *my* side of the fence." She never expressed envy over anyone else's life.

One of my mother's strongest beliefs was in "Reading a newspaper every day." My mother, who was very smart, read the *Los Angeles Times* from cover to cover daily. And I've come to believe in reading a newspaper every day to understand your community and your world. *Hey, Mom, I write for the papers now; what do you think of that?*

She loved politics, which led to some lively discussions. I remember one election when each of us was backing a different candidate. The arguments we had! My mother supported Shirley Chisholm for president that year. She never stopped surprising us.

My mother was a lot like her aunt, my great-aunt Annie. Aunt Annie was the first person who showed me you could get younger as you got older. The first time I met her, she was already in her sixties. That day, she had just finished some class: foreign language, piano playing, I don't recall. Aunt Annie was always taking classes, always learning. She outlived four or five husbands; I think even she lost count. She never let age or infirmities get in the way of her keeping active. This runs on my father's side, too: my aunt Lillian went to clown college at age sixty-nine! I guess I have a lively future to look forward to.

My aunt Annie taught me a lesson from her mother, who would have been my great-grandmother, and it's a saying I've in turn taught my niece, Adeena: "If it means having only one dress to wear, always have help in the house." It's not that anyone in my family was a snob, and we certainly didn't have money. It was more a recognition that you don't have to do every job yourself, especially jobs you're not good at. This has been an important lesson in my business life, too: hire the help you need, don't try to do everything yourself. And I don't have to be good at everything. That's why I need help in the house, and seeing my siblings and my nieces and nephews, I can tell you that we have five generations—*five generations*—of bad housekeepers! Hey, every family has to have its traditions.

Finally, my mother taught me perhaps the most important lesson of all: life is to be lived fully, *now*. I learned this lesson partially from her sudden and early death, but also because she didn't wait for the good things to come to her. She enjoyed her life, she enjoyed what she had, even something as simple as a hot-fudge sundae or a night out with friends. She had a wonderful time. She may have died young, but she lived the time she had with gusto. Since none of us can control how many days we get, only how we will spend those days, my mother showed me the importance of savoring and enjoying your life.

So I know what she'd say to me and to you now, as we finish this book. My mother would tell us that life shouldn't be so serious; we should have more fun and not work so hard. I can almost hear her voice, telling both of us . . .

. . . "Now, go outside and play!"

Acknowledgments

It takes a lot of assistance and support to create a work like this. I was fortunate to have the aid of so many good people.

Research Information

I'd like to thank all of those who helped me identify and research backgrounds on companies for possible inclusion in this book. The list grew to hundreds of potential companies. Thanks to these individuals and organizations:

Kathleen Meyer, Stephanie Weiss, Suzanne Allen, Marilyn Turner, The Business Enterprise Trust, Palo Alto, California

Elizabeth Elliott McGeveran and Alisa Gravitz, Coop America, Washington, D.C.

Robert Levering, Great Place to Work Institute, San Francisco

Jerry Porras, Stanford University Business School

Sam Stern, Oregon State University

Gail Work, Berkeley, California, independent consultant

Carl Neal, Heartland Institute

Stephen Lydenberg, Kinder, Lydenberg, Domini & Co. Inc., Cambridge, Massachusetts

Lloyd Kurtz, Harris Bertall Sullivan & Smith, L.L.C., San Francisco, California

David Birch, Cognetics, Cambridge, Massachusetts

Michael Jantzi, Canada

Daniel Watson, Minnesota Center for Corporate Responsibility, Minneapolis, Minnesota

And for all the many friends and colleagues who also suggested companies, including Bill Rollinson, Andrew Anker, Mark Gorenberg, Susan Buffett, Helen Ingerson, and many more. I appreciate what you've given me more than I can say.

At the Companies

Thanks to all the public relations and folks at the companies I visited. I have rarely seen a group of PR people less eager to get press. Thank you all for putting up with my unrelenting pursuit and for arranging the details of my visits and making them so pleasant.

John Schroeder, 3M

Kristin Nelson and Linda Rutherford, Southwest Airlines

Paula Stanley and Brooke White, Nordstrom

Laura McCormick, Kinko's, and Lisa Lewis and John Cannon in Dallas

Linda Fiorentino, Zingerman's

Lu Setnicka and Hal Thomson, Patagonia

Isabel Siegel, Cumberland

And a special thank-you and apology to Kathy Murtallo of Hewlett-Packard, which didn't get nearly the coverage they deserved—that's what comes from being just down the street.

Personal Support

I particularly want to thank my staff, friends, and colleagues for all the help they've given me. Without them, none of this would have been possible.

My first thank-you goes to Erin Wait for maintaining my Web site, www.rhondaonline.com. Erin's a great writer, thinker, and nag (the best!) and wishes I'd stop telling her how wonderful she is. Sorry, Erin. I think you're terrific.

Next, my gratitude to Chris Young, research assistant, who spent hours on the Internet, in libraries, and on the phone. Thanks, Chris. Mary Bergner gets my thanks for maintaining my mailing list and database.

Thank you, Jennifer Long, an incredibly talented graphic designer, who did such a great job on my identity graphics and Web design. Next book, I promise, Jennifer!

And my personal assistants get my undying gratitude for putting up with me and keeping me the little bit of organized that I'm able to manage:

Ann Smitherman: Ann, you were right about Zingerman's but wrong about leaving just to have a baby. Come back and bring M.C.! He can copyedit.

Melissa Klumpar: Melissa, thanks for being so patient, flexible, and capable. I'll lighten up one day, I'm sure.

And after all these years of rescuing me from airports and rebooking schedules, I'd like to thank my friend and travel agent, Nancy "Jane" Weir of Simone International in San Francisco.

My thanks to Eugene Kleiner, one of the founders of Silicon Valley: my mentor and friend, the one who got me into all this. And who taught me that you always invest in *people,* not plans.

I'd like to thank my colleagues and friends at Gannett. Gary Strauss at *USA Today*—see, Gary, look what you started. To Mark Rohner (now of Bloomberg), the most patient man in the world. Thanks to Jerry Langdon, my new editor. And a warm, fond, heartfelt hug and thank-you to Craig Schwed, my editor for five years, who generously hardly ever touched a word!

I also want to thank my friends at the *Costco Connection*: David Fuller, my dear friend and editor, and Anita Thompson, Tim Talevich, and the others at Costco.

Thank you also to Gary Chappell, a client, of Gallery Records, for supplying me with a complete collection of CDs to keep me company these long hours. How about putting out *Music to Write Books By?*

And finally, to my personal support network who have to put up with me—and do it so graciously, while having to pull their hair out from my antics:

My family: Janice Hill, my sister and friend, who puts up with me telling her, "I can't talk now." And thanks, Michael, Aaron, and Seth—next year, I promise I'll have more time. My brother, Arnie Abrams, and Mary, Brendan, and Kayley, okay, I'm coming for a visit now. And thanks to my sister and "brother," Karen and Scott Colbert, for all you've given me over the years. And to my niece, Adeena Colbert, a wonderful woman and friend.

Thanks to my dear friends for their help and understanding:

Edward Pollock, who not only has such a great mind but also such a kind heart (I promise I won't tell anyone).

Freddi Gerard, for being an unceasing source of song titles and popular culture, even at two A.M.

June Rose Buch, my friend for so many, many years. No matter how long it's been, it always seems just like yesterday.

Raquel Newman, personal freelance editor, chef, and errand runner.

Matthew Abergel, wordsmith, editor, friend, and therapist. And maybe we can find some other synonyms.

Mary "Andi" Compton, my personal daily support system, without whom I'd be five times crazier and ten pounds heavier. And our constant canine companions, Cosmo, Meagan, and Tali (stop barking!). We'll get through it together, Andi.

Cathy Goldstein, my dear friend, lawyer, and support. Truly one of the finest people I know. How are *your* puppies?

Daniel Greenberg, my agent, of James Levine Communication. What a mensch. Who else could have held my hand so well for so long? Bruce is right, he's "the best agent in New York." And thanks to Jim Levine and all the others there.

A final huge thank-you to the incredibly patient people at Villard Books, especially Oona Schmid. Adam Rothberg and Brant Janeway, whom I'm just about to start driving really crazy. A huge hug to Brian DeFiore. And a special *muchas gracias* to my terrific editor, Bruce Tracy. Relax now, Bruce. More See's chocolate's on the way.

BIBLIOGRAPHY

Allen, Oliver E. "Sticky Business." *American Heritage of Invention & Technology Magazine,* winter 1995.

"America's Most Admired Companies: Where Companies Rank in Their Own Industries." *Fortune,* March 2, 1998.

Armstrong, J. Scott, and Fred Collopy. "Competitor Orientation: Effects of Objectives and Information on Managerial Decisions and Profitability." *Journal of Marketing Research,* vol. 33, May 1996.

"Baptists Vote to Boycott Disney over Gay Benefits." *The Wall Street Journal,* June 13, 1996.

Bartmess, Andrew D. "The Plant Location Puzzle." *Harvard Business Review,* March 1, 1994.

Beason, Tyrone. "Automated-Defibrillator Industry Gets a Boost from Hewlett-Packard." *Knight-Ridder Tribune Business News,* December 30, 1997.

Beattie, Bonnie, and Linda DeBlanco, eds. *Poker, Cooking, and Pearls of Wisdom: The Biography of Virginia Orfalea.* Ventura, Cal.: Paul Orfalea, 1988.

Bennis, Warren, and Patricia Ward Biederman. *Organizing Genius: The Secrets of Creative Collaboration.* Reading, Mass.: Addison-Wesley, 1997.

"The Best Corporate Citizens." *Business Ethics,* May/June, 1996.

Bollier, David. *Aiming Higher: 25 Stories of How Companies Prosper by Combining Sound Management and Social Vision.* New York: AMACOM, 1996.

Branch, Shelly. "Smart Managing: So Much Work, So Little Time." *Fortune,* February 3, 1997.

"A Brief History of People Express." The Airline History Archives, 1996.

Briskin, Alan. *The Stirring of Soul in the Workplace.* San Francisco: Jossey-Bass, 1996.

Britt, Russ. "Leaders & Success: Bill Hewlett and David Packard." *Investor's Business Daily,* October 14, 1997.

Buber, Martin. *I and Thou,* translation by Walter Kaufman. New York: Touchstone, 1996.

Burrows, Peter. "Lew Platt's Fix-It Plan for Hewlett-Packard." *Business Week,* July 13, 1998.

Byrne, John A. "The Horizontal Corporation: It's About Managing Across, Not Up and Down." *Business Week,* December 20, 1993.

Carey, Pete. "Odwalla Settles 5 Juice Lawsuits: Sincere Talks Impress Poisoned Survivor's Day." *San Jose Mercury News,* May 27, 1998.

Caudron, Shari. "The Only Way to Stay Ahead." *Industry Week,* August 17, 1998.

Chan, Yvonne. "Hewlett-Packard Recycling Programme Draws Fire from Some Environmental Groups: Printer Maker Switches to Green." *South China Morning Post,* January 20, 1998.

Clary, Mike, and James Bates. "Religious Right Shuns Benefits to Gays." *Los Angeles Times,* December 26, 1995.

Collins, James C., and Jerry I. Porras. "The 3M Story." *Audacity,* vol. 4, no. 2, winter 1996.

———. *Built to Last: Successful Habits of Visionary Companies.* New York: Harper-Business, 1996.

Comfort, Mildred Houghton. *William L. McKnight, Industrialist.* St. Paul: Minnesota Mining and Manufacturing Company, 1962.

Conger, Jay A. "How 'Gen X' Managers Manage." *Strategy & Business.* Booz, Allen & Hamilton, Inc., First Quarter, 1998.

Cooper, Robert K., and Ayman Sawaf. *Executive EQ: Emotional Intelligence in Leadership & Organizations.* New York: Grosset/Putnam, 1996.

Crown, Judith, and Glenn Coleman. *No Hands: The Rise and Fall of the Schwinn Bicycle Company, an American Institution.* New York: Henry Holt and Company, 1996.

"Does It Pay to Be Ethical?" *Business Ethics,* March/April 1997.

Eisner, Michael, with Tony Schwartz. *Work in Progress.* New York: Random House, 1998.

Fikac, Peggy. "Texas School Board Members Fear Slippery Slope After Disney Stock Dump." Associated Press, July 11, 1998.

Freiberg, Kevin, and Jackie Freiberg. *Nuts! Southwest Airlines' Crazy Recipe for Business and Personal Success.* New York: Broadway Books, 1998

Fulmer, Melinda. "Investing in Bonds: Firms Embrace Socializing Trend." *Los Angeles Times,* April 25, 1998.

Gerlin, Andrea. "How a Jury Decided That a Coffee Spill Is Worth $2.9 Million." *The Wall Street Journal,* September 1, 1994.

Godsey, Kristin Dunlap. "Slow Climb to New Heights: Combine Strict Discipline with Goofy Antics and Make Billions." *Success,* October 1996.

Grant, Linda. "Happy Workers, High Returns." *Fortune,* January 12, 1998.

Gruner, Stephanie. "Have Fun, Make Money: How Herb Kelleher Parties Profitably at Southwest Airlines." *INC.,* May 1998.

Halbfinger, David M. "Former Executives Guilty." *The New York Times,* November 26, 1997.

Hall, Cheryl. "Still Crazy After 25 Years: Southwest's Culture Committee Keeps Tight Reins on Staying Loose." *The Dallas Morning News,* June 9, 1996.

Hasek, Glenn. "Stretch Before Exercising Genius." *Industry Week,* August 17, 1998.

Hewlett, William R. "The Human Side of Management." Eugene B. Clark Executive Lecture, University of Notre Dame, March 25, 1982.

Hochshield, Arlie Russell. *Time Bind.* New York: Metropolitan Books, 1997.

"The HP Way." Brochure from Hewlett-Packard Company, 1997.

Huck, Virginia. *Brand of the Tartan: The 3M Story.* St. Paul: Minnesota Mining and Manufacturing Company, 1995.

Izumo, Gary. "Inspiring Loyalty Makes Good Business Sense." *Los Angeles Times,* July 16, 1996, Ventura County edition.

Jacobs, Joanne. "Apple Juice Poisoning: The Panic That Wasn't." *San Jose Mercury News,* November 14, 1996.

Jesitus, John. "On the Road Again: New Top Management Uses a Teamwork Approach to Put Schwinn Back into the Bicycle-Industry Race." *Industry Week,* vol. 245, November 4, 1996.

Katz, Jesse. "Southwest Is the Zaniest, Savviest Company on Earth." *Los Angeles Times,* June 9, 1996.

Kearney, Robert. "Bright Work." *3M Today,* vol. 15, no. 1, January 1998.

Kelleher, Herb. "Today's Issue: Putting Humor in the Workplace; Guest CEO: Herb Kelleher," interview by Donna Rosat, *USA Today,* February 23, 1998.

Labich, Kenneth. "Is Herb Kelleher America's Best CEO?" *Fortune,* May 2, 1994.

Langberg, Mike. "House of Fry's." *San Jose Mercury News,* August 24, 1997.

———, and Larry Slonaker. "Workers Kept on Tight Leash, but Some Praise the Practices." *San Jose Mercury News,* August 24, 1997.

Levering, Robert. *A Great Place to Work: What Makes Some Employers So Good (and Most So Bad).* New York: Random House, 1988.

———, and Milton Moskowitz. "The 100 Best Companies to Work for in America." *Fortune,* January 12, 1998.

———. *The 100 Best Companies to Work for in America.* New York: Plume, 1994.

Lindahl, Laurel. "A Scholar and a Gentleman." *3M Today,* vol. 15, no. 1, January 1998.

Mall, Elyse. "A Look Back: Brooklyn's Cumberland Packing Corp. Has Survived the Artificial-Sweetener Wars by Sticking to Its Founding Principles." *Your Company,* June/July 1998.

Martin, Douglas. "Nice 'n Easy at the Factory: A Family Business That Tries to Treat Workers Like Family." *The New York Times,* April 2, 1997.

Memmott, Carol. "A Starter, a Surfer, and an Ex-Secretary Reform Travel; Colleen Barrett, Southwest Airlines." *USA Today,* March 17, 1998.

Miller, Michael. "It All Comes Down to a Viable Strategy and a Defensible Niche: Low-Fare Airlines: A New Bar Has Been Set." *Aviation Daily,* January 6, 1998.

Miller, Mike. "How Schwinn Bike Company Pedaled into Bankruptcy." Reuters Business Report (on-line), December 18, 1996.

Morris, Tom. *If Aristotle Ran General Motors: The New Soul of Business.* New York: Henry Holt and Company, Inc., 1997.

Moskowitz, Milton. "That's the Spirit." *Mother Jones,* vol. 22, July/August 1997.

Munk, Nina. "The New Organization Man." *Fortune,* March 16, 1998.

Myerson, Allen R. "Air Herb." *The New York Times Magazine,* November 9, 1997.

"Odwalla's Costly Penance the Issue: Juice Company Fined $1.5 Million; Our View: A Penalty or a Message?" *Rocky Mountain News,* July 27, 1998.

Oppedahl, Rachel, ed. *The Squeeze: An In-House Publication for Odwallians,* November/December 1996.

Packard, David. "Eleven Simple Rules." Unpublished Packard Speech Files in the Hewlett-Packard Archives, Sonoma Meeting, 1958.

———. *The HP Way: How Bill Hewlett and I Built Our Company.* HarperBusiness, 1995.

Reingold, Jennifer. "Executive Pay: Special Report." *Business Week,* April 21, 1997.

Reuter, Madalynne. "Judge Rules Kinko's Infringes Copyrights." *Publishers Weekly,* April 12, 1991.

Robertson, Edward A. "America's Most Admired Companies." *Fortune,* January 1997.

Robinson, Alan G., and Sam Stern. *Corporate Creativity: How Innovation and Improvement Actually Happen.* San Francisco: Berrett-Koehler, 1997.

Ruddick, Sara. *Maternal Thinking: Toward a Politics of Peace.* New York: Ballantine Books, 1989.

Ryan, Michael. "They Call Their Boss a Hero." *Parade Magazine,* September 8, 1996.

"St. Louis CEOs Pocketed $430 Million Last Year; Here Are the Five Highest Paid." *St. Louis Post-Dispatch,* July 19, 1998.

Schine, Eric. "McDonald's Hot Coffee Gets Her Cool Cash." *Business Week,* September 5, 1994.

Schmid, Randolph E. "Southwest Holds Top Airline Quality Rating." Associated Press, April 21, 1997.

Seipel, Tracy, and Jennifer Mena. "Odwalla Workers Rely on Company Values During Crisis, Juice Maker Falls Back on Openness and Integrity." *San Jose Mercury News,* November 17, 1996.

Slonaker, Larry, and Mike Langberg. "Expansion into New Markets Will Test Fry's Spotty Record on Customer Service." *San Jose Mercury News,* August 24, 1997.

Smith, Wendy. "Shifting Gears at Schwinn." *Newsday,* December 22, 1996.

Spector, Robert, and Patrick McCarthy. *The Nordstrom Way: The Inside Story of America's #1 Customer Service Company.* New York: John Wiley & Sons, 1995.

Spock, Benjamin, M.D. *Dr. Spock on Parenting.* New York: Simon and Schuster, 1988.

Stewart, Thomas A. "Gray Flannel Suit—*Moi?*" *Fortune,* March 16, 1998.

Stewart, Thomas. "3M Fights Back." *Fortune,* February 6, 1996.

"Sweet 'n Slow." *The Wall Street Journal,* August 4, 1997.

Taninecz, George. "Gates Wins Respect." *Industry Week,* November 20, 1995.

3M Stemwinder, vol. 12, no. 7, February 18, 1998.

Tully, Shawn. "Why to Go for Stretch Targets." *Fortune,* November 14, 1994.

Waddock, Sandra A., and Samuel B. Graves. "Finding the Link Between Stakeholder Relations and Quality of Management," abstract in *Business and Society,* vol. 36, no. 3, September 1997.

Welsh, Tricia. "Best and Worst Corporate Reputations." *Fortune,* February 7, 1994.

Yankelovich, Daniel. "Got to Give to Get." *Mother Jones,* July/August 1997.

ABOUT THE AUTHOR

RHONDA ABRAMS writes the nation's most widely read small-business column, distributed by Gannett News Service. Her bestselling book, *The Successful Business Plan: Secrets & Strategies,* was acclaimed by *Forbes* as one of the two best books for small business and by *Inc.* as one of the six best for start-ups, and it was a Main Selection of the *Business Week* Book Club. Rhonda doesn't just write about business; she lives it. In 1986, she founded a management-consulting practice that has clients ranging from one-person start-ups to Fortune 500 companies. In 1995, she was an Internet pioneer, founding a Web-content company, which she later sold. Rhonda is a popular public speaker and frequent commentator on business topics. She lives in Los Altos Hills, California.

Visit Rhonda Abrams at www.RhondaOnline.com